Public Policy under Thatcher

Public Policy under Thatcher

Edited by

Stephen P. Savage

and

Lynton Robins

MACMILLAN

First published 1990 by
THE MACMILLAN PRESS LTD
Houndmills, Basingstoke, Hampshire RG21 2XS
and London
Companies and representatives
throughout the world

ISBN 0–333–53659–2 (hardcover)
ISBN 0–333–53660–6 (paperback)

A catalogue record for this book is available
from the British Library.

Printed in Hong Kong

Reprinted 1991, 1992

Contents

Acknowledgements

The editors would like to thank all of the contributors to the book for their tolerance towards what has been a very demanding timetable of delivery. Their responsiveness to the various forms of inducement employed to meet deadlines, some of which bordered on the illegal, has made the editors' task that much more manageable. We would like to give special thanks to Rob Atkinson who, in addition to writing one and co-authoring two of the chapters, was of great assistance in advising the editors on other aspects of the book. We would also like to express our gratitude to all of those who have assisted the authors in the preparation of manuscripts. In particular, we would like to acknowledge the contribution of Carol Knight, who undertook important work on the Bibliography, and to thank Olive, Lorraine, Nicky and Heather, of the School of Social and Historical Studies, for their invaluable work on the manuscripts.

Stephen P. Savage
Lynton Robins

Notes on the Contributors

Rob Atkinson is a Senior Lecturer in Politics in the School of Social and Historical Studies at Portsmouth Polytechnic. He has recently completed a Doctorate on housing and local government which, together with industrial policy, constitute his primary research interests. He has published a variety of articles on trade unions, urban politics and local government.

John Bradbeer is Senior Lecturer in Geography, Department of Geography, at Portsmouth Polytechnic. His interests are in environmental planning and policy, with particular emphasis on natural resources and the coastal zone, rural planning and leisure and recreation. His main publications include chapters in books on the future of mineral extraction in the British countryside; the problems of nuclear power station location in the United Kingdom; the Heritage Coasts of England and Wales; defence heritage and tourism development.

Fergus Carr is a Principal Lecturer in International Politics in the School of Social and Historical Studies at Portsmouth Polytechnic. His primary research interests are contemporary strategy and international politics in the Middle East. He is also currently pursuing Doctorate research into the American Doctrine of Limited War.

Mike Dunn is Head of the School of Economics, Portsmouth Polytechnic, and lectures in the area of industrial and resource economics. He has published widely in the field of resource economics and has published *Fisheries Economics: An Introduction* (with S. Cunningham and D. Whitmarsh) (Mansell/Cassell, 1985).

Paul Durden is a Senior Lecturer in Social Policy in the School of Social and Historical Studies at Portsmouth Polytechnic. His research interests focus on housing and education policy, particularly in the field of comparative social policies. He has published mainly in the area of housing policy.

Neil Evans is a Senior Lecturer in Social Work in the School of Social and Historical Studies at Portsmouth Polytechnic. Prior to this post he has worked in a variety of capacities for Social Services. His current research interests focus on provision for elderly people, and he has published articles on medical services in the community.

xi

David Farnham is a Principal Lecturer in Industrial Relations at the Business School, at Portsmouth Polytechnic. He has written widely on industrial relations, personnel management and employment legislation. He is author of *The Corporate Environment* (IPM, 1990) *Personnel in Context* (IPM, 1986) and co-author of *Understanding Industrial Relations* (with John Pimlott) (Cassell, 1990) and *Public Administration in the UK* (with Malcolm McVicar) (Cassell, 1982).

Sylvia Horton is Principal Lecturer in Public Sector Studies in the School of Social and Historical Studies at Portsmouth Polytechnic. Her major research interests are in local government and the civil service, and she has published a variety of articles in these areas.

Kelvyn Jones is Senior Lecturer in Geography, in the Department of Geography, at Portsmouth Polytechnic. His specialist interests lie in medical geography and quantitative methods. He is author (with Graham Moon) of *Health, Disease and Society: A Critical Introduction to Medical Geography* (Routledge & Kegan Paul, 1987) and holds a Doctoral thesis for work on the exploratory analysis of mortality information.

Ian Kendall is Senior Lecturer in Social Policy in the School of Social and Historical Studies at Portsmouth Polytechnic. He has recently completed editing a collection of Fabian Society papers on the NHS and co-authoring a book on complaints procedures and health services in the UK.

Carol Lupton is Senior Research Officer in the Social Services Research and Information Unit (SSRIU) within the School of Social and Historical Studies at Portsmouth Polytechnic. In addition to her research in the Unit, evaluating the quality of personal social services provided to a range of client groups, she has written and published in a range of areas including: post-war unemployment policy, feminist research practice and the development of performance indicators within local authority social service departments. She is currently editing a book on the dilemmas of feminist community work.

Frank Lyons is a Senior Lecturer in Sociology in the School of Social and Historical Studies at Portsmouth Polytechnic. His major research interests are in the area of the politics of Ireland and educational development.

Francis McGlone lectures in Social Policy in the School of Social and Historical Studies at Portsmouth Polytechnic, and also at the Polytechnic of Central London. His research interests focus on state policy, poverty and social security, and social policy with specific reference to elderly people. He has worked previously with Age Concern.

Malcolm McVicar is Dean of the Faculty of Humanities and Social Science at Portsmouth Polytechnic. His primary research interests are in the area of education policy, particularly higher education. He has written extensively on performance monitoring in higher education, and is co-author of *Public Administration in the UK* (with David Farnham) (Cassell, 1985).

Frances Millard is Principal Lecturer in Politics in the School of Social and Historical Studies at Portsmouth Polytechnic, where she specialises in Soviet and Eastern European Politics. Her research interests focus on social policy and issues of civil liberties. Among her major publications are *Pressure Politics in Industrial Societies* (with Alan Ball) (Macmillan, 1986) and editor of *Social Policy and the Market* (London School of Economics, 1990).

Graham Moon is Senior Lecturer in Health Studies, in the School of Social and Historical Studies at Portsmouth Polytechnic. His current interests focus on community health planning, public health and health informatics. He holds a Doctoral thesis on urban political geography and has published work in the areas on urban and local government studies, services for elderly people and health planning and policy. He is author (with Kelvyn Jones) of *Health, Disease and Society: A Critical Introduction to Medical Geography* (Routledge & Kegan Paul, 1987), and is currently working (with Liz Twigg and Kelvyn Jones) on the development of consultancy work with various health authorities.

Lynton Robins is Course Leader in Public Administration at Leicester Polytechnic. He is co-author (with Bill Coxall) of *Contemporary British Politics* (Macmillan, 1989), editor of *Talking Politics*, and is currently researching aspects of post-war British politics.

Dave Russell is Senior Lecturer in Sociology, School of Social and Historical Studies at Portsmouth Polytechnic. His major research interests are in the areas of race and anti-racism, states and society and professions and public policy. He has published various articles in journals and books on South Africa, and on British racism.

Stephen P. Savage is Senior Lecturer in Criminology and Police Studies at Portsmouth Polytechnic. His Doctoral work was in the area of social theory, and his current research interest focuses on criminal justice and policing policy. He has written variously in the area of sociological theory, social policy and criminology, and he is author of *The Theories of Talcott Parsons* (Macmillan, 1981) and co-author of *Education and Social Policy* (Macmillan, forthcoming).

Sandy Smith is a Senior Lecturer in the School of Economics at Portsmouth Polytechnic, and has a particular interest in the economics of central planning and market socialism. He has published a number of papers in the area of economic theory, and particularly on the Soviet economy.

Liz Twigg lectures in Social Statistics in the School of Social and Historical Studies and the Department of Geography at Portsmouth Polytechnic, and also holds a Research Fellowship in health and health care information. She is currently working on a public health database for Winchester Health Authority and completing her Doctoral thesis on geographical aspects of health information. She has published on geographical information systems, official health statistics and statistical methods.

Glossary of Acronyms and Political Terms

ACAS   Advisory Conciliation and Arbitration Service
ANC   African National Congress
ASI   Adam Smith Institute

BA   British Airways
BAA   British Airports Authority
BES   Business Expansion Scheme
BT   British Telecom
BTG   British Technology Group
BUPA   British United Provident Association

CAP   Common Agricultural Policy (EC)
CBI   Confederation of British Industry
CC   Community Charge
CEC   Commission of the European Communities
CFCs   Chlorofuorocarbons
CHB   Child Benefit: a non-means-tested allowance payable to the main carer of a child, usually the mother
CHOGM   Commonwealth Heads of Government Meeting
CO   Certification Officer/Office
COI   Central Office of Information
CPAG   Child Poverty Action Group
CPS   Centre for Policy Studies
CRE   Commission for Racial Equality
CRTUM   Commissioner for the Rights of Trade Union Members
CSO   Central Statistical Office
CTC   City Technology College

DE   Department of Employment
DES   Department of Education and Science
DHA   District Health Authority
DHSS   Department of Health and Social Security
DOE   Department of the Environment
DOH   Department of Health
DOI   Department of Industry
DPR   Data Protection Registrar

DSS	Formerly DHSS, responsible for the administration of social security
DTI	Department of Trade and Industry
EC	European Community
EEC	European Economic Community, now known as EC
e-i-a	environmental-impact-assessment
EMS	European Monetary System
EO	Equal Opportunity
EOC	Equal Opportunities Commission
EPG	Eminent Person's Group
ERM	Exchange Rate Mechanism (of the EMS)
ESA	Environmentally Sensitive Area
ET	Employment Training
EZ	Enterprise Zone
FC	Family Credit: a means-tested benefit payable to families on low wages, replacing FIS (see below) from April 1988
FO	Foreign and Commonwealth Office
FIS	Family Income Supplement
FMI	Financial Management Initiative
FPA	Family Practitioner Authority
FPC	Family Practitioner Committee
GCHQ	General Communications Headquarters
GLC	Greater London Council
GNP	Gross National Product
Go7	Group of 7 (economic powers)
GSS	Government Statistical Service
HAT	Housing Action Trust
HB	Housing Benefit: a means-tested housing subsidy for people in rented accommodation and owner-occupiers (general rates only) administered by the local authority
IBA	Independent Broadcasting Authority
IEA	Institute for Economic Affairs
IHSM	Institute of Health Service Management
ILEA	Inner London Education Authority
IMF	International Monetary Fund
INF	Intermediate-Range Nuclear Forces
INLA	Irish National Liberation Army

IS	Income Support: a means-tested benefit for people not in full-time employment replacing SB (see below) from April 1988
IT	Industrial Tribunal
ITC	Independent Television Commission
LEA	Local Education Authority
LFA	Less Favoured Area (agriculture)
MAFF	Ministry of Agriculture, Food and Fisheries
MCC	Metropolitan County Council
MINNIS	Management Information Systems for Ministers
MOD	Ministry of Defence
MSC	Manpower Services Commission
MTFS	Medium Term Financial Strategy
NATO	North Atlantic Treaty Organisation
NCC	National Curriculum Council
NCCL	National Council for Civil Liberties
NEB	National Enterprise Board
NHS	National Health Service
NIB	National Insurance Benefit: benefit based on a record of contributions into the National Insurance scheme
NIMBY	'Not in my back yard'
NNDR	national non-domestic rate
NSPCC	National Society for the Prevention of Cruelty to Children
OFGAS	regulatory agency for British Gas
OFTEL	regulatory agency for British Telecom
PCFC	Polytechnics and Colleges Funding Council
PF	Popular Front (Zimbabwe)
PIRA	Provisional Irish Republican Army
PPP	Private Patients Plan
PRC	People's Republic of China
PSBR	Public Sector Borrowing Requirement
QGA	Quasi-governmental Agency
QUANGO	Quasi-autonomous Non-governmental Organisation
QUELGO	Quasi-elected Local Government Organisation
RHA	Regional Health Authority
RPI	Retail Price Index

RSG	Rate Support Grant
RUC	Royal Ulster Constabulary
RWA	Regional Water Authority
SB	Supplementary Benefit (see IS above)
SDI	Strategic Defense Initiative (US)
SDLP	Social Democratic and Labour Party (N. Ireland)
SEA	Single European Act
SEAC	Schools Examination and Assessment Council
SERPS	State Earnings Related Pension Scheme: a National Insurance contributory additional state pension for employees only
SF	Social Fund: a cash-limited discretionary fund of loans and grants for exceptional needs, replacing single payments from April 1988
SNF	Short-Range Nuclear Forces
SPZ	Simplified Planning Zone
SSD	Social Services Department
SSSI	Site of Special Scientific Interest
TC	Training Commission (formerly MSC)
TEC	Training and Enterprise Council
TUC	Trades Union Council
TVEI	Technical and Vocational Education Initiative
UDC	Urban Development Corporation
UDI	Unilateral Declaration of Independence (Rhodesia)
UDR	Ulster Defence Regiment
UFC	University Funding Council
UNESCO	United Nations Economic and Social Council
WCC	Welsh Curriculum Council
YOP	Youth Opportunities Programme
YTS	Youth Training Scheme

Introduction

This book is concerned with the study of developments in the field of
public policy throughout what has been to many people a distinctive if
not remarkable political period in British politics – the three Thatcher
Administrations of 1979, 1983 and 1987. Few other periods of
government have attracted so much attention and created so much
controversy, for despite open disagreement over the actual impact of
Thatcher's policies and the extent to which there is some coherent
ideology of 'Thatcherism' (Riddell, 1989), virtually all would agree that
the politics and policies which have emerged since 1979 constitute a
distinctive phase in the history of post-war British politics. This should
hardly be surprising, given the context of the political environment
from the late 1970s onwards. Not since the first post-war government
of 1945 has a political party set out on such a radical programme as
that which emerged within the Conservative Party under the leadership
of Margaret Thatcher, and which, if anything, has gained momentum
during the 1980s. Coupled with the fact that the Conservatives have
been able to enjoy more than a decade of continuous government, and
been faced with, until recently, a weakened and divided opposition, the
recipe for a period of rapid political change had been created. The
extent to which this has happened, in the sense of its impact on public
policy as a whole, is one of the central questions which the chapters
which follow seek to address.

As a basis for approaching such questions it is useful to draw some
general comparisons between the central post-war themes of British
politics, pre- and post-1979. Without assuming that there are two
clearly identifiable and opposed phases along these time-scales – as will
be seen, there are many areas of continuity and similarity between the
two periods – it is possible nevertheless to speak of a number of repects
in which the political horizon has shifted. Certainly when looked at
from the standpoint of contemporary politics, the comparisons
between pre- and post- 1979 Britain seem marked.

Post-war Politics and Policy Prior to 1979

It is clearly impossible in this context to provide a full overview of the complex and variable nature of politics and policy during what was itself a period of substantial political change – post-war politics up to the late 1970s. However, it is possible to identify a number of themes and features of the stance taken by both Labour and Conservative governments which, at least with the benefit of hindsight, paint a picture of a very different political landscape to that increasingly familiar in contemporary Britain. Indeed, Thatcher and her followers have set out their political stall very much in direct opposition to these characteristics of post-war politics. The phrase which best encapsulates such characteristics, despite the need to treat it with caution, is the 'post-war consensus'.

The notion of a 'post-war consensus' is a relative one. It addresses the relationship between the two major polical parties in the post-war period (up to the 1970s) on matters of policy and style of government, in which, so the idea goes, there were substantial areas of cross-party agreement on fundamental aspects of politics. It does not imply an absence of political opposition and conflict as such, rather the broad agreement over the parameters of public policy and the proper role of government on economic and social affairs. It is probably fair to say that it appears to be more of a 'consensus' now than it did at the time! Three features are most commonly cited as the framework of public policy underpinning this consensus.

The Role of the State in Economic Affairs

Both Labour and Conservative governments have, for most of the post-war period, considered that central government should play a key role in economic management, normally referred to as the 'mixed economy'. This has taken a variety of forms, from state ownership of particular units or sectors of the economy by nationalisation (coal-mining, steel production, public utilities, and so on), through government subsidies to industry, to the manipulation of specific economic mechanisms such as prices and income controls, credit controls and exchange controls. Furthermore, such instruments of economic policy were used as a means of attempting to achieve a general policy of maintaining full employment (see Chapter 2).

In other words, a key feature of the post-war period has been the acceptance by governments of Keynesian economic management, in which the state was to play the role of partner to the private sector of the economy. Political differences over the extent of that role did clearly exist. The ambitions of the Labour Party to operate economic mechanisms, particularly fiscal policy and nationalisation, in the pursuit of greater economic equality, while never that notable in practice, were nevertheless opposed by the Conservatives, whose main justification for the mixed economy rested in its belief that, without, state intervention and regualation in the economy, the market simply would not survive (see Gilmour, 1977, and Russell, 1978). Despite these differences in the logic of support for the partnership role of the state, the broad principle that this was a proper function of the state was accepted by all post-war governments up to 1979.

The Welfare State

Both Labour and Conservative governments had accepted that the state should also play a key role in the provision of 'welfare', i.e. health care, education, income support, personal care for the elderly, children in need, and the disabled, and housing. This went well beyond the idea of providing a 'safety-net' for the destitute, to one in which the state would guarantee a basic entitlement to a reasonable standard of living and the provision of suitable social resources, such as schooling and health care. One commentator referred to this as 'social citizenship', the establishment of basic social rights to parallel those of civil and political rights, (Marshall, 1981). It is known more popularly as the 'Welfare State', formed in large part in the period immediately following the Second World War, but expanded in scope and levels of expenditure substantially during the next three decades. Its most notable features have been the National Health Service, state provision of secondary, further and higher education, provision of the 'personal social services' (care for the elderly, disabled, mentally ill, children), local authority or 'council' housing, and state provision of pensions and social security. This did not mean that no bodies other than the state were involved in the welfare services, on the contrary, the private sector (private schools, residential homes, private beds in hospitals, owner occupied residences, and so on), and voluntary agencies (e.g. charitable bodies), both played important roles in the overall provision of services (Titmuss, 1976); indeed the relative balance of state to private/voluntary sector services was an issue on which the main parties were often divided – the Conservatives typically in favour more, rather than less, of the latter. Again, the dispute was over the extent to which the Welfare State should be used in pursuit of wider objectives, with Labour supporting the goal of social egalitarianism through social welfare policy (Crosland, 1956), in contrast with the Conservatives more modest aims of 'social justice' (Russell, 1978). What was not in dispute in mainstream politics at least was the notion that the state should play a central role in the provision of social and welfare services.

Corporatism

A third feature related to the manner in which government approached decision-making on central aspects of policy, often referred to as 'corporatism' (see Plant, 1988, p. 11). Across a range of areas of decision-making, from economic and industrial policy to plans for the health service, post-war governments have tended to adopt an approach in which key interest-groups in the field were allowed to play influential roles in the decision-making process, either on a consultative or participative basis. For example, both the Wilson and Heath governments of the early 1970s accepted the view that industrial and industrial relations policies could be arrived at only after some form of tripartite negotiations between government and the two major interest groups to be affected, the trade unions, through the TUC, and the employers, through the Confederation of British Industry (CBI). This was known in popular parlance at the time as 'beer and sandwiches' negotiation. At a local level, another example was the form of 'consensus' management which to be found in NHS hospitals, whereby decisions affecting hospital staff, particularly the medical staff, would be reached only after the relevant professional bodies had been represented at board level. Both forms of approach to decision-making have been defined as 'corporatist', the participation of the major interest groups in the policy-making process which affects them. Inevitably, it presumes that decisions, whether at government or local level, can only benefit, (or at least can only be workable with the cooperation of) those most centrally involved, and in effect it is a strategy which accepts that most decisions thus reached will be some form of compromise.

Politics and Policy Since 1979

It is precisely these sorts of approaches to government which the Conservatives under Thatcher have sought to undermine and discard (and as much vitriol has been directed at previous Conservative as Labour governments). The particular directions which this strategy has taken are very much the concern of this book. It will consider not just the substance of policy during the Thatcher years, but also the nature of the policy process itself, and the style of government it has entailed. However, at this stage it will be useful to draw out a number of general features of politics and policy since 1979, particularly in terms of the comparisons which can be drawn between this period and the pre-1979 era.

Of central concern here is the ideological context within which the Thatcher period has developed, and not least the ideological stance of Thatcher herself. What types have thinking have underpinned the policies and strategies of the Thatcher leadership? The problem here is that the issue of the 'meaning of Thatcherism' has now itself become a hotly contested one; it has become an area of study in its own right (see Jessop *et al.*, 1988). One debate is whether there is, or has been, such a thing as 'Thatcherism', in the sense of a coherent consistent set of ideas and principles. To some commentators Thatcherism is an identifiable ideological movement which has all of the consistency of a 'project' to restructure Britain (Gamble, 1988). To others, the very term 'Thatcherism' is misleading, for if, it is argued, there has been an identifiable politics behind the Thatcher governments, it is one made up of 'an instinct, a series of moral values and an approach to leadership rather than an ideology.' (Riddell, 1989 pp. 2–3). Another, and closely related, debate, is over the relationship between the rhetoric and reality and the politics of Thatcher. Are the radical messages of Thatcher and her followers implemented in actual policies and reforms? Again, there are marked differences in the responses to such a question (see Holmes, 1985, and Riddell, 1989). These are, of course, concerns also of the chapters that follow. These points should not, however, prevent us from being able to identify at least a number of themes which, even in erratic form, have characterised the ideological context of the politics of Thatcher.

The Virtues of the Market

In economic affairs, a belief in the virtues of the market. The Thatcher governments have been committed to the neo-liberal view that the market is by far the best mechanism for producing and distributing resources. They have embraced the ideas of the 'New Right' on the superiority of the market over state run or state regulated processes (see King, 1987, pp. 70–91). The market is seen to be more efficient, responsive to people's needs, and ultimately more productive than any state system could be (Green, 1987). Increasingly, it would seem, the Conservative governments have come under the influence of neo-liberal think-tanks such as the Adam Smith Institute and the Institute of Economic Affairs (IEA), which have acted as advisers on a wide range of public policies. The acceptance of neo-liberal principles has been a feature in the government's avowed strategy of 'rolling back the state' in economic affairs (see Chapter 2), and it has also been apparent in the policies of deregulation and encouragement of competition and markets in a variety of areas of the public sector (see Chapters 3, 7 and 8). Most certainly, it has been a key component in the virtual abandonment of Keynesian economic strategy as one pillar of the post-war consensus.

An Emphasis on 'Individualism'

Closely linked to the neo-liberal ideology of the primacy of the market is the belief that the individual is to be seen as self-reliant and responsible for her or his own actions. If it was a mistake to involve the state in economic affairs, it was also, so it is argued, a mistake for the state to become to involved in people's lives, and most certainly if that means the state taking away from people their self-reliance and individual responsibility to themselves and to their families. This view is particularly apparent in two areas. Firstly, it is expressed in many of the attacks by Thatcher and the radical Right on the 'Welfare State' (see Anderson *et al.*, 1983).

A major criticism made of state welfare, whether provision of services such as social work (see Chapter 10), or benefits (see Chapter 11), is that it has created a 'dependency culture', whereby many individuals and even whole communities have become reliant on the state to provide for them. The post-war welfare state had damaged individual self-responsibility; it was to be the task of government to rekindle that individualist ethos, and one way of doing this was to 'roll back the welfare state'. A second expression of this notion is in relation to policy on dealing with criminal offenders (see Chapter 6). The trend of post-war governments was seen as one in which offenders were increasingly sheltered from learning the consequences of their actions by 'progressive' methods of treatment. The only alternative is a 'get tough' approach to offenders, which teaches them that crime does not pay, and this involves the use of more, and not less, punishment. It is another reflection of the idea of individual responsibility.

A Belief in 'Strong Government' and 'Authority'

Despite Thatcher's commitment to the market and to individualism, many authors have commented on the theme of 'social authoritarianism' which permeates many of her leadership's policies (Gamble, 1988; Jessop, *et al.*, 1988). It is associated with notions of 'firm' or 'resolute' government, and contrasted unfavourably with the 'consensus' politics of previous administrations. Again, it is expressed in a variety of ways. Firstly, it is linked to a campaign for more 'law and order'(see Chapter 6). Secondly, it is associated with a tightening of the security services and controls on information (see Chapters 14 and 15). Thirdly, it has, on a number of occasions, taken the form of a patriotic if not openly nationalistic approach to international affairs, both in foreign policy and defence (see Chapter 16). On the domestic front, it has in general been reflected in a confrontational rather than consensual style of government (see Chapter 1), which is far removed from the corporatist approaches of earlier administrations: another pillar of the post-war consensus undermined.

These constitute, it must be emphasised, ideological themes rather than necessarily consistent political strategies. Again, there is debate as to whether the rhetoric which surrounds them is matched by policy. However, even those who, like Riddell, question the ideological strength of the Thatcher programme for British politics, accept that, as the 1980s progressed, the radicalism of the Thatcher governments if anything became more apparent (1989, p. 12).

This leads us to what are the central concerns of this book as a whole. It seeks, through a detailed study of a wide range of areas of public policy, to make an assessment of the impact of the Thatcher governments on British politics and policy. In doing this, it will provide discussion on issues such as the extent to which radical principles have been expressed in radical policies, the extent to which policy during the three Thatcher administrations has evolved in the direction of greater radicalism, and, with an eye to the future, the prospects of policy in each area as we move further into the 1990s.

The first three chapters of the book address issues which are both aspects and areas of policy in their own right, and features of public policy which are of major significance to many of the other areas of policy dealt with in later chapters: the nature of government under the Thatcher administrations (Chapter 1); economic policy and privatisation policy (Chapter 2); and enterprise policy (Chapter 3). On that basis, the following chapters then set out to outline and discuss policy in a range of discrete areas, which together constitute the full package of public policy under Thatcher.

1

Government During the Thatcher Years

ROB ATKINSON

Introduction

The election of a Conservative government in 1979 with Mrs Thatcher at its head meant that for the first time since 1945 Britain had a government which seriously questioned the post-war consensus. However, the arrival of a 'radical' government signalled not only changes in policy but also changes in the institutions/organisations which governed Britain. Mrs Thatcher, like many of her supporters, was strongly opposed to the growth of government which had taken place during the thirty years preceding her election.

Indeed, she and her supporters may be described as 'anti-statist', believing that the state's role should be reduced to a minimum and that *a priori* the private sector was a more efficient and effective provider of goods and services. This superiority derived directly from the market which was seen as the most efficient allocator of resources and provider of goods and services. As a result the public sector was seen as inherently wasteful and inefficient, particularly when compared to the private sector (see Introduction; and Drucker *et al.*, 1988, ch. 1, for these arguments in greater detail). The solution was simple – return as many of the state's functions as possible to the market.

Not only was government seen as inefficient and wasteful, but Mrs Thatcher went so far as to hold the organs of government and those who staffed them at least partly responsible, if not directly culpable, for Britain's post-war decline. Thus there was a strong impetus to reform the government of Britain from the moment Mrs Thatcher became prime minister.

In those cases where the state could not be withdrawn then the government's task was to introduce management methods based upon those found in the private sector, emphasising in particular cost control and value for money. It will be the task of this chapter to assess the extent to which, and why, reform has actually taken place over the last ten years. Accordingly the chapter will be split into four sections:

1. Government at the centre, dealing with (a) The position of the prime minister; and (b) Whitehall and the civil service.
2. Government at the local level.
3. Non-traditional forms of government, e.g. Quasi-governmental Agencies (QGAs) and Quasi-autonomous Non-governmental Organisations (QUANGOs).
4. The implications of the European Community (EC).

Government at the Centre

The Position of the Prime Minister

Mrs Thatcher is perhaps the 'strongest' Prime Minister (PM) since Lloyd George and she is widely perceived as the driving force behind reforms since 1979. She is clearly not afraid to set, and maintain, the pace of reform, nor to dispense with the services of ministers whom she feels have outlived their usefulness or are not truly committed to radical change. As a result a great deal of attention has focussed on Mrs Thatcher's role, relationship with ministers and Parliament. Broadly speaking, it has been argued that Mrs Thatcher has: (1) undermined cabinet government and collective responsibility; (2) this has produced a form of prime ministerial government; and (3) established an 'electoral dictatorship' (*pace* Lord Hailsham). These then are the major issues with which this sub-section will concern itself.

On the issues of prime ministerial government or Cabinet government the argument begins from the proposition that Mrs Thatcher dominates her Cabinet to such an extent that it no longer acts as the key decision-making body in government, but more as a rubber stamp for decisions taken elsewhere.

Constitutionally speaking the relationship between the PM and the rest of the Cabinet is expressed by the phrase *primus inter pares* ('first among equals'). It is argued that Mrs Thatcher has subverted this relationship. However, the extent to which *primus inter pares* has *actually* been the case under previous PMs is questionable. To begin with the PM has always had the power to appoint or sack ministers. It is s/he who sets the Cabinet agenda and sums up at the end of discussions as well as possessing wide powers of patronage (e.g. to award honours or appoint individuals to key positions and committees of inquiry). The PM is also the elected leader of the party. Thus the PM has always been more than simply 'first among equals'.

In Mrs Thatcher's case the argument is not simply that she is dominant but that this dominance has been used to subvert Cabinet government and the doctrine of *collective responsibility*. The latter assumes that all key issues are discussed in Cabinet, that a majority view prevails and once a decision has been taken all members of the Cabinet support the decision in public. This raises the issue of Cabinet committees, which, constitutionally speaking, do not exist. It is argued that under Mrs Thatcher Cabinet meets less frequently than under any other post-war PM and that many key decisions are taken in committees (e.g. on the economy, the European Monetary System (EMS) etc.) dominated by Mrs Thatcher and/or those who agree with her. As a result it is contended that the majority of important decisions are taken before they ever reach Cabinet and ministers are prevented from fully and frankly expressing their views on policies to which they must be publicly committed.

Finally it is argued that Mrs Thatcher has been gathering around herself a number of advisers (e.g. on the economy, foreign affairs, etc.) and researchers who provide the PM with alternative policies on almost every issue. Thus rather than simply appointing ministers to departments and leaving them to get on with the job Mrs Thatcher is constantly intervening, attempting to impose her chosen preferences and publicly undermining those ministers who do not agree with her. In particular it has been argued that through 'unattributable' briefings by her personal press secretary, Bernard Ingham, she has publicly attacked and queried the policies of Cabinet colleagues, even going so far as to describe one minister as a 'semi-detached member of the government' shortly before sacking him.

Taken together do these charges amount to conclusive proof of the emergence of prime ministerial government? As already pointed out the PM is more than simply 'first among equals', s/he has powers which other ministers do not possess. Yet even these exclusive powers are circumscribed. The power to appoint or sack ministers cannot be used in a cavalier fashion. Sacking ministers on a regular basis not only leads to governmental instability, creating unease on the back benches and giving the opposition ammunition, it also questions the judgement of the person who first appointed them.

Appointments to Cabinet must also reflect and try to balance out the various political tendencies within the party; any PM considering consigning a Cabinet colleague to the back benches must also consider whether or not they are creating a focus for opposition within the party. In this instance it may be better to retain an opponent within the Cabinet but neutralise him/her by marginalising him/her. This is precisely what Mrs Thatcher did to Jim Prior when she moved him from Employment to Northern Ireland in 1981. Thus much will depend on the political skills of the PM, and on this criterion Mrs Thatcher appears to rank well above most of her Cabinet colleagues. However, the point is that the PM, and that includes Mrs Thatcher, is by no means free to act as s/he wishes regarding the appointment of ministers. Even after ten years as PM it would be difficult to call her Cabinet 'Thatcherite' in any meaningful sense.

Cabinet committees are not new nor is their use to bypass Cabinet entirely unheard of. During the 1974–79 Labour Administration the politically sensitive decision to modernise the guidance system of Britain's nuclear missile (Polaris) was taken by a small committee without the knowledge of the majority of Cabinet members. What is specific to Mrs Thatcher's period as PM is the charge that while Cabinet meets less frequently more committees, taking more decisions, have been set up. In this instance there would seem to be more substance to the charges, although a definitive view is not possible given the secrecy which surrounds such committees. In particular Mrs Thatcher appears to have placed herself and her supporters in certain key committees (e.g. on the economy) to ensure that the decisions she wants are reached. In this sense there does seem to be real grounds for questioning whether Cabinet government and collective responsibility truly exists (although it would be tempting to question whether it ever has really existed).

To turn to the question of advisers the point which needs to be made here is that once again Mrs Thatcher is not departing from the precedents set by her predecessors Harold Wilson and Jim Callaghan. Both, as did other PMs, appointed advisers, yet they were not accused of undermining Cabinet government. The question here is partly one of extent, and it would seem that Mrs Thatcher has more advisors than any previous PM. In a sense this may be seen as a good thing allowing the PM to exercise independent judgement, although Mrs Thatcher's use of advisers seems to reflect, at least in part, her distrust of civil servants. The problem is that the use of such advisers may actually undermine the position of ministers.

Perhaps the most notable example of this came to a climax in October 1989 when Nigel Lawson, the then Chancellor of the Exchequer, resigned as a result of a series of disagreements between himself and Mrs Thatcher's Economic Adviser, Sir Alan Walters, over economic policy in general and the question of Britain's entry into the

European Monetary System in particular. Mr Lawson was in favour of entry while Mrs Thatcher and her adviser opposed entry. Mr Lawson felt that Sir Alan was undermining his position, both in public and private, and demanded that Mrs Thatcher either sack her adviser or he would resign. Mrs Thatcher refused to do so, and Mr Lawson resigned, creating one of the most significant political crises of Mrs Thatcher's premiership. Many commentators felt that this reflected badly upon Mrs Thatcher's style of government and that the particular issue, entry into the EMS, had never been put before the Cabinet as a whole, yet ministers were expected not to express public views on the issue.

Generally speaking it would appear that Cabinet's importance as a key decision-making centre has declined since 1979. However, it would be wise to note that it is doubtful if the Cabinet has ever truly fulfilled this function or that collective responsibility has ever functioned in the manner constitutionally envisaged. Nor does the evidence cited prove that a form of prime ministerial government has been created and we certainly do not have a situation similar to the USA where the President has an army of advisers (for more detail see Jordan and Richardson, 1987, ch. 6).

It would be sensible to bear in mind Jones's (1985) point that one of the strengths of the prime ministership is its flexibility and that the power potentials inherent in the post require exercising, thus developments at any time reflect the strengths and weaknesses of the PM. In Mrs Thatcher's case she appears to stand head and shoulders above most of her colleagues and her determination to achieve radical change has led to the ruthless use of mechanisms, such as committees, unofficial press briefings, etc, to achieve those aims. The main point is that were Mrs Thatcher to be replaced tomorrow the changes she has made would not be permanent; subsequent developments would depend very much upon the individual occupying the position, the attitudes and attributes of his/her colleagues and the wider balance of political forces.

Finally, in this subsection I turn to the question of Mrs Thatcher's relationship with Parliament. Constitutionally it is assumed that Parliament, in particular the Commons, is the supreme policy-making body; however, once again constitutional conventions bear little relation to reality. With the rise of the modern party system and the development of party discipline it is doubtful if the Commons has ever acted as more than a scrutineer of legislation emerging from the executive. This is not to belittle Parliament's role, but simply to recognise that back bench influence works mainly through threatened revolts and via the party Whips conveying disquiet to the PM. In fact given the traditional loyalty of Conservative MPs and the size of the current government's majority the Whips have acted as an important transmission belt for back bench disquiet. This has often led the government to revise or drop contentious pieces of legislation. Somewhat ironically it has been the House of Lords which has most frequently frustrated the current government's policy wishes (see Drucker *et al.*, 1988, ch. 3 for more detail on these issues).

On the whole given the size of the current government's majority, the fact that Mrs Thatcher has won three consecutive elections, her forthright style of leadership and the disorganised state of the opposition parties it should come as no surprise that the Commons has on the whole operated largely as a rubber stamp. This has produced a situation which at times has come close to Lord Hailsham's definition of an 'elected dictatorship'. However, were the next election (in 1991/2) to produce a much reduced Conservative majority with a considerable number of Conservative marginals it is highly likely that at the very least back benchers would extract more concessions from the executive and possibly, in traditional Conservative style, dispatch a group of Tory 'grandees' to tell Mrs Thatcher to make way for a new and more flexible leader. Thus while noting the relative quiescence of Parliament during the 1980s, this should not be assumed to be a permanent state, nor should Parliament's role be underestimated.

Whitehall and the Civil Service

As already noted in the Introduction, Mrs Thatcher came to power believing that government was inherently inefficient and wasteful. In particular she saw civil servants as a privileged group largely concerned to preserve their own position – thus they needed to be 'deprivileged'. In addition the civil service was one of the few constants in government during the post-war era, therefore it was seen as a key part of the post-war consensus which Mrs Thatcher wished to overthrow and thus it was held at least partly responsible for Britain's decline. Given these factors it is hardly surprising that reforming the civil service has been high on Mrs Thatcher's list of priorities since 1979. However it should be noted that she was not the first PM to set out to do this, and her aims were similar to her predecessors (Harold Wilson and Ted Heath), i.e. to introduce greater managerial efficiency into the service (see Greenwood, 1989).

Unlike her predecessors Mrs Thatcher, perhaps having learned from their failures, did not initially set out to bring about wholesale reform from the top down. Instead she began a process of introducing new working procedures from inside departments which could then be generalised, gradually, throughout Whitehall, changing the culture of Whitehall from an administrative to a managerial one.

Her first step was to bring in Sir Derek Rayner from Marks and Spencer, set up an Efficiency Unit with Sir Derek at its head reporting directly to her and, perhaps most importantly, threw her full political weight behind him. Sir Derek and his team's task was to promote efficiency and eliminate waste in Whitehall departments by carrying out Scrutinies (known as Rayner Scrutinies) of particular activities in departments. The Scrutinies were carried out over a 90-day period by members of the department under investigation, the reports were produced quickly and some were even presented to the PM. It has been estimated that between 1979 and 1983 these exercises identified potential savings of £421m a year (Fry 1987). The Scrutinies are an on-going process intended to make ministers and civil servants more cost conscious.

Two other programmes have also emerged: MINNIS (Management Information Systems for Ministers) and FMI (Financial Management Initiative). MINNIS reputedly had its origins in Michael Heseltine's period of office at the Department of the Environment and was designed to provide information for ministers about what was happening in their department and thus provide the information necessary for decision-making. FMI was designed to given managers more power to manage and to emphasise the importance of management over the senior civil servants' more traditional, and highly valued, role as policy advisers to ministers. Like earlier attempts at reform this was designed to introduce greater cost consciousness; however, what was unique about this initiative was its attempt to devolve financial management as far down line management as possible, essentially to middle managers. These individuals then became 'budget-holders' responsible for the use of funds (see Fry, 1987; Jones, 1989, for more detail).

Through these initiatives it was hoped gradually to bring about a change in civil servants' attitudes to costs, making them more aware of the cost implications of policies. While there is no doubt that these initiatives have been generalised throughout Whitehall their effects are more contentious. In some cases it has been argued that Rayner Scrutinies have largely been steered into blind alleys and their results ignored (Ponting 1986, ch. 7; see Hennessey, 1989 for a different view). In the case of MINNIS the argument has been that much depends upon the attitude of ministers and senior civil servants; thus while every department has a variant of MINNIS its effectiveness and role are questionable. In some cases a system is in place for show purposes to demonstrate to Mrs Thatcher that an effort is being made (Ponting 1986). In the case of FMI it has been argued that the 'budget-holders' have little or no power over their key costs, such as salaries (Fry 1987), and thus can do little to control costs. Nor do many of the civil servants intended to be 'budget-holders' have the necessary training to carry out this function. As such, the impact of FMI is unlikely to be as great as was initially hoped. Moves have also been made to reinforce these changes by altering personnel within the service. In particular this has operated through Mrs Thatcher taking an active role in the appointment of senior civil servants. However, this does not necessarily mean a politicisation of the civil service. Rather than ask 'is he one of us' Mrs Thatcher seems more concerned with whether or not people are 'doers', i.e. individuals who can be relied upon actively to pursue policies and concern themselves within issues of efficiency and effectiveness. A further development has been the, limited, recruitment of individuals from the private sector on fixed term contracts, often at salaries higher than the service norm. However, the effects of this are as yet marginal on overall recruitment and staffing policy. Indeed Mr Kinnock has intimated that should he become prime minister he would have no difficulty working with the individuals appointed since 1979.

The other major elements of 'staff policy' have been the reduction of numbers and reform conditions of service. By 1988 Mrs Thatcher hoped that there would have been a cut from the 1979 figure of 732,000 to 593,000, yet, as Fry (1987 and in Drucker *et al.*, 1988: ch. 4) points out, these cuts have mainly affected the highest and lowest grades and industrial civil servants. The great mass of civil servants have not been affected and future reductions seem likely to be achieved via further cuts in industrial civil servants.

Nor has any major progress been made in the area of conditions of service; civil servants still retain their pension rights and index linked pensions. Attempts to hold down wages have led to strikes and a generally antagonistic relationship between workforce and employer, culminating in the government's unilateral decision to withdraw trade union rights at GCHQ in Cheltenham. As a result of these developments service morale has declined.

Taken together have the various initiatives described above fundamentally altered the civil service's and Whitehall's working methods and culture? Opinions are divided on the degree of success achieved (see for instance Fry, 1987; Hennessy, 1989, ch. 15; Ponting, 1986, ch. 7; Jones, 1989), for while civil servants have reacted more favourably to these initiatives than to previous reforms the hostility produced by Mrs Thatcher's antipathy towards the civil service may well have nullified any gains. Additionally, fundamental change would seem unlikely while Whitehall remains in its current state and the civil service continues as a unified body with national pay negotiations, promotion regulations, etc. which effectively curtail managers' freedom of action and control over costs. It should, however, be noted that most of the above has largely been concerned with altering processes while radical change also involves the changing of structures (see Jones, 1989).

Indeed the publication of the Ibbs Report in 1988 (Jenkins *et al.*, 1988) may indicate the limits to 'process change' and that the PM and her advisers are well aware of the need to reform both processes and structures if truly radical change is to be achieved. Ibbs represents an implicit acknowledgement that Raynerism, FMI, MINNIS, etc. can bring about only partial, relatively small scale, changes. If change is to be truly radical much more wide-ranging reforms are necessary.

The Ibbs Report acknowledges that the ethos which dominates the civil service, particularly its senior levels, is that of policy adviser while management skills come a poor second. Thus most attention is placed on the advisory function rather than the service delivery function. In order to breakdown this division the Report advocates splitting up the functions of policy advice and service delivery/management. In essence this is to be achieved by 'hiving-off' the service delivery function into 'independent' agencies while the senior civil servants remain attached to ministerial departments. Thus the vast majority of civil servants would be transferred into agencies whose managers would have, within budget limits, total control over wages, conditions of service, staff levels, etc. and where management issues would predominate. If Ibbs were to be implemented it would, at a stroke, break up the unified civil service and Whitehall.

How successful has Ibbs been? By July 1989 only eight agencies had been created. Why has this been the case? Firstly, the Treasury, perhaps the most powerful of departments, has been unwilling to see its control over costs reduced. Secondly, agencies create real problems for the doctrine of ministerial responsibility, leaving ministers 'responsible' for agencies yet with little control over their activities (see Jones, 1989). As such these are powerful impediments to the hiving-off of other than peripheral, largely self-contained and uncontentious areas of work. Furthermore a contentious division between policy-making and policy implementation underlies the Report; whether this distinction is workable is open to dispute (for views on how a version of Ibbs might work see Hencke, 1988; Ponting, 1989).

To sum up, while changes have taken place since 1979 they do not add up to radical change, as Fry (1987) has argued, 'the old "Civil Service" recognizably survives'.

Government at the Local Level

In 1979 the then Secretary of State for Environment, Michael Heseltine, declared his intention to reduce central controls on local government, leaving locally elected councillors to decide on policy. In fact, exactly the opposite has happened. Since 1979 the financial control which the centre exercises over local government has greatly increased (via reforms of the Rate Support Grant, rate-capping, the Community Charge and the Unified Business Rate), thus considerably limiting the decision-making powers of local authorities (see chapter 12 below; Stoker 1988, ch. 7; Drucker *et al.*, 1988, ch. 5).

This increase in financial control is only part of the story; central government has increasingly intervened directly to force local authorities to pursue particular courses of action. What should be remembered is that during the post-war era the vast majority of legislation emerging from Parliament giving local government powers and responsibilities has been 'permissive'. Such legislation rarely lays down clearly defined standards, leaving authorities with a great deal of room for manoeuvre and discretion over how they actually carry out their duties. However, legislation such as the Housing Act, 1980, left authorities with no choice other than to sell council houses and the Local Government Act 1988 forced the 'contracting-out' of particular services (see Stoker, 1988, ch. 8). There has thus been a reduction in the independent decision-making powers of locally elected councillors.

In some areas local discretion was further eroded by the abolition of the Greater London Council (GLC) and the Metropolitan County Councils (MCCs) in 1986. The government's declared aim was to save money and devolve powers and responsibilities from these upper tier authorities to the lower tier London Boroughs and Metropolitan Districts. In reality it is questionable if any money has been saved and up to 70 per cent of the services (in cost terms) have not been devolved to the lower tier. These services (such as fire, police, transport) are administered by Joint Boards, indirectly elected bodies often chaired by government appointees (often referred to as QUELGOs, see p. 18), with budgets, during their first three years of existence, subject to central control. Once again the decision-making power of localities has been limited.

Some authorities have had their powers further undermined by the setting up of a large number of organisations such as Urban Development Corporations (UDCs), Enterprise Zones (EZs) and Housing Action Trusts (HATs) which, to varying extents, replace local government within specified areas. UDCs, EZs and HATs are examples of QUANGOs (see pp. 18–19) which effectively by-pass local authorities and electorates, and provide government with a way of pursuing particular policies regardless of local wishes, London Docklands is perhaps the best example of such a development (see Drucker *et al.*, 1988, ch. 5; Stoker, 1988, ch. 8 for more detail).

Without wishing to give the impression that local government is about to disappear the various developments outlined above add up to

a considerable diminution of local government's powers and discretion in decision-making (though authorities have not taken this lying down, see Stoker, 1988, ch. 9). This is surely a strange turn of events when compared to the 1979 declaration by Michael Heseltine referred to at the start of the section. Why has this come about? Essentially there are three reasons.

First, central government believed the control and reduction of public expenditure was vital to its economic strategy and local authorities, particularly Labour ones, were seen as wasteful. Thus greater control over finance was required.

Second, Mrs Thatcher has been unwilling to tolerate challenges to her authority and the GLC in particular was prepared to flaunt that authority on a regular basis. It is arguable that between 1981 and 1983 when the parliamentary Labour opposition was in total disarray Labour controlled authorities such as the GLC constituted the effective opposition in the country. As such this could not be tolerated so a body which Sir Keith Joseph had set up in 1963 was abolished as were the MCCs, bodies set up by a Conservative government of which Mrs Thatcher was a part.

Third, following on from the above, UDCs, EZs and HATs provide an effective means of by-passing local authorities and electorates. It is hoped that businesses will then be allowed to flourish without interference from local government.

Non-traditional forms of Government

In this section the focus will be on bodies such as Quasi-governmental Agencies (QGAs), Quasi-autonomous Non-governmental Agencies (QUANGOs) and Quasi-elected Local Government Organisations (QUELGOs), some of which have already been referred to above.

First of all we need briefly to define the nature of such organisations. This is a contentions area, however, generally speaking, this chapter will follow the definitions offered by Dunleavy and Rhodes (in Drucker *et al.*, 1988, ch. 5). QGAs are usually national level organisations, concerned with a particular issue, funded in part by government and having an 'arm's length' relationship with parliament – public corporations and the Arts Council are good examples. QUANGOS are part of the public sector and are funded in part by government, but are not subject to direct central or local government control and are left very much to run themselves. UDCs and the National Rivers Authority are good examples of QUANGOs. Finally, QUELGOs are bodies which usually cover more than one local authority, have only a limited number of places and election to them is indirect. The Joint Boards referred to on p. 17 are examples of such bodies. There are thus literally hundreds of these bodies.

When elected in 1979 Mrs Thatcher expressed considerable hostility towards these forms of organisation, seeing them as products of a past which she wished to repudiate, part of Britain's problem. Thus their numbers were to be slashed. Initially there was a 'QUANGO cull' carried out by a Treasury official. However since then a whole range of these organisations have been set up, e.g. UDCs, HATs, Joint Boards, the Office of Electricity Regulation, and spending on them has increased greatly. The exact increase in cost varies depending upon which category of organisations one looks at. One report in the *Guardian* (28 August 1989) suggested that between 1979 and 1988 spending on QUANGOs rose from £2,970m to £5,930m while a wider definition stated that spending rose from £6,150m in 1979 to £9,100m in 1987 (Greenwood and Wilson, 1989, Table 11.1, p. 219). Whichever definition is adopted it is clear there has been no overall reduction in such organisations and that there has actually been an increase in their numbers which has frequently led to the displacement of locally elected bodies.

Why has this occurred? First, it should be noted that these organisations can focus their attention on a particular issue (e.g. UDCs and the economic regeneration of rundown urban areas). Second, by giving tasks to such organisations the centre can effectively 'wash its hands of' responsibility for them, e.g. the Commission for Racial Equality and race policy. Third, they provide a way of by-passing troublesome local authorities, e.g. UDCs and HATs. Fourth, decision-makers within these organisations are at best only indirectly accountable to Parliament or local authorities, thus providing them with a virtual free hand to pursue the 'policy brief' given them by the centre.

Given these facts, it seems likely that these non-traditional forms of government will continue to grow, further reducing the control which those elected to public office and those who elected then have over significant areas of public life.

Extra-national Forms of Government

This section will be concerned with the European Community (EC) and the implications of Britain's membership of that body. However, it should be borne in mind that many other international organisations affect policy in the UK, in particular on economy policy organisations such as the World Bank, the International Monetary Fund (IMF) and the Group of Seven (Go7), exercise a considerable and pervasive influence.

On 1 June 1973 Britain officially became a member of the EC; the process of entry and continued membership has been a source of constant controversy, with politicians from both sides of the political divide (e.g. Tony Benn and Enoch Powell) arguing for withdrawal because membership represented a loss of sovereignty for Britain in general and Parliament in particular. However, since the referendum of 1975 withdrawal has not been a serious option and most debate has concerned the degree to which Britain should become integrated with the EC. In policy terms the essential issue has been to what extent decision-making powers have inexorably drifted away from Parliament and Whitehall to the European Parliament and in particular to bodies such as the European Commission (Brussels bureaucrats) (see Nugent, 1989 and Daltrop 1982, Part II for more detail).

Initially Mrs Thatcher was preoccupied with the high level of contributions Britain was making to the Community budget, but with that problem's resolution the focus has been on issues referred to in the previous paragraph. The situation began to come to head in 1986 with the signing of the Single European Act (SEA); this effectively legalised EC's ability to intervene in a wide range of areas affecting environmental, economic and social policy. Thus the EC has the power, for instance, to set water purity standards which could have serious implications for the privatisation of the water industry, to prevent British governments paying subsidies to industries in financial difficulties for other than restructuring purposes, to set health and safety standards in the workplaces, etc.

However, it would be wrong to give the impression that directives simply emerge from Brussels which are then forced upon national assemblies. In practice, Community Laws provide a great deal of discretion for their interpretation and adaptation to particular national conditions and provide lengthy time periods for their adoption and implementation. So, while in the long term legislation will have to be accepted, the time scale over which this takes place is often considerable.

More recently the agreement to create a Single European Market in 1992 has given these issues a new and intensified lease of life. While fully supporting the creation of a single market Mrs Thatcher seems unwilling to accept some of the other developments which have preceded or are accompanying it. From her perspective what she perceives is an ever growing state bureaucracy and socialism being reintroduced by the 'back door'.

The European Monetary System (EMS), which has been in existence for several years, and is designed to provide a stable framework within which community currencies can operate has created serious problems for Mrs Thatcher. She has adopted a rather 'arm's length' attitude towards the EMS, initially refusing to join and more recently agreeing to do so only at some unspecified date in the future. For Mrs Thatcher the issues at stake are vital as she sees membership of the EMS as the first step towards the creation of a common EC currency and the setting up of a Central European Bank. Such developments would severely restrict the ability of British governments to pursue an independent economic policy and would probably also have implications for decisions on public expenditure.

For Mrs Thatcher, and many others, this would mean the establishment of a highly centralised European State which would mark the beginning of the end for national sovereignty. In a speech given at Bruges in September 1988 she firmly set her face against such a development. The great danger inherent in this attitude is that with the wider introduction of majority voting in 1986 the other eleven members of the EC will press ahead setting the agenda and creating the policy framework which Britain will find itself forced to join at a later date on unfavourable terms, much as happened when the EC was established in 1957. Thus the dilemma is whether or not to remain outside and preserve 'national independence' or to join and try to influence the formation of the institutions which develop.

Another key issue which has emerged concomitantly with that of a single European Market is that of the Social Charter. The Charter assumes that the creation of a single market should be accompanied by the setting up of Community wide workers' rights to strike, health and safety regulations, minimum wage levels, etc. For Mrs Thatcher this represents a pernicious attempt to 'introduce socialism by the back door' after she has done so much to remove it. The fact that the TUC and Labour Party have firmly embraced the Charter (and reversed their long standing hostility to the EC) is, for her, additional evidence of its 'socialist' nature.

It is undoubtedly true that even without a common currency, a Central European Bank and the Social Charter Britain has already ceded key elements of its independence to EC institutions (see Nugent, 1989). Whether or not this is something to be regretted remains a matter of judgement, although it should be borne in mind that Britain's much vaunted independence was shown to be an illusion as long ago as 1956 when Britain was forced into a humiliating withdrawal from Suez by the USA. Given the weakness of Britain's economy, perhaps membership of a 'United States of Europe' represents our only long-term opportunity to retain a seat, however peripheral, at the 'top table'.

Conclusion

At the end of each section I have tried to pull together conclusions, thus only a brief overall review will be attempted here. How great have the changes in government been since 1979? As the first section illustrated Mrs Thatcher has tried radically to restructure central government, yet to date the judgement must be 'has tried hard but still has a long way to go before anything lasting is achieved'. In the case of local government its scope, discretion and responsibilities have been reduced, yet it has not disappeared and local government still retains the ability to pursue its own chosen courses of action and to frustrate (even thwart) central government. The resort to an increased use of non-traditional forms of government perhaps proves the point that fundamental changes have not yet been brought about at either central or local government. In fact I would go as far as to argue that were Mrs Thatcher to leave office tomorrow many of the reforms she has pioneered would not survive her. In the long run it is membership of the EC which will bring about the greatest and most long-lasting changes in British government and decision-making.

2

Economic Policy and Privatisation

MIKE DUNN and SANDY SMITH

The 1970s in Britain were marked by an important change in the priorities of government economic policy, and by a growing disillusion with the Keynesian approach on which much of postwar policy had been based. Increasing importance was attached to the problem of controlling inflation rather than holding down unemployment, and Keynesian policies were increasingly perceived to be ineffective. The product of this disillusionment was the 'monetarist revolution' and a new economic approach in the 1980s that came to be known as Thatcherism. This chapter analyses the economic conditions that gave rise to Thatcherism, how this approach developed and changed in the 1980s, and why privatisation became a dominant feature.

The Keynesian Approach

The Keynesian approach had emphasised the role of spending (aggregate demand for goods and services) in determining the level of economic activity. By regulating the level of spending, governments controlled the level of unemployment and the rate of inflation; and by maintaining a steady increase in spending, the government stimulated increases in productivity and in standards of living. Furthermore, the theory suggested that, while the supply of money had some influence, the most effective way of regulating spending was by adjusting the relationship between government spending and government revenues – that is, by means of fiscal (budgetary) policy. Thus government spending, employment and rising standards of living were seen to be closely interconnected.

This view of the important role of fiscal policy complemented a radically different view of the role of the government brought about by the experience of the 1930s' depression and of planning during the second world war. In the period after 1945, there was a consensus that the government ought to be the main agency providing certain goods and services. Not only did this include the development of a 'welfare state', with the provision of payments for the old, the sick, the disabled and the unemployed through government-backed insurance schemes, but also a much extended role in the provision of certain market goods and services. The essential arguments for government provision were, and remain, threefold:

- *merit goods*: to prevent the underprovision of certain goods and services, especially where consumers are not the best judges of their own welfare or where information flows to them are imperfect. Here the government takes a paternalistic and normative position. Examples of this are particularly in the provision of health and education services.
- *public goods*: where provision by the private sector may be sub-orbital, especially where provision is 'non-rival' and 'non-excludable'. Examples of this include defence and law and order activities.
- *natural monopoly*: where the costs of provision are lower with one single provider than with more than one. Here, even allowing for the potential benefits of competition in encouraging efficiency, the monopoly provider is potentially more efficient, due primarily to economies of scale. Examples of this might include water supply, electricity transmission (but not necessarily generation), and some areas of transport.

It was generally considered that the government provision of 'merit' and 'public' goods was best financed from taxation. With 'natural monopolies' the solution typically adopted was nationalisation under a government corporation, financed by revenue from sales and subsidies from the government. The main political argument was over whether state ownership should be extended also into other commercial activities that were not necessarily monopolistic (road haulage, steel, shipbuilding, etc.), and the extent to which the government should intervene to manage the restructuring of important industries as economic conditions changed.

During the twenty years after 1945, the Keynesian policy of demand management based on fiscal policy appeared to work tolerably well. Throughout this period, the value of the £ sterling was tied to that of the US $ at a fixed exchange rate, and the US government pursued very conservative policies with respect to regulating spending in their domestic economy. As a result, the main constraint facing successive British governments was that if they allowed spending to increase too rapidly, more imports were 'sucked in' as demand rose, causing a deficit in the external Balance of Trade. In order to maintain the exchange rate, governments were then forced to dampen down spending, hence slowing down growth (the 'stop-go' problem). Consequently, 'excess' demand tended to show itself in the form of a weakening £ sterling exchange rate, rather than as inflation. Hence, for twenty years the British economy managed to combine low levels of unemployment with low inflation. However, these went alongside constrained economic growth compared to other countries, due to a persistent tendency towards a Balance of Trade deficit, reflecting the declining relative competitiveness of British industry and the consequently increasing propensity to import other nations' outputs. This was largely attributed to a lack of investment in the non-defence sector of the economy hand to poor industrial relations.

Growing Disillusionment

During the 1960s and the 1970s, inflation throughout the world economy began to accelerate. Many governments, including that of Britain, found that increased spending tended to feed through in the form of higher prices, rather than increased output (or, in the case of Britain, increased imports). The key to this seemed to be the effects of increased spending on money wages. In a market economy, companies will increase output and employ more workers only if it is profitable so to do – that is, if the value of what the additional workers will produce exceeds the cost of employing them. This value depends upon the amount they produce (i.e. their productivity) and the prices received for outputs. The cost of employing workers depends on the level of money wages and the level of employment taxes (such as National Insurance contributions). If the result of an increase in spending is that money wages rise faster than productivity (so that the labour costs per unit of output rise), then the effect is rising prices (that is, inflation); if the result is that productivity rises faster than money wages, then the effect is rising output and employment.

Until the end of the 1960s, the rate at which money wages increased was closely related to the level of unemployment. Consequently, when unemployment was relatively high, increased spending resulted in higher output and employment. But when unemployment was relatively low the outcome was inflation. This relationship seemed to break down in the late 1960s and into the 1970s, when rising unemployment seemed to have less and less effect on the rate of increase of money wages and prices.

Keynesians argued that the main reason for this was that, as a result of the long postwar boom, there had been a fundamental change in the way that the economic system functioned. This was due to the emergence of large companies, with the power to control prices, and of powerful trade unions with the power to control how work was organised and the money wages paid. Prices were no longer established on the simple basis of supply and demand. As levels of spending changed, companies would tend to adjust output, rather than prices: a fall in the level of spending resulted in lower output and employment, rather than reduced prices. At the same time, the emergence of powerful trade unions had made money wages less responsive to changing conditions in the labour market. Rather, money wages were determined on the basis of the 'going rate' for other workers, which in turn was largely determined by the observed rate of inflation and expectations of rising standards of living, unrelated to levels of productivity achieved. High rates of unemployment had only a small effect on money wages.

The consequences of these twin effects was, according to the Keynesians, that the economic system now had a built-in 'inflationary bias'. If, for whatever reason, costs increased in one sector of the economy, the companies affected had sufficient market power to pass these on in the form of higher prices, thereby raising other peoples costs and prices. As prices rose, trade unions would demand higher money wages, thereby further increasing costs and prices. Thus an inflationary spiral would set in, and this could happen almost irrespective of the levels of spending and unemployment. Government attempts to control this by reducing spending might succeed, but only if it was prepared to raise unemployment to levels that seemed socially and politically unacceptable. Moreover, such a policy could succeed only if the level of spending and economic activity was maintained at persistently depressed levels. According to Keynesians therefore, the appropriate policy for controlling inflation was to impose controls over money wages and prices, by means of some form of prices and incomes policy.

However, government attempts to introduce such policies proved largely ineffective and, particularly in Britain, led to confrontations between successive governments and a trade union movement that was increasingly perceived as being over-powerful, particularly in 1978–79 ('the winter of discontent'). Indeed, some held the movement responsible for Britain's relative economic decline because, by imposing various restrictive practices, it reduced productivity and the competitiveness of British industry in international markets. This in turn reduced profits and discouraged investment.

This growing disillusionment with economic policy was heightened by a further perceived consequence of the Keynesian approach, namely that although the government appeared to be too weak with respect to the trade unions, in other respects it had become too dominant. Rising inflation and the social problems associated with it had led to rising government spending. This in turn had resulted in relatively high levels of taxation. Workers with incomes below the level of benefits paid to the unemployed were having to pay income tax, creating a 'poverty trap' where there was no incentive to work harder (and some incentives to work less hard). At the same time, rates of taxation on high incomes had reached levels which gave rise to a huge 'tax avoidance' industry, and which many felt was acting as a disincentive to top businessmen and entrepreneurs. The limits of taxable capacity had been reached. As J. K. Galbraith put it, Britain had reached the unenviable position of needing to encourage people to work harder and increase productivity , but seeing itself as able to do so only by *reducing* the incomes of the less well-off whilst *increasing* those of the better-off. As a consequence of all this, increased government spending was increasingly financed by increased government borrowing. This tended to force up interest rates, and to 'crowd-out' investment by the private sector or, to the extent that it was financed by selling government bonds to the commercial banks, to cause a rapid increase in the money supply.

The view that the government had become too dominant was reinforced by a growing perception that nationalised industries, and the public sector generally, were inefficient in terms of controlling costs, in meeting public demand and in labour relations. Throughout the 1960s and the 1970s successive governments had struggled with defining the objectives and constraints of the nationalised industries; the general direction was towards a more 'commercial' approach, especially in pricing, but this had proved impossible to define satisfactorily. The root cause of the problem, it was argued, lay in the form of ownership itself. With their 'bottomless pit' of public funding, these public sector enterprises could never go bankrupt, so that there were few incentives for managers to be efficient, responsive to demand and competitive and there were plenty of opportunities for the public sector unions to manipulate restrictive practices and seek high wage settlements. For as long as these industries lacked the discipline of market competition, and the need to convince the capital markets to supply them with funds, then they would remain a drain on the public purse and one of the main causes of the country's economic problems. This contributed to a perception that the government sector reduced welfare, and that higher standards of living could be achieved by 'freeing the private sector'.

The Monetarist Challenge

From this disillusionment arose a widespread acceptance of 'monetarism' and the so-called 'Thatcher revolution'. In the aftermath of the 'winter of discontent' in 1979, the new Thatcher government took office with three basic economic objectives, which they perceived to be complementary: to reduce inflation, to curb the power of trade unions (see Chapter 4), and to reduce the economic role of the government. That these were seen as complementary reflected the Monetarist approach they adopted, an approach most closely associated with the American economist Milton Friedman.

The essential basis of this approach was that the level of spending depended upon the amount of money in circulation (the money supply) and on the extent to which people wanted to hold their wealth in the form of money (cash and bank deposits) as opposed to property, goods or income-yielding financial assets. Due to the rapid development of the financial system, it had become very easy to convert money (bank deposits) into income-yielding financial assets and back again into money. Consequently, the amount of money people wanted to hold was mainly determined by the level of their income and spending. If therefore the government reduced the money supply, people found they were holding less money than they would like to and consequently they reduced their spending. Thus, by controlling the rate of growth of the money supply, the government could control the rate of growth of spending.

The Monetarists further argued that increased costs could cause accelerating inflation only if there was a corresponding increase in spending. If costs and prices rise faster than spending, this would cause falling sales and increased unemployment. By controlling the money supply and thus spending, the government could hence control inflation. Whether or not this caused unemployment was something that the government could not control directly, because this depended on decisions taken by companies and workers (trade unions). Succinctly, governments were responsible for inflation: trade unions and monopolistic firms caused unemployment.

The proposition that controlling inflation depended on controlling the money supply was complemented by the Monetarist view of the effects of 'excessive' levels of government spending and taxation. Money takes the form of cash and deposits with commercial banks: bank deposits are largely created by people (and companies) borrowing from banks, so that the growth of the money supply depends on the extent to which people want to borrow from banks, and on the banks' ability to make such loans. In turn the banks ability to lend depends on the quantity of assets that the banks hold to 'back' these loans. These assets consist largely of government bonds, which are sold to finance the government's 'borrowing requirement' (the difference between government spending and government income, normally called the Public Sector Borrowing Requirement or PSBR). Thus, the government could try to control the growth of the money supply in two ways: by raising interest rates to reduce the demand for bank loans, or by reducing the banks' ability to extend loans by reducing the government's borrowing requirement. For most Monetarists, the optimal way to control the money supply was to reduce government borrowing by cutting government spending.

The Thatcher Revolution

These Monetarist ideas were central to the Thatcher governments economic policy when it took office in 1979. The primary economic objective was (and remained throughout the 1980s) to bring inflation under control. This they believed could be done only by reducing the rate of growth of spending by controlling the money supply. This meant reducing the public sector borrowing requirement (PSBR). The government accepted that a short-term cost of bringing spending under control was that, as markets adjusted, there would be a transitional increase in unemployment. But it believed that the more quickly people (firms and trade unions) adjusted to lower rates of growth of spending, the smaller would be the increase in unemployment during the transition to price stability – and the more quickly would markets adjust to eliminate this transitional unemployment. Since the speed with which markets adjusted depended on the effectiveness of market incentives, and since high rates of taxation (particularly on incomes) reduced the effectiveness of these incentives, then the reduction of the borrowing requirement meant reducing government spending and taxation.

This approach gave rise to the Medium Term Financial Strategy (MTFS), which linked targets for the growth of the money supply to targets for government borrowing which were consistent with monetary targets. The criterion for determining government spending became not (as had been the case in the 1950s and 1960s) 'What effect will the particular level of spending have on output, employment and the balance of trade?', but rather 'How can we finance government spending?'. The government imposed 'cash limits' on the budgets of the main spending departments, and sought to impose tight controls on spending by local government and investment by nationalised industries, since borrowing by these were included in the borrowing requirement targets. Finally, in order to reduce central government spending, it substantially increased the charges for public services and prices set by the commercially-based government corporations.

Despite its rhetoric, between 1979 and 1982 the government found itself unable to reduce either the rate of growth of the money supply (mainly because it proved in practice to be too difficult to define usefully, to predict or to stabilise), or indeed to control the overall level of government spending. However, despite this the rate of inflation did fall dramatically, from 21.9 per cent p.a. in 1980 to 3.7 per cent p.a. just before the 1983 Election. This led to a gradual reappraisal of the entire approach to economic policy.

One problem was that the rapid expansion of credit availability within the expanding and innovatory banking system made the whole concept of controlling 'money' supplies very difficult, and by 1985 the government decided it could not really tell what was happening to the money supply anyway. More significantly, although the government consistently failed to bring the rate of growth of the money supply within its target range, its attempts to do so caused a large increase in interest rates, which in turn attracted funds from abroad. Consequently the exchange rate of sterling rose, despite rapidly rising domestic costs and prices. This inflow of funds was reinforced by a rapid rise in oil exports based on the North Sea oil boom, and by the fact that foreign investors were impressed by the government's policy approach and by its firm resolve to 'be tough' by sticking to its principles even though unemployment had doubled. The rising exchange rate increased the price competitiveness of foreign imports into Britain, and reduced the competitiveness of British-produced exports in overseas markets. The effect on manufacturing industry was devastating, coming as it did on top of a deep-rooted neglect of investment requirements for innovation in many sectors: the number of manufacturing jobs fell by almost a quarter between 1979 and 1983, and 'de-industrialisation' became a political as well as an economic issue. The effect of this shake-out on less efficient firms, and of the heavy cuts in the labour force, was to produce a large rise in productivity, together with a notable weakening of trade union power, especially as the severest effects were felt in those sectors where union membership was traditionally high.

However, the steep rise in unemployment undermined the government's attempts to control its expenditure. Overall government spending barely changed over the period 1979–83, although there was a change in its composition. Cuts in areas like education, housing and the Civil Service were largely offset by increased spending on defence, 'law and order', and especially on social security (mainly because of the increased levels of unemployment). Moreover, the quality of government services declined significantly because of the combined effects of the 'cash limits' on spending and the fact that trade unions in the public sector remained relatively powerful. The high exchange rate most directly affected those sectors of the economy exposed to foreign competition – that is, primarily the manufacturing sector. Employment in the public sector (with the notable exceptions of steel and ship-building) was maintained, so that to hold spending within cash limits, it was necessary to reduce the 'quality of provision' and investment in public services, and to increase substantially the charges made for services. Consequently, the government became increasingly concerned to find ways to deliver public services more cheaply and more effectively. This involved especially a search for ways of transferring government activities to the private sector through subcontracting ('contracting-out') and denationalisation. This was seen as a way of imposing the 'discipline of the market' on workers which the government itself was unable to impose without becoming embroiled in politically damaging confrontations. Moreover, this seemed a relatively painless way of reducing government spending and borrowing. Thus privatisation became increasingly important among government policy objectives.

Changing Emphasis

The increasing emphasis on privatisation complemented another significant change in overall policy. The original Monetarist position which had been adopted was that inflation was caused by the direct effect of excessive increases in the money supply on the level of spending. A variation of this view was that if the money supply in one country is growing faster than in other countries, this 'excess' money will flow out through the foreign exchange markets, causing the exchange rate to fall. This in turn causes the price of imports to rise, which then causes prices generally and money wages to rise. Thus, it was the effect of changes in the money supply on the exchange rate that determined what happened to inflation.

This version seemed to provide a more convincing explanation of what had happened in Thatcherite Britain between 1979 and 1983 than did the original Monetarist approach. Moreover, with the widespread acceptance of Monetarist thinking within the international financial community from the late 1970s onwards, it became a self-fulfilling proposition. Since international financiers believed that excessive increases in the money supply caused inflation, if 'market sentiment' held that the growth in the money supply *was* indeed 'excessive', then foreign and domestic investors would transfer funds abroad. This would cause the exchange rate to fall and the price of imports (and hence prices generally) to rise accordingly. Furthermore, because of this outflow of capital, the flow of funds into domestic money markets would fall, causing interest rates to rise. This approach implied that the key to controlling inflation lay in maintaining the exchange rate, and this depended on pursuing policies that encouraged an appropriate flow of funds across the foreign exchanges. This marked a significant change from the original Monetarist position of 1979.

By 1985, the government's policy was no longer based on targets for the rate of growth of the money supply, but on using interest rates to maintain a strong exchange rate. With this, import prices were held down, and companies competing with foreign producers were compelled to control costs, especially wage costs. However, to maintain the exchange rate, the government was compelled to maintain interest rates at relatively high levels (to persuade foreign and domestic investors to 'invest in Britain'). The key to maintaining the exchange rate and reducing interest rates was seen to be reducing government borrowing. In this respect, privatisation as means of reducing government spending and increasing government revenue again offered an attractive way of achieving economic objectives.

However the policy of controlling inflation by controlling the exchange rate led to problems in the period 1987–89 when rising spending and demand by the private sector, based on borrowing, led to a fall in unemployment and increased output. It also led to a rapid increase in imports, aggravated by the loss of the manufacturing capacity that had occurred during the 1979–83 period. But despite this, relatively high interest rates in the UK caused a significant net inflow of funds from abroad which put upward pressure on the exchange rate. Thus the rise in imports and the rapid increase in domestic spending suggested that interest rates were too low and should be raised, whilst simultaneously the strength of the £ sterling suggested that interest rates were too high and should be reduced. Chancellor Lawson opted to reduce interest rates. This created the buoyant economic conditions during the 1987 Election campaign, but in due course led over 1988–89 to rising inflation as a result of accelerated demand and spending, together with in 1989 the most massive Balance of Trade deficit ever encountered in the UK. Government economic policy seemed to have lost direction.

Supply-side Economics

Meanwhile, the increased emphasis on privatisation from 1984–5 onwards was reinforced by another consequence of basing economic policy on a strong exchange rate. As unemployment rose in the early 1980s, the rate at which money wages were rising fell by about a half, and the rate of increase fell significantly below the rate of increase of productivity, so that unit labour costs fell. However, once economic growth began to pick- up after the 'recession' of the early 1980s, the rate of increase of money wages stopped falling even though unemployment continued to increase (albeit at a slower rate than during 1980–82). More significantly, money wages began to increase faster than productivity so that, by the mid-1980s, unit labour costs in British manufacturing industry were again rising, whilst in other countries they were falling, leading to rising imports. The government hoped that, by maintaining the exchange rate, companies would be compelled to hold down costs to remain competitive. But as costs in Britain rose relative to those overseas, then the consequence was that as imports increased, unemployment remained at relatively high levels, and there was a relatively slow recovery of the British manufacturing base that had been decimated by the 1979–81 recession.

As the government saw it, workers were 'pricing themselves out of jobs'. Their view was that the key to increasing output and employment was to change, by appropriate 'supply-side' policies, the response of individuals and firms to changing conditions in the market.

When, in the mid-1980s, unemployment showed little sign of falling despite increasing economic activity, the Thatcher government shifted the emphasis of its policy towards improving the supply-side of the economy. Central to this approach was the belief that the role of the government should be largely limited to creating the conditions in which markets can function efficiently – and, to a very limited extent, dealing with the occasional undesirable outcomes of these processes. The overall supply-side strategy was summarised by Chancellor Lawson in 1989:

> Strong sustainable growth is achieved not through any artificial stimulus, but by allowing markets to work again and restoring the enterprise culture; by removing unnecessary restrictions and controls and rolling back the frontiers of the state; by reforming trade union law and promoting all forms of capital ownership; and by reforming and reducing taxation (Budget Speech; 20 March, 1989).

The process of 'rolling back the frontiers of the state' had moreover a forceful ideological basis. The electoral success of 1983 had seemed to confirm widespread popular support for the view that Keynesian welfarism had resulted in the over-extension of the state and hence the violation of individual freedoms and particularly the freedom to exercise undistorted 'choice', a word which came to dominate government economic thinking. Where previous governments, especially Labour, had sought to develop various forms of positive industrial strategy, Thatcherism had no specific strategy except a trust in the efficacy of market forces.

There were two main aspects of the supply-side approach: first to improve the way the labour market functioned by improving incentives to work and reducing any 'distortions' which prevented the labour market from working efficiently, and second to make markets for goods and services function more efficiently, through privatisation in the broadest sense.

Privatisation

From 1983 onwards, privatisation developed to become the corner-stone of the Governments emerging emphasis on improving the supply side of the economy. Simultaneously it extended from tentative beginnings to become the main tactic of a political strategy aimed at reversing the post-1945 growth of 'collectivism' in general and socialism in particular.

The broad privatisation policy has involved three main areas:

1. 'de-nationalisation – by the sale of publically owned assets and equity (shares) to the private sector, e.g. British Rail hotels, British Telecom, British Gas.
2. 'contracting-out' subcontracting the provision of government financed goods and services to private contractors, e.g. refuse collection, hospital cleaning.
3. 'de-regulation' – removing inhibitions and regulatory restrictions on enterprise and competition, e.g. the opticians' dispensing monopoly, coach transport regulations.

The Thatcher government has in fact concentrated mostly on 1 above, even though it is arguably 3 which is the most important in economic theory, as it is not clear that the change of industrial ownership from government to private shareholder is always particularly significant in itself. The government's emphasis on de-nationalisation has been due to the influence of other broader policy objectives.

The government was impressed by various evidence (for example, see Pryke, 1980) that contrasted the relatively poor performance of the public sector industries with the private sector, particularly in terms of efficiency, meeting public demand, self-financing and labour relations. In fact, the evidence is not conclusive, mainly because of the difficulties of deciding what are the relevant 'performance indicators' that should be used for such comparisons, and then making valid comparisons between industries with different basic objectives and subject to very variable degrees of government regulation, intervention and interference. Further, even accepting a balance of evidence (nationally and internationally) against public ownership, it is not clear that it is the ownership as such that matters, but rather the lack of actual or potential competition facing the publically owned firms. It certainly seems likely that it is the latter that explains why some nationalised industries in Britain have shown poor technological responsiveness (e.g. telecommunications), used excessive cross-subsidisation (coal), or have not met public demand (railways). For there can be little doubt that by the 1970s some nationalised industries had become unacceptably inefficient and unprofitable, even allowing for their unspecified 'social' obligations.

The government's interpretation of the persistently poor financial performance of the nationalised industries, and indeed of many parts of the public sector generally, was that the root cause lay in the ownership form itself, and the lack of incentives to managers to be efficient, 'thrusting' and competitive – plus the considerable opportunities for the unions to manipulate restrictive practices, seek high wage settlements and block technological innovations that sought to raise productivity (or reduce manning levels).

A further factor influencing policy priorities was partly economic, partly political: this was the drive towards wider share ownership, or 'popular capitalism'. In this respect, the apparent objectives of privatisation have tended to change throughout the 1980s. Wider share ownership was not a prominent feature of the early years. However, by the mid-80s the popular success of privatisation supported a dual governmental aim: first, wider share ownership to obtain more involvement, more commitment, and more popular understanding of the process of creating wealth – the 'enterprise culture'; second, to make the re election of a (renationalising) Labour government less likely and also the renationalisation process itself extremely difficult . This was not least because it would then have to be costed in terms of increases in personal taxation – it was estimated that each 1 billion of renationalisation costs would put 1p in the £ back on personal income tax. Moreover, denationalisation would undermine the Labour movement politically, to the extent that the nationalised industries were 'flagships' of socialism, with highly organised and powerful (and Labour-voting) trade unions.

To these factors was added the not inconsiderable financial benefit arising from the denationalisations. The share sales themselves (see Table 2.1) raised substantial government revenue (even allowing for the costs of 'preparing' and actually selling off the companies), and the floated-off firms would no longer require government financial support which added to the PSBR. The accusations of 'selling off the family silver' were swamped by the popularity of the process, arising partly from the profits that large numbers of small shareholders were able to make, as well as the tax cuts made possible (in part) by increased government revenue and reduced government spending.

TABLE 2.1   *The Main Privatisation Sales Since 1979*

Date	Company	Proceeds (£ m)
A Sales by share offer		
1981	Cable and Wireless (49%)	224
1982	Amersham International	71
	Britoil (51%)	549
1983	Associated British Ports (52%)	46
1984	Enterprise Oil	392
	Jaguar	294
	British Telecom (51%)	3,916
1986	British Gas	5,434
1987	British Airways	900
	Rolls Royce	1,363
	British Airports Authority	1,226
1989	British Steel	
	Water Boards (10)	5,240
B Private sales		
1980	Ferranti	54
1982	National Freight Corporation	7
1983	B.R. Hotels	45
1984	Wytch Farm	80
	Sealink	66
	Inmos	95
1985	Yarrow Shipbuilders	34
1986	Vickers Shipbuilding	60
	Royal Ordnance	201
	National Bus Company	250
1987	Unipart	30
1988	Rover Group	150
C Flotations of government holdings		
1979	British Petroleum	290
1981	British Aerospace	50
1983	British Petroleum	15
	British Petroleum	566
	Cable and Wireless	275
1984	Associated British Ports	52
	NEB/BTG	142
1985	British Aerospace	363
	Britoil	449
	Cable and Wireless	602
1987	British Petroleum	5,727

Overall, then, not only did privatisation, especially denationalisation, fit into the supply-side macroeconomic policy package, but it also met a number of other government objectives. The catchphrase became 'the business of government is not the government of business' (Nigel Lawson, 1985).

The Phases of Privatisation 1979–90

As suggested already, the policy of privatisation has evolved as the Thatcher years have unfolded. Little was made of privatisation in the 1979 Conservative Manifesto. In the early years of the Monetarist approach privatisation mainly involved the sale of council houses, of certain publically owned assets, and of firms already in competitive markets. This was accompanied by deregulation to increase competitive pressures generally and especially on publically owned firms (e.g. in telecommunications and road transport). The emphasis was clearly stated:

> The long-term success of the privatisation programme will stand or fall by the extent to which it maximises competition. If competition cannot be achieved, an historic opportunity will have been lost (John Moore, Financial Secretary to the Treasury. November 1983).

A major switch was however evident after the 1983 Election, with much greater weight thereafter on share ownership and redistributional objectives. This led to the sales of the major public monopolies, notably British Telecommunications (BT), British Gas and British Airways (see Table 2.1). In selling these public companies that had enormous market power, the government rejected the possibilities of splitting them up in order to create separate competing units, and instead maintained large units with considerable potential for making profits. This was simpler and also made them attractive to small investors, thus encouraging wider share ownership. Instead, the monopoly powers of these large units were to be controlled mainly by regulatory agencies such as OFTEL to control British Telecom (with one small competitor, Mercury) and OFGAS to control British Gas (with no competitors) – whilst British Airways (BA) moved from being a public monopoly to being a private one. Despite the very mixed experience of similar regulatory agencies in the USA, the government felt that effective and meaningful regulations could be developed which would influence or control the firms' output decisions, especially prices, whilst still exposing the firms to the competitive forces of the capital markets.

In this phase, it was more difficult to see how the change of ownership would achieve much in terms of making the firms more responsive to market pressures, apart from freeing them from the restrictions of governmental ownership as such. Most of the hopes for improved performance rested on regulation, rather than with John Moore's commitment in 1983, quoted above, to competitive forces. However, the government itself felt that much was being achieved. In particular, the 'process' of privatisation proved spectacularly successful in terms of wider share ownership involving a wide cross-section of the community: 4m separate applications were received for British Gas shares. Share ownership extended rapidly, reaching over 9m people by 1988, and after the flotation of Abbey National in 1989, reached an estimated 11.5m. Part of this success was based on the speculative opportunities created, even for small investors, by the relatively low prices at which shares were offered. Substantial oversubscription of share issues was seen by the government as evidence of successful marketing rather than inaccurate pricing. If the critics said that the shares were underpriced deliberately, the government could point to the difficulties of pricing such unprecedented share issues amongst the unpredictable vagaries of the financial markets (demonstrated forcefully by the stock market 'collapse' in October 1987). Interestingly, whilst there were many willing to criticise, during this second phase privatisation carried the weight of public opinion with it, and it was the Labour Party that found considerable difficulties convincing the general public that denationalisation might be to the net disadvantage of ordinary people.

The third and current phase of denationalisation may be said to have started in 1989, with the move to privatise the huge public utilities, particularly water supply and electricity generation and supply. Not only does the sheer scale of these sales differ, but also a significant change in public attitudes became apparent. Whilst water privatisation in December 1989 was (again) substantially oversubscribed by the public as investors, public opinion was no longer nearly so much in favour of these privatisations, fearing the consequences of the creation of such powerful private monopolies. The record of OFTEL and OFGAS, whilst not itself poor, had seemingly failed to convince the public as consumers that regulation would prevent prices rising and services declining. This was hardly surprising, as economists have long believed that regulation can only prevent the worst excesses of monopoly, and is not a substitute for competition. Moreover, the much-discussed extension of the policy into more sensitive public service areas such as health, prisons and roads seemed to fail to find the support that the sales of the more obviously 'commercial' companies had revealed.

It is also in this third phase that questions began to be asked about 'popular capitalism' itself. Although the number of people owning shares trebled between 1984 and 1987 alone, in 1987 more than a third of shareholders overall held only shares in privatised companies. The depth of individual share ownership remained very shallow (in 1987, 78 per cent of shareholders held shares in only one or two companies), and the widespread resale of shares after each privatisation process had in fact concentrated share ownership relatively amongst the largest owners (30 per cent of the £5.24bn of Water Companies shares changed hands on the day of issue in December 1989). As some issues had a free share bonus after three years, the true extent of resale will become apparent only in the early 1990s: will such investors widen their holdings, or sell their shares in privatised companies and revert to traditional accounts in Building Societies and suchlike ? If they do, and the shares are bought by the large financial institutions, the policy will simply result in further wealth-concentration, after an initial burst of redistribution. Overall the proportion of company shares held by individual investors actually *fell* during privatisation, from 28 per cent in 1981 to 20 per cent in 1988. Even amongst remaining shareholders, the General Household Survey (HMSO, 1989) revealed that whilst the proportion of the population owning shares trebled from 7 per cent to 21 per cent between 1981 and 1987, the typical shareholder was a middle-aged professional man in the south-east with an income 66 per cent above the average (or 42 per cent above, if he just held privatised industry shares).

Questions were also being asked by sceptics about the continued delay in the privatisation of the unprofitable or less profitable parts of the nationalised industries. If privatisation was so successful, and so worthwhile from the national point of view, why was it not being applied to areas most in need? Another awkward question was that if nationalised industries could be prepared for privatisation by being made more efficient and profitable *before* being sold off, why could this not be done anyway under public ownership, rather than only in the run-up to privatisation ? And was it not indeed a strange strategy that argued, as seemed to be the case in electricity in 1989–90, that disproportionately high price rises had to be endured prior to privatisation, so that price rises would be lower afterwards?

The Impact on Industrial Performance

There has been much speculation as to the extent that the change of ownership and, in fewer cases, the environment of increased competition and/or regulation, has improved the performance of the privatised industries. It is not easy to draw conclusions: not only is it too soon to disentangle causes and effects, but conclusions depend on which measures of performance are chosen and over which time periods. In particular, simple indicators like prices, partial productivity (e.g. output per man), and profits are influenced by a host of factors other than ownership. The most comprehensive overall study, by the London Business School (Bishop and Kay, 1988), suggested that the privatised utilities (BT 1984, BAA 1987, and British Gas 1986) had not performed notably better since being privatised, nor indeed better than comparable state owned concerns. The comparison looked especially at average annual changes in total factor productivity: both public and private companies as a whole did better over 1983–88 than during 1979–83, with the state-owned British Steel the best performer, but with no clear bias towards either state or private ownership forms. However, an imponderable element here is the impact on performance of the 'threat' of potential privatisation, affecting all public industries. These now have much clearer commercial objectives and often a changed management culture, both of which have improved their performance even without a change in ownership as such.

There is plenty of partial evidence also: unacceptable price discrimination in industrial gas markets by British Gas and the neglect of telephone call boxes by British Telecom were widely recognised abuses of power by the newly privatised companies. Against these might however be set the much accelerated rate of introduction of modern telephone exchanges and the widespread publication by British Gas of 'consumer ratings' for all its services, ironically never considered necessary under public ownership. Similarly, the contracting-out of services such as refuse collection has invariably reduced the costs of operation, but the impacts on quality of service and conditions of work are much less easily assessed. On such matters, judgement must be deferred as yet. The overall impacts will probably not be assessable until a full business cycle has passed and the impact of investment decisions taken under private ownership take effect.

Overall, it is perhaps not in the individual firms and industries that the impact on performance should be assessed anyway, for privatisation has much wider objectives, as we have suggested. If it is 'successful' then this will be reflected in the performance of the economy as a whole. If it is not successful, then as a policy it cannot be adjusted or 'tweaked' as other governments have adjusted policies in the past. Thatcherism has no other industrial strategy: there is no active agency to direct or even influence the long-term direction of the British industrial economy. After the privatisation of the 1980s, arguably there is nothing, only an unknown balance between market forces and regulation.

The Beneficiaries

If we cannot yet assess the overall impact of privatisation, we can at least identify who has benefited from the move to privatisation. Certain groups have visibly been advantaged: most obviously, the initial shareholders, who have usually obtained their investments at a discount, and whose privatisation shares have performed better over the period 1982–90 than the Stock Market as a whole. The government's financial and legal advisers have earned large sums working for the companies but being paid by the taxpayers (likewise, some advertising agencies!). The salaries of senior managers of privatised companies have risen very rapidly – on average, some 250 per cent in real terms over 1979–88, although much of this was a 'catching-up' process.

Apart from these obvious beneficiaries, other benefits are less distinct. Arguably, taxpayers have benefited by a combination of reduced spending on public funding (although few persistent loss-making industries as such have yet been privatised) and from the increased government income from sales. However, the 'preparation' for sale has often involved substantial writing-off of debts, advertising, fees, etc. This reached a peak with Water privatisation in 1989, when it was calculated that the writing-off of debts, cash injections, fees, underwriting, incentives and other provisions amounted to £8.5bn, for an issue totalling only £5.24bn, such an obvious loss to the taxpayer that for a while the government preferred to stress the environmental aspects of this privatisation.

As for the firms themselves (and their owners) the act of privatisation seems to have been neither necessary nor sufficient to improve their performance – although the threat or preparation for it does seem to have had an impact. The message here seems to be that it is the state of competition that matters – in all markets – rather than ownership for itself. There can be little doubt that the *process* of privatisation has been one of the success stories of the 1980s: whether the *performance* will be as successful is still unclear.

The Thatcher Economic Experiment

The economic policies of Thatcherism developed out of disillusion with the Keynesian view that rising prosperity, full employment and low inflation could be achieved by demand management based on government spending on the welfare state and by establishing a policy 'consensus' between government, industry and the trade unions. With its emphasis on controlling the money supply, reducing the power of trade unions, and 'rolling back the frontiers of the state', together with its willingness to replace consensus with confrontation, Thatcherism appeared to mark a radical break with postwar Keynesian policies: other governments may have done such things at times under pressure of circumstances, but the Thatcher government took these as its main tenets.

Yet the basic elements of 'Thatcherism' itself changed significantly during the period 1979–89. From 1985 onwards, there was a growing emphasis on maintaining the exchange rate through interest rate policy, together with the redistribution of income in favour of the better-off, and privatisation became a central part of policy. Overall, the degree to which this was truly a 'revolution' is debatable: the extent of privatisation achieved during the 1980s was a radical break with the post-1945 consensus but was essentially a reversion to earlier approaches, fuelled in part by political ideology. The use of interest rates has a long antecedence, but the Thatcher government was unique in that this seemed to become the only policy instrument it was prepared to use to regulate economic activity – the 'only golf club in the bag' syndrome.

What, then, have been the results of Thatcherism? By 1988, central government expenditure as a share of GDP was just over 38 per cent (HMSO, 1990). This was significantly lower than during the 1970s when it approached 50 per cent, but was still notably higher than during the 1950s and early 1960s. Taxes (particularly those on high incomes) had been reduced, and public sector borrowing had been transformed into substantial public sector debt repayment, estimated at £14.2bn for 1990. But arguably much of this change was made possible by tax revenue from North Sea oil, and by a significant reduction in investment in, and the quality of, public services. It is debatable whether further reductions are politically and economically sustainable. The policy of privatisation has introduced more competition into the provision of public services (possibly at the expense of quality), and has led to the replacement of certain powerful public sector monopolies by private sector ones, making necessary the establishment of regulatory agencies. These developments have tended to reinforce the view that growth and development in modern industrial economies are still dependent on a powerful government sector, and that it is impossible to 'turn the clock back' to the economically less complex world of the eighteen and nineteen centuries. But, at the same time, the experience of Thatcherism, and particularly of contracting-out, has led to a more critical appraisal of how the government should organise the provision of 'essential' public services.

With regard to the overall performance of the British economy, it could be argued that the most significant changes have been due not to the policies of Thatcherism but to the effects of the severe recession of

1979–81 (albeit the latter being made worse by these policies), and of more fundamental long-term changes in the technologies and techniques of production. In the period 1979–81 many relatively inefficient plants were closed down, and companies, unable to compete internationally because of the lack of appropriate investment and the high exchange rate, were sold off or closed down. This contraction left British industry with a critical shortage of capacity to meet domestic demand in several important sectors, so that when demand increased from 1985 onwards, goods previously produced in Britain had to be imported. Furthermore, while increases in exports pointed to some improvement, rapidly rising imports suggested that the government's supply-side policies had had little significant effect on the relative non-price competitiveness of goods produced in Britain.

Significant changes did, however, take place within production units. Strikes were reduced, and the 'right of managers to manage' was partially restored (see Chapter 4), although arguably this may have been as much the result of high unemployment than of any fundamental change in labour relations or attitudes. To survive the recession of the early 1980s, companies were forced to become more efficient by reducing restrictive practices and overmanning. The result was significant 'one-off' increases in productivity. However longer-term improvements required a sustained increase in the rate of investment, and this was held back by the flow of investment funds overseas brought about by the deregulation of financial markets, and by the relatively high interest rates needed to maintain the exchange rate. It is one of the most basic dilemmas of Thatcherism in 1990 that these high interest rates, needed to control the inflationary tendencies of the late 1980s, will also depress much needed overall investment on the supply-side of the policy.

Nevertheless, between 1983 and 1989 the British economy grew at a rate of about 3.5 per cent per annum, compared to a rate of about 1.5 per cent per annum in the period 1973–79. However, in 1966–73 the growth rate had been some 3 per cent per annum. The growth performance of the 1980s was not significantly better than that in the 1960s. Moreover, by the end of the 1980s manufacturing capacity had no more than recovered to the level at the end of the 1970s. Despite significantly higher levels of unemployment compared to the 1970s, wage costs increased at about 7.5 per cent per annum from the early 1980s, rising to over 9.0 per cent per annum in 1989, almost double the rate of the major continental economies. Thatcherism had failed to suppress wage growth pressures sufficiently to permit rapid productivity growth without large wage increases. This was compounded by the absence of any active policy towards the manufacturing sector, and in particular towards industrial investment. British industry became increasingly less competitive relative to its international competitors. The consequences were a record Balance of Trade deficit and accelerating inflation, accompanied by high interest rates that were a direct result of a failure to reshape the economy so as to sustain a reasonable rate of growth without a trade deficit or inflation.

By the end of the 1980s, the advocates of Thatcherism were once again fighting battles over economic ideas and policies which they thought they had won ten years previously.

3

Towards an Enterprise Culture? Industrial and Training Policy under the Conservatives

ROB ATKINSON and CAROL LUPTON

When the Conservatives came to power in 1979 one of the major problems they faced was the effect of Britain's long-term economic decline on industry and employment. This already bad situation was moreover greatly exacerbated by the downturn in the world economy which occurred in 1980 and by the policies pursued by the new government. The result was a massive decline in manufacturing industry and a dramatic rise in unemployment levels. The depth of the recession created serious problems for the Conservative government: for political and long-term economic reasons it had to be seen to be doing something, even though it remained strictly opposed to state intervention in these matters. Somewhat ironically therefore the government was caught on the 'horns of a dilemma' of its own making: either it followed its free-market principles and did nothing or it intervened to ameliorate the effects of recession using the very interventionist methods which it had diagnosed as being part of the problem.

The government's answer was to argue that the depth of the decline vindicated its critique of the weakness and uncompetitiveness of British industry. The causes of this decline could be traced back to excessive state intervention and the behaviour of the trade unions; in particular to the corporatist economic interventions of previous Labour and Conservative governments. In this way the government welcomed the 'shake-out' caused by the recession as old, unproductive and unprofitable plant was scrapped and businesses were forced to adapt or go under. Here was the market restructuring industry much more radically than any government could or would have dared.

The solution was to unleash the entrepreneurial spirit which Mrs Thatcher believed had been shackled by years of excessive state interference in the affairs of industry. A new 'enterprise culture' had to be created in the country which would stimulate a more efficient and productive market. The government's role would be restricted to ensuring that the right external conditions for the self-revival of the market prevailed and that any constraints over its full and unrestricted operation – particularly on the 'supply' side – were effectively removed.

This chapter will examine the success or otherwise of the government's attempt to stimulate an effective enterprise culture by examining the development of policy in two key areas centrally affecting the 'supply-side' operation of the market: industrial and training policy. In its efforts to maintain and expand the industrial skill-base, and in its strategy for industrial regeneration and regional development more generally, how successful has the government been in creating the framework within which Britain's 'new enterprise' can flourish?

Industrial Policy – Pre-1979

For much of the post-war era the existence of an industrial policy has seemed a self-evident truth. In essence this has meant that successive governments have attempted to provide frameworks for, and encouragement of, the sustained industrial growth which would produce a modern and internationally competitive industrial sector. Policy largely took the form of selective intervention where potential growth areas were identified and firms encouraged to invest or to merge, sometimes with financial assistance. The form of intervention however was such that the firms themselves were largely left to their own devices once funds and advice had been made available. This 'limited interventionism' was a central characteristic of industrial policy pre-1979.

Industrial policy up to 1979 thus followed the largely familiar pattern of limited, selective intervention and the maintenance of declining but important industries in politically sensitive areas (Mottershead, 1978; Skuse and Jones-Owen, 1983). What is perhaps most striking about the whole period is that, as Wilks (1983) has noted, there was no intellectual framework to guide intervention nor administrative machinery to carry out interventions. Generally speaking industrial 'policy' was an ad hoc bundle of initiatives responding to specific crises; it was reactive rather than pro-active.

Industrial Policy Since 1979

The First Two Thatcher Administrations: 1979–87

Given the Conservatives' opposition to state intervention, it was logical to expect them quickly to reduce industrial policy as pursued before 1979. This was particularly so as Sir Keith Joseph, Mrs Thatcher's free-market guru, was appointed Secretary of State for Industry with David (later Lord) Young as his advisor.

Yet things were not quite so simple as free-market theories suggested. In the context of a major economic crisis Sir Keith found it politically impossible to institute a wholesale withdrawal of the state from the industrial arena. Thus after much agonising Sir Keith found himself continuing massive state aid to industries such as British Leyland. The *quid pro quo* for maintaining this aid however was the acceleration of restructuring projects along the lines which Michael Edwardes had already begun at British Leyland and Ian McGregor was to carry out at British Steel. Thus there were clear elements of continuity with pre-1979.

The major distinctive element of post-1979 industrial policy which began to emerge was the aim of making aid more selective, directing it towards firms and industries which 'genuinely' needed it, where development would not take place without state funds. At the same time the Department of Industry (DOI) stressed the importance of market discipline. These two trends were emphasised when Kenneth Baker, a 'wet' supportive of industrial policy, and Norman Tebbit, an advocate of market discipline, were appointed to the DOI as Ministers of State in January 1981.

The Joseph, Baker and Tebbit team was to be relatively short-lived when in September 1981 Joseph and Tebbit were moved out of Industry and Patrick Jenkin became Secretary of State. In many ways Jenkin was a much more 'traditional' Industry Secretary, encouraging the department to continue its support of new industries in information technology (begun by Kenneth Baker), though at the expense of 'lame ducks'. In addition he also placed much more emphasis upon the development of skills and training.

The major problem which faced the DOI was the government's general hostility to state intervention and the Treasury's particular wish to limit public expenditure and reduce inflation via strict monetary policy, regardless of its effect on British industry. Generally

groups such as the CBI felt that industry's interests were being under-
represented by the DOI during this period, a perception confirmed
when in June 1983 the DOI was merged with the Department of Trade
to form the Department of Trade and Industry (DTI) (Wilks, 1985). As
the emphasis on controlling public expenditure and reducing inflation
continued throughout Mrs Thatcher's second term of office, it seemed
to industrialists that the government lacked any explicit policy for
industry (Holdsworth, 1986). This was particularly problematic given
the rapid decline of British manufacturing industry since 1979
(Aldington, 1986).

It would be wrong to say that government had no strategy towards
industry during this period. If anything its policy was increasingly to
leave market forces to determine which firms survived and prospered.
However there is no doubt that the major developments taking place at
this time were outside the DTI. Firstly, the growth of training
programmes administered by the Manpower Services Commission
(MSC) (see later in this chapter) and the privatisation programme (see
Chapter 2) represented key elements in the government's 'supply-side'
revolution from which the DTI was largely excluded. During this
period the fortunes of the DTI and industrial policy generally were to
reach their nadir. In a sense this period was something of an
interregnum where elements of previous policies were continued
alongside the emerging free-market policies which had yet to be
clearly formulated in policy terms.

The Third Thatcher Administration: 1987–

The DTI's fortunes were to be revived when one of Mrs Thatcher's
favourites, Lord Young, and his deputy, Kenneth Clarke, were moved
from the Department of Employment to the DTI. Young's return to
the Department was to produce a radical reappraisal of its role,
thrusting it back into the political limelight. Instead of being seen as a
prop to Britain's ailing industries it was to become a key purveyor of
free-market ideas, i.e. of supply-side doctrines. In June 1987 Lord
Young was quoted as saying that he saw the DTI as the 'Department of
Wealth Creation', which would represent the 'Power Station of the
Economy', and create the conditions and confidence within which the
economy could flourish (*Financial Times*, 17 June 1987). These
objectives were reflected in the title of the White Paper published in
January 1988: *DTI – The Department for Enterprise* (Cm 278).
Henceforth the DTI was to be at the cutting edge of Mrs Thatcher's
revolution, championing the free-market cause and encouraging
industry to adopt new attitudes and practices. Discussing the White
Paper Kenneth Clarke argued:

the main role of the DTI... must be... to influence attitudes and to encourage open markets in order to promote enterprise and prosperity. *(Hansard,* vol. 125, col. 145, 12 January 1989).

Increasingly the DTI's role was to become that of market regulator; the guarantor of competition and thus of efficiency (Cm 278, ch. 2). This was to be achieved by emphasising the importance of management, education and the use of technological innovations in manufacturing. An essential element was the creation of a Single European Market which would provide new opportunities for British exports and force British industry to become more efficient and competitive. The new role of the DTI was launched in a blaze of publicity.

The 1988 White Paper also placed considerable emphasis on the importance of small businesses as one of the key growth sectors of the economy, and introduced a range of new incentives to encourage their formation. The long-term decline in their number was seen as a key cause of Britain's economic problems and policy was influenced by the example of expanding economies such as Japan where it was argued there was a direct correlation between economic growth and a dynamic and expanding small business sector.

While a great deal of attention was being lavished on small business, very little was given to the plight of manufacturing industry. There was to be no attempt to 'direct' growth into any particular sector; the market would be left to decide where and in what form investment should take. Thus in June 1989, shortly before he was to retire from political life, Lord Young said of the DTI:

We inherited a highly interventionist department. But we have seen that the less government interferes, the better things get moving (*Financial Times*: 29 June 1989).

In effect the industry wing of the Department had been downgraded and much greater emphasis given to trade and competition policy and to regulation of the City. As Young noted when speaking of the DTI: 'Fundamentally now it is the old Board of Trade with bits added on'. (*Financial Times*, 29 June 1989), an attitude which Young's successor, Nicholas Ridley, seems determined to extend to the point of virtually dismantling the DTI.

Industrial 'policy' thus became essentially negative, largely concerned with creating the free-market frameworks within which business could operate more effectively. Central to this was the reform of the tax system and the privatisation programme. Taken together these moves represented steps in the supply-side revolution which the Thatcher government sought to bring about. The question is whether they have been part of a wider strategy to create an enterprise culture or simply a series of ad hoc attempts to realise general free-market ideas. Certainly it would seem difficult to portray developments in the industrial sphere as part of any wider coordinated strategy. Developments since 1979 have alternated between a desire to withdraw the state altogether, a recognition of the need to encourage the development of certain 'key' industries and skills and a recognition of the necessity of 'supporting' declining, but politically important, industries.

Regional Policy Pre-1979

Regional policy has its origins in the 1930s when attempts were made to compensate those regions of Britain which were experiencing particularly high unemployment rates. In the post-war era it has been an important element in all pre-1979 governments' attempts to iron out regional imbalances in industry and jobs. On the one hand a wide range of grants and subsidies were automatically offered to firms if they located in specified regions. On the other hand if firms wished to expand or establish new factories in relatively prosperous areas such as the South-East or the Midlands they were discouraged from doing so by government controls over industrial and office development: a system of Industrial Development Certificates and Office Development Permits (Smith, 1989; Damesick and Wood, 1987). Thus a 'carrot and stick' approach was employed to persuade firms to locate in the 'depressed regions'.

During the 1950s and 1960s it appeared that regional policy was having a major effect in persuading firms to locate in depressed regions such as the North-East of England. However in the 1970s, as firm closures and unemployment began to rise nationally, regional policy was increasingly questioned. By the late 1970s when unemployment was over 1.5m and growing, evidence seemed to suggest that the costs of regional policy were disproportionate to its achievements. It became increasingly difficult to justify favourable treatment for specific regions at the expense of others – particularly when many of the firms set up in the 1960s and early 1970s using regional incentives were closing down. In addition one has to acknowledge that regional policy was essentially an attempt to ameliorate the uneven distribution of jobs and industry in the British economy rather than to tackle the underlying causes of that unevenness. This central limitation was exposed during a period of recession. When the Conservatives came to power therefore regional policy was under severe pressure.

Regional Policy Since 1979

As might be expected the newly elected government was strongly opposed to the intervention in the market which regional policy represented. In addition its concern to control and reduce the level of public expenditure boded ill for the future of regional policy from the start. Initially Sir Keith and his ministers used the ineffectiveness of pre-1979 regional policy as an excuse to run it down. Industrial Development Certificates and Office Development Permits were abandoned (the 'stick' side of the equation) and the areas eligible for regional assistance were dramatically reduced. However within designated areas automatic eligibility for grants and subsidies etc. remained.

These initial attempts to remove regional policy altogether were thwarted by the riots of 1981 which focussed national attention on run-down areas of the country. Arguably the 'urban problem' began to replace the 'regional problem' at this time, having the advantage of being smaller and cheaper to deal with. As a result until the 1983 election the emphasis remained on the need for regional policy to be more selective.

In 1983 regional policy underwent a review which produced a White Paper – *Regional Industrial Development* (Cmnd 9111) – recommending a further reduction of grant availability and the removal of the automatic right to grants for firms locating in certain areas (Smith, 1989). This process was carried further in the review initiated by Lord Young upon his return to the DTI in 1987. The White Paper which emerged – 'DTI – The Department for Enterprise'. (Cm 278) – stated that automatic eligibility for grants would end in those areas which still retained development area status. Assistance would henceforth only be provided to firms which could demonstrate that development would not take place without grant aid. Thus the marginalisation of regional policy was complete.

The downgrading of regional policy should come as no surprise: the government believed that investment decisions should be made by business without government interference. If there were regional imbalances (or a North–South divide) they would be rectified if the market were left to its own devices: high costs in the South-East would lead firms to rethink investment strategies causing them to look to regions where costs were low. 'Automatic' market adjustments were to be preferred to state intervention.

Thus in both industrial and regional policy the 1980s have witnessed elements of continuity with pre-1979 policies as the political and social ramifications of a declining manufacturing base, rising unemployment and increasing regional differences in levels of economic activity have forced the government to maintain some degree of involvement in the market. At the same time, both policy areas have witnessed the emergence of greater selectivity, initially to reduce expenditure, accompanied by a growing emphasis on the role of the market.

Training and Enterprise Policy – Pre-1979

A central precondition for business growth is the supply of an appropriately skilled and adequately motivated workforce. Despite rapidly rising levels of unemployment evidence was emerging in the early 1970s of serious inadequacies in the nation's industrial skill-base. Increasingly the then Conservative government was subject to growing pressure, from both sides of industry, actively to intervene to ensure a better fit between the supply of and demand for labour. The government's response came in the 1973 Employment and Training Act which established the Manpower Services Commission (MSC) to develop and coordinate training and employment services on a national basis. One of the many publicly funded 'QUANGOs' (Quasi-autonomous Non-governmental Organisations, see Chapter 1) which were established during these years, the Commission was loosely corporatist in composition, comprising representatives from both sides of industry and from local authorities and educational organisations. Ironically, given that it was introduced by an avowedly non-interventionist government, the MSC was to represent one of the most significant extensions of central intervention in the operation of the labour market which occurred in the post-war years.

Under the 1974–79 Labour government the Commission expanded dramatically in both size and ambition, quickly setting out to establish itself as the 'authoritative centre' of a unified and comprehensive labour power policy which would underpin the government's wider industrial strategy. The deepening of the economic recession in the late 1970s however rather diverted the MSC from this strategic planning role as the Labour government pressed it to develop a range of temporary schemes to alleviate the plight of those hardest hit by rising unemployment. By 1978 it became obvious that these 'special measures' were not to be a temporary feature of the Commission's work but a permanent and increasingly central one. The balance of emphasis within the MSC was thus tipped away from the development of longer-term labour market strategies to the administration of short-term, politically useful responses to rising levels of unemployment.

The 1979–87 Thatcher Administrations

With the election of the Conservatives in 1979 the future of the MSC
looked uncertain. Mrs Thatcher announced in the Commons that there
would be no more creation of artificial jobs; what the nation needed
now was genuine new jobs in productive industry. These could be
created only if the state got off the backs of individual producers. In
particular she promised her government would get rid of the expensive
and meddlesome 'QUANGOs' of which the MSC was a prime
example. The June 1979 budget announced cuts of over £170 million
to the training and employment programmes administered by the
Commission and the Department of Employment.

Such cuts notwithstanding – and the Commission's funds were
further pared both at the end of 1979 and again at the end of 1980 – the
bulk of the Commission's schemes and programmes remained intact.
Plans to transfer its central responsibilities to the Department of
Employment were shelved and, after some initial retrenchment,
expenditure in almost all areas of the Commission's activity
increased. Despite its obvious ideological distaste for such an agency,
in the face of still rising levels of unemployment, the government was
forced to acknowledge its political usefulness.

What the Conservative government was concerned to do in the
shorter term was to introduce a greater degree of political scrutiny of,
and control over, the activity of the Commission and to align its
operations more closely with the government's wider political and
economic strategies. As with its industrial policy more generally the
Conservatives attempted to introduce a greater degree of selectivity
into the Commission's operations.

In line with the more general restructuring of social welfare taking
place during this period (see Chapters 10 and 11) there was an attempt
to effect a central readjustment in the balance of responsibility between
the state and the individual. Those who remained without work, the
government argued, must accept some responsibility for their plight.
The state should not support these individuals with benefits or employ
them on schemes of 'make-work', but help them improve their
employability. The role of the Commission was to encourage this
process of self-responsibility: to refit and remotivate individuals for the
world of work. Interestingly, the problem facing the nation was in this
way redefined: from the economic problem of insufficient jobs to the
social problem of poorly skilled or badly motivated unemployed
people.

Through its involvement in youth training the MSC played a central
role in what has been termed the new 'educational settlement' which

characterised these years (Rees and Atkinson, 1982). In this settlement
the educational priorities of school and the post-school 'transition'
became increasingly geared to the needs of industry, with a resultant
blurring of the distinction between 'training' and education. In the
belief that there was a central 'mismatch' between the needs of
employers and the skills and attitudes possessed by young school
leavers, emphasis was placed on the need for the more extensive
vocational preparation of youngsters. Through programmes such as
TVEI (Technical and Vocational Education Initiative) within secondary schools and the YTS for school leavers, the aim was to create a
flexible and adaptable new generation of workers:

> To develop and maintain a more versatile readily adaptable highly motivated
> and productive workforce which will assist Britain to compete successfully in
> the 1980s and beyond. (Youth Task Group Report, MSC, 1982, p. 5).

For those perceived as less deserving – the older, longer-term
unemployed – the government was keen to reduce the degree (and cost)
of state responsibility whilst maximising their availability for work. In
contrast to the increased expenditure on youth schemes, expenditure on
work creation programmes for the longer-term unemployed was cut
substantially. Within a wider political and ideological onslaught on the
'workshy' new programmes for the adult unemployed were characterised by the emergence of the American 'workfare' approach. This
approach requires that those without work be made to pay in some
way – typically by participating in government training or employment
schemes – for the benefits they receive. It introduces thus a greater
degree of compulsion into the operation of such schemes, whereby
refusal to participate may result in loss of benefit. This period saw the
growth of a number of programmes which 'offered' longer-term
unemployed people the opportunity to undertake some form of
'socially useful activity' in return for a 'wage' which was little more
than benefit levels.

Although it had stopped short of removing the Commission, the
government nevertheless made clear its continuing dislike of its
corporatist structure and of its relative autonomy from central state
control. The early 1980s thus witnessed a series of attempts by the
government to control the activities of the MSC. In this as in industrial
policy more generally the government particularly objected to the
participation of the trade unions in the development of policy.
Growing concerns on the part of TUC representatives that the
government was attempting to circumvent the powers of the
Commission were exacerbated by the proposals in the 1987 Election
Manifesto to change the nature and composition of the MSC. Its new

name – the Training Commission – signified a reduced responsibility, with administration of the public employment services being returned to the Department of Employment. The number of employers represented on its new governing body moreover was significantly increased at the expense of the representatives of organised labour.

The Conservative Administration Since 1987

The development of training policy under the third successive Conservative government in many ways brought to a head all of the emergent tendencies described above. As with its industrial strategy more generally the government's approach to training became increasingly single-minded in its third term. Industry, it warned, should not assume that the government would always be prepared to shoulder responsibility for industrial training or reskilling. While the closer alignment of training opportunities with the operation of the benefit system would ensure a ready supply of available and motivated workers, employers themselves must begin to accept greater responsibility for the production of a flexible and adaptable work-force. Two White Papers were produced early in this third term which established clearly the parameters of a what was now to called the new 'training and enterprise policy'.

In *Training for Employment* (Cm 316) the government set out its plan for a new training programme for the adult unemployed which, as with the schemes for young people, would combine all existing adult training schemes into one unified vocational programme. Launched in September 1988, *Employment Training* (ET) was presented as the 'largest and most ambitious training programme ever undertaken...anywhere in the world' (Norman Fowler, Secretary of State for Employment, *Guardian*, 6 September 1988). It would transform the training of the adult unemployed, ensuring a better fit between the need for and supply of labour: 'training the workers without jobs to do the jobs without workers' (*Guardian*, 6 September 1988).

In addition to overcoming the skill shortages and inflexibilities which the government felt were undermining Britain's industrial performance, there were indications that ET was also designed to play a central role in managing the continuing political problem of the unemployed. To its critics, ET represented a considerable extension of the 'workfarist' approach: trainees were to be paid a benefit-related 'allowance' and, despite the government's initial assurances to the contrary, keen consideration was quickly given to ways in which attendance could be made compulsory for the 'more poorly motivated clients'. (Unemployment Unit, 1989, p. 1). Combined with the tightening of the 'actively seeking work' test under the 1989 Social Security Act, the offer of a place on a training scheme appeared to many to be an 'offer' that unemployed people could not afford to refuse.

The concern over the extent to which ET represented a compulsory work-for-benefit scheme led to considerable political opposition from the trade unions. In September 1988 the TUC voted by a narrow margin not to cooperate with the scheme. The government's response to this decision was decisive: the Training Commission would be abolished. It was simply not possible, the government argued, for the Commission to administer a scheme to which a significant minority of its Commissioners was actively opposed. Although the TUC subsequently reconsidered its decision, and agreed to cooperate with schemes on a selective basis, the damage was done: the Secretary of State took back the Commission's functions and responsibility for its training programmes was transferred to the Department of Employment. Given its dislike of the relative autonomy of the Commission and its corporatist structure, the confrontation over ET may have merely hastened the government down a route it was already preparing to take. It provided the perfect opportunity to weaken the participation of the unions and increase the degree of central political control over this area of politically sensitive policy.

The second White Paper to emerge in this policy area set out the Government's alternative to the Manpower Services/Training Commission; an alternative which was much more in line with its general industrial strategy. *Employment for the 1990s* (Cm 540) announced the government's intention to place the 'ownership of the training and enterprise system' firmly with employers. The vehicle for this shift in responsibility was to be the Training and Enterprise Councils (TECs) : independent companies which entered into a commercial contract with the Secretary of State for Employment to develop training and enterprise within a particular area. Over the three or four years following the White Paper a series of these TECs was to be established throughout the country, each with a budget of between £20–£50 million. Two-thirds of their membership was to be culled from the chief executives of private companies, with representatives from education, the voluntary and public sectors and the trade unions together comprising the remaining third.

The general aim of the TECs was to transfer the 'prime responsibility for investment in the 'skills and knowledge of our people' to employers (Norman Fowler, Introduction to the TEC Prospectus). Their central objective was to administer the YTS and ET programmes at a local level and ensure that enough places were made available to meet the government's guarantees to school leavers and the long-term unemployed. TECs were able to provide some training and enterprise programmes directly, but would predominantly sub-contract to a range of existing agencies. They had scope to adapt the rules of existing training schemes to meet local needs and to achieve better value for money. Above all the TECs were to be organisations. . . 'born of the enterprise culture' (Introduction, TEC Prospectus, p. 4), tackling the boundaries that fragment training and enterprise development and focussing their investment to' secure . . . the broader aims of community revitalisation' (Introduction, TEC Prospectus, p. 4).

In the autumn of 1989 the government announced cuts of £250 million to the ET budget, and a reduction in the places it provided of between 150,000 and 450,000. (*Guardian*, 16 November 1989) Soon after, it revealed that the YTS would be scrapped; 'market discipline' would provide for the effective training of the young in the future. A pilot scheme would be introduced to give individual unemployed young persons training credits to spend on private training schemes of their choice (*Guardian*, 22 November 1989). These decisions – not unrelated to the falling numbers of young unemployed people – marked the beginning of the end of the interventionist 'special measures' of the 1970s and early 1980s. As with its industrial policy more generally, the approach of the government's new training and enterprise 'policy' has proved to be ultimately a negative one, characterised by the fairly systematic attempt on the part of the centre to divest itself of the responsibility for ensuring the right quality and quantity of available industrial skills.

Conclusion

In this chapter we have examined the development of industrial and training policy under three successive Conservative administrations. In both areas we can see that the general policy objective has been to reduce the extent of direct state intervention, and to stimulate economic regeneration indirectly by ensuring the unimpeded operation of the market. In the first two administrations however this disengagement was only partially achieved, thwarted by rising levels of unemployment and increased political unrest. Until late 1987 remnants of previous interventionist policies continued alongside emergent free-market strategies, with the government limited to increasing the selectivity of its interventions. In its third term the government's industrial and training policies became more explicit and single-minded as it attempted to stimulate a more positive 'enterprise culture' within the market. How successful has the government been in this attempt? How coherent have the policy developments been in respect of training and industrial development? To what extent indeed do the different policy strands add up to a coherent and coordinated 'policy for enterprise?'.

The dictates of a 'hands off' enterprise policy have meant that, in terms of its general industrial strategy, the DTI in effect increasingly abandoned the manufacturing sector, leaving it to the whims of the market. Implicit in this approach was the belief that manufacturing industry no longer had a key role to play in generating economic growth; that the oil and service sectors could be left to achieve this end. There seems to be no evidence however that the growth of small firms which the DTI has been so eager to promote will make up for the loss in manufacturing jobs over the past ten years. Indeed research suggests the opposite: the socio-economic structures of regions which have been heavily dependent upon manufacturing industry for employment over the last hundred years are unlikely suddenly to change and develop a thriving small business sector.

The development of regional policy similarly saw the state attempting to reduce the scope of its involvement and introduce a greater degree of selectivity in the allocation of funds. It is difficult in this way to see the government's industrial strategy as 'policy' in the positive sense; few of the proposals in the DTI White Paper (Cm 278) will do much to help either manufacturing industry or the regions. Indeed, in their eagerness to stimulate a wider enterprise culture, it seems that the Conservatives have been prepared to sacrifice both industry and the regions.

In the area of training policy, similar doubts must obtain about the effectiveness of recent policy developments in establishing an appropriate framework for a more entrepreneurial approach. There must be a major question mark, for example, over the extent to which the unimpeded operation of market forces, aided and abetted by the work of up to 80 individual TECs, will be able to deliver the necessary quality and quantity of industrial skills on a national basis. There is evidence moreover of the only very limited extent to which the TECs have connected with the particular economic needs of their local communities: their membership has been dominated by the representatives of large companies not the small local firms so desired by the government, and there has been little involvement on the part of local economic development agencies.

There is also a central issue concerning the extent to which the development of a national enterprise policy can overcome the problem of departmentalism, and whether the mechanisms established to coordinate the activities of the DTI and the Department of Employment (DE) (and other departments) have enabled a united approach at central, regional and local level. Certainly at a central level it is highly questionable whether such mechanisms have functioned to overcome the traditional rivalry of different Whitehall departments and there is no evidence of any close cooperation between the 'representatives' of various departments at regional or local levels. The establishment of the TECs indeed has resulted in an increased tension between the DE, the Department of Education and Science (DES) and the DTI about the scope and impact of their operation.

The examination of developments within both training and industrial policy thus reveals a central tension within the Conservatives' wider strategy for stimulating a market based enterprise culture: the creation of the preconditions for a more efficient and competitive economy may require a significant degree of state intervention. It may simply not be enough for the state to withdraw. In particular there would appear to be a strong case for major investment in infrastructure, yet the Treasury remains unwilling to sanction such active intervention. Despite all the publicity and hyperbole therefore it would seem that the government's enterprise policy is in danger of remaining a stylishly designed and expensively promoted but largely empty policy package: something of a smokescreen to cover its more general retreat from the development of effective industrial and training policies.

4

Trade Union Policy 1979–89: Restriction or Reform?

DAVID FARNHAM

The central argument of this chapter is that governmental policy towards the trade unions since 1979 has been to displace the industrial relations consensus of 1945–79 with a new policy. The former consensus was based on supporting collective bargaining and trade union organisation, within a voluntarist framework of trade union law. The new policy stresses individualism, market forces and the legal regulation of trade unions and trade disputes.

Another main argument of this chapter is that the real impetus of governmental policy on the trade unions since 1979 is not necessarily the official version it espouses. This version stresses the government's vital role in reforming outdated industrial relations and trade union practices primarily by using the law. The claimed objectives and outcomes of this policy include: removing trade union legal privileges in trade disputes; providing legal safeguards for individuals in closed shop situations; giving the unions back to their members by extending their legal rights in union decision-making; and tackling the problem of unofficial strikes by requiring the unions to repudiate unofficial action and enabling employers to dismiss those participating in unofficial action, without allowing them recourse to an industrial tribunal (DE 1981, 1983, 1987, 1989a and 1989b).

More specifically, governmental policy towards the unions since 1979 appears to have four underlying implicit aims. These are: (1) to weaken collectivism and the role of trade unions in industrial relations; (2) to strengthen the right to manage amongst employers; (3) to regulate and reduce union power and influence in the labour market; and (4) to depoliticise trade unions and industrial relations. The specific instruments being used to effect this policy include: legislation;

governmental example in its own spheres of responsibility; economic measures, the creation of the Commissioner for the Rights of Trade Union Members (CRTUM); and governmental propaganda.

The Conservative Party and the Unions

The Conservative Party's attitudes to British trade unions have always been ambivalent, ever since the emergence of the early unions towards the end of the nineteenth century. On the one hand, with the extension of the franchise, the Conservatives needed to court working class men and then working class women for their votes in local and national elections, and some of these individuals were trade unionists. On the other hand, ever since the last quarter of the nineteenth century there have been determined elements in the modern Conservative Party which have been distinctly hostile to trade unionism. This hostility has derived from three sources: 'intellectual conviction; the economic interests of powerful groups in the party; and the institutional interests of the party itself' (Movan, 1977, p. 13). To some Conservatives, the unions seek to distort the free working of the labour market in their members' favour, they oppose employer power in the workplace and they provide financial and organisational support to the Labour Party.

More substantively, the Conservative Party generally distrusts trade unions on three counts: as organisations; their leaderships; and the activities of trade unionists as groups of workers collectively defending their employment interests against employers. In general, unions challenge employers, in both the private and public sectors, which resist demands for union recognition, reject what the unions regard as reasonable wage and conditions claims on behalf of their members, and treat their members unfairly at the place of work. There have always been individuals and pressure groups amongst Conservative MPs, and within Conservative governments, therefore, who want policy measures, to varying degrees, to tackle the so called 'trade union problem' and to reduce union power.

This debate has continued throughout the history of the Conservative Party. The Party has always wanted working people's votes and those of trade unionists but it has also wanted to contain the unions. Yet whilst the party normally agrees that something 'has to be done' to deal with the unions, it is generally divided on the best way to do it. Even today, opinion is split between the 'restrictionists' and the 'reformers' in the party. The restrictionists want to change the emphasis away from collectivism and trade union rights in industrial relations to individualism and union members' rights. The reformers are softer on union power. They are prepared to support the principle of collectivism in industrial relations but feel that the balance of industrial power is too often skewed in favour of the unions and their members in the employment relationship. They believe that this needs to be redressed in favour of managerial power, whilst wanting a basic floor of legal rights for individual employees at the workplace. In the 1980s, however, the 'restrictionists' views dominated the political agenda.

Weakening Collectivism and the Role of the Unions

Governmental policy on industrial relations and towards trade unionism between 1940 and 1979 was complementary and reciprocal. It was also bipartisan, apart from the duration of the Industrial Relations Act from 1971 to 1974. Policy was rooted in the belief, underwritten by the Donovan Commission set up in 1966 to enquire into the state of British industrial relations, which reported in 1968, that collective bargaining was the best method of conducting industrial relations (Donovan, 1968, para. 203). Since effective collective bargaining depends on the existence, strength and recognition of trade unions, it was governmental policy to encourage the growth of trade unions and their recognition by employers as partners in the joint negotiation of terms and conditions of employment.

This was done by example in the public sector and, over the years, by providing a series of legal props to collective bargaining in the private sector. These props included: setting up wages councils as an intermediate step to collective bargaining where union organisation was traditionally weak; establishing conciliation and arbitration services; passing fair wages resolutions in the House of Commons; providing certain legal rights for trade unions and their members; and establishing a basic floor of individual employment rights capable of extension through collective bargaining. The major feature of the industrial relations consensus was the centrality and legitimacy of collective bargaining, between autonomous employers and independent unions, as the prime means of determining wages.

Three other limbs of governmental policy were commitment to full employment (certainly up to the mid-1970s), willingness to consult national union leaders on economic and social policy issues and a wish as far as possible to keep the law out of trade disputes and trade union affairs. In practice, there were difficulties in supporting collective bargaining as the main method of conducting industrial relations and operating a full employment policy. With increased union bargaining power, and low unemployment, cost-push inflation (see Chapter 2, p. 26) became a continuous feature of the post-war economy. In response to this, a series of prices and incomes policies was instituted to contain wage bargaining within national productivity limits and planned pay guidelines.

Since 1979, one of the government's major policy goals has been to encourage employees, and employers, to move towards a more individualist model of industrial relations and away from collectivism. One set of policies is directed at weakening the solidarity of union members and delegitimising collective bargaining. One way in which the government has tried to do this is by changes in the law. The statutes currently operational are: the Employment Acts 1980, 1982 and 1988 (EA 1980, 1982 and 1988) and the Trade Union Act 1984 (TUA 1984). There are also proposals to legislate further on closed shops and industrial action, including unofficial action (DE, 1989a and 1989b).

One set of legal changes affects union balloting arrangements. The TUA 1984, as amended by the EA 1988, for example, provides that trade unionists must elect, by postal ballot at least once every five years, all those who take part in decision-making on union executive committees. Ostensibly, these legislative changes in union election procedures stem from the government's desire, stated in its 1983 Green Paper, to ensure that trade union leaders are truly representative of their memberships. Because the unions did not reform themselves voluntarily, the government claimed that it had 'reluctantly come to the conclusion that some legislative intervention is necessary' (DE, 1983, p. 16). Another interpretation of these provisions, however, is that they are seen by government as a means of weakening the collective links amongst trade unionists, and between them and their union, thereby loosening internal union cohesion and collective solidarity.

Since 1980, the law has also severely constrained the legality of closed shop arrangements between employers and unions. Under the EA 1980 and EA 1982, secret ballots are promoted for closed shops and specific protections are provided for non-union members in closed shop situations, especially protection against dismissal for not being union members. Individuals are also entitled to increased compensation if they are dismissed because of not joining a closed shop. In its Green Paper published in Spring 1989, the government proposes further restrictions on the closed shop. This would give individuals a statutory right not to be refused engagement on the ground of non-membership of a trade union, or refusal to become a member after starting employment, thus effectively outlawing all closed shop arrangements (DE, 1989a, p. 9).

Whilst the government's case against the closed ship is defended on the grounds that it both infringes personal liberty and is economically inefficient, legally removing it could have another purpose. Namely, it is seen as a further means of weakening collectivism and the role of trade unions in industrial relations. Outlawing the closed shop, in other words, helps to loosen the links between employers and the trade unions in the collective bargaining process and to delegitimise joint approaches to resolving conflict at work.

Other government actions in the 1980s reflecting its antipathy to collectivism in industrial relations, and its preference for more unitary employment practices, are demonstrated by example in the public sector. These include: the derecognition of civil service unions at the General Communications Headquarters (GCHQ) at Cheltenham; the setting up of a pay review body for nurses and midwives in the National Health Service; and the removal of collective bargaining arrangements for school teachers in England and Wales by the Teachers Pay and Conditions Act 1987. Amongst the nursing and teaching professions alone, over 800,000 state employees have been removed from pay bargaining machinery by government directive, despite union resistance to this policy. And, by Summer 1989, the last remaining trade unionist had been dismissed at GCHQ.

Strengthening the 'Right to Manage'

The 'right to manage' is that area of corporate decision-making which managers consider to be theirs alone and is not constrained by collective bargaining. Managerial prerogative 'carries with it the implication that there are actions or areas for action so essential to management that these must remain unilaterally the property of management if management itself is to continue to exist' (Marsh, 1979, p. 186). The boundaries of the right to manage are the interface between unilateral managerial control and the ability of employees to influence or counterbalance those decisions most affecting their daily working lives. For this reason what comes within the scope of 'managerial rights' is at the centre of industrial relations controversy.

Given the government's commitment to the so called enterprise culture and the free market economy, it is not surprising that one of its policy goals is to strengthen the right to manage. It is a policy which is complementary to its aim to weaken the union role in industrial relations. The idea behind strengthening the right to manage is to provide managers with more autonomy in enterprise decision-making. This in turn, it is claimed, should enable managers to react more swiftly to changing product market forces, to obtain greater flexibility from their human resources and to have more control over workforce productivity. In consequence, companies should become more efficient and more competitive in the marketplace, thus boosting the economy and leading to economic growth.

One way in which government has strengthened the right to manage is by adopting private sector managerial models and employment practices in the public sector, including the local authorities, the National Health Service, the educational services, the civil service and other public services. According to Gray and Jenkins (1986, p. 171), managerialism in the public sector is where:

> The guiding principles are the pursuit of efficiency, effectiveness and value for money: responsibility is . . . decentralised, lower level operatives [are] made aware of and accountable for the costs of their operations, targets are . . . established and individuals assessed according to their ability to achieve them.

This contrasts with the public administration model emphasising bureaucratic procedures, the avoidance of mistakes, equity and fairness in dealing with clients, and accurate record keeping to ensure public accountability. The private sector employment practices imported into the public sector in the last decade include: performance related pay; performance appraisal; employee flexibility; new patterns of working; and decentralised collective bargaining.

Since 1979, the government has also initiated a series of legal changes which have had the effect of strengthening the right to manage. In industrial tribunals, for example, prehearing assessments have been introduced, with the possibility of costs being awarded on the grounds of unreasonable, frivolous or vexatious claims. In unfair dismissal cases, the length of service requirement has been increased to two years, the burden of proof no longer rests with the employer but equally with the applicant, and a one-year period is now sufficient for an employee to agree to waive rights to claim unfair dismissal or redundancy.

The powers of Wages Councils to set wage levels for those under 21 years of age, non-wage conditions and above minimum differentials have been abolished. Wages Councils' powers are now limited to setting minimum adult hourly rates and overtime rates. In addition, the Fair Wages Resolutions have been rescinded and the comparable terms and conditions arbitration procedure (Schedule 11 of the Employment Protection Act 1975) has been repealed. Whilst female employees retain a right to reasonable time off work for ante-natal care with pay, their right to return to work has been modified. Extended written notice is now required to retain this right, whilst employers with less than five employees can refuse to take employees back. All these provisions enable employers to be more flexible and autonomous in determining the terms and conditions of their employees.

The right of unions to seek employer recognition through the 'claims procedure' embodied in sections 11–16 of the Employment Protection Act 1975 has been abolished. Where 10–99 employees are to be made redundant, the minimum period for trade union consultation has been reduced to 30 days. Further, 'union only' or union recognition and consultation clauses in commercial contracts are now void in law. It is also unlawful to discriminate against or victimise contractors on these grounds. Here, too, the legal emphasis is on strengthening the right to manage, at the expense of employee and trade union rights.

Regulating and Reducing Union Power and Influence in the Labour Market

Complementary to the government's policy of strengthening the right to manage is its aim to reduce union power and organisation in regulating the labour market. The freedoms to organise members, to negotiate terms and conditions with employers and to withdraw their members' labour when in dispute with employers are fundamental for trade union effectiveness. Organised collectively, employees are generally in a much stronger position to protect, defend and extend their employment interests than each person is able to do individually. At the root of the government's economic policy, however, is the objective of opening up markets, including the labour market, to free competitive forces to facilitate economic efficiency and effective resource utilisation. Since trade unions are viewed by supporters of free markets as labour cartels, they are to be weakened to enable wages and conditions to be determined by free-market forces, rather than by institutional ones.

One arm of governmental policy which has undermined union power in the labour market is its approach to economic management (see Chapter 2). This has been distinctly non-Keynesian throughout the 1980s, eschewing any attempt to keep unemployment levels low by the use of demand management policy instruments. On the contrary, successive Conservative governments have preferred monetarist and supply-side approaches, primarily aimed at controlling price inflation. Whilst monetarist policy focuses on attempts to control money supply to maintain price stability, supply-side economic policy focuses on impediments to the supply of and efficient use of the factors of production. Because of government policies in the 1980s, unemployment was allowed to rise to unprecedented levels for the post-war period, reaching over 3m in the mid-1980s, thus severely constraining union wage bargaining power and leading to large leakages in union membership.

Another way in which government attempted to reduce union power is by changing the law relating to trade disputes. As a result of the new legislation of the 1980s, the freedom of individuals, trade unionists and unions to take part in lawful industrial action has been severely curtailed. Legal immunities are at the root of the issue. Where employees take industrial action, they are normally in breach of their contracts of employment. Under common law it is unlawful to induce people to break a contract, to interfere with the performance of a contract or threaten to do so. Without some sort of legal protection or 'immunity', unions and their officers could face legal action for inducing breaches of contract when organising industrial action. Legal immunities provide, in effect, that unions and individuals cannot be sued for damages for inducing breaches of contract when furthering industrial action in certain circumstances. The EAs 1980 and 1982, however, have withdrawn immunities from certain types of industrial action, opening up the possibility of unions and individuals having injunctions issued against them, or being sued, where their actions are unlawful.

The law also provides that those organising industrial action, thus interfering with contracts, are protected only if they are acting 'in contemplation or furtherance of a trade dispute'. To remain within the law, those calling industrial action must show that there is a dispute and that the action is to support it. As a result of the EAs 1980 and 1982, to be lawful disputes must be between workers and their own employers and must be concerned 'wholly or mainly' with matters such as terms and conditions, negotiating machinery and so on. Disputes 'only connected' with matters like pay and conditions are now excluded from the definition of a lawful dispute. Several types of dispute, which were previously lawful, are now unlawful as a result of the EA 1982. These include: inter-union disputes; disputes between a union and an employer where none of that employer's workforce are in dispute with it; disputes relating to matters occurring overseas; disputes with employers not recognising unions or employing non-union labour; and 'secondary' or 'sympathy' disputes between workers and employers other than their own.

There is also no legal protection for those organising or taking part in secondary picketing at a place other than the picket's own place of work, whether or not the picketing is 'in contemplation of furtherance of a trade dispute'. Lawful picketing enables persons to picket only at or near their own place of work. It must be peaceful and its purpose must be to obtain or communicate information or persuade other persons to work or not to work. The only three exceptions are: union officials accompanying members picketing their place of work; mobile workers picketing where their work is administered; and unemployed persons picketing their former place of work.

Where trade unions act unlawfully, such as supporting sympathy action or secondary picketing, they lose their legal immunity. The EA 1982 establishes that a union is liable for any unlawful act authorised or endorsed by its executive committee, general secretary or president or any other person with power under union rules to call industrial action. A union is also liable for any unlawful act authorised by an official employed by the union, or by a committee to which such officials report. This is unless the authorisation is disowned by the executive, general secretary or president, is in writing and is delivered as soon as reasonably practicable.

The effect of removing legal immunities from certain kinds of industrial action is to provide those damaged by the action, such as employers or union members, with the right to take civil proceedings in the courts against the union, or in some cases the individual, that is responsible. There are two remedies available to those going to court about unlawful industrial action. First, those damaged can seek a court order or injunction preventing the action taking place or having it stopped. Where such an order is disobeyed, those seeking it can return to court which will declare the action in contempt of court. Any party found in contempt may face fines or even imprisonment. Second, it is possible to claim damages from those responsible for the unlawful acts. There are upper limits to the damages which can be awarded in any proceedings against a union, according to its size. But failure to pay fines or damages can lead to the union's assets being sequestrated and taken out of its control.

Linked with these legal restraints on the ability of trade unions to use their collective power in the labour market are a series of legal rights for individual union members. These provisions appear to be aimed not only at reducing union bargaining power but also at weakening the collective identity and solidarity of employees as trade unionists. Under the TUA 1988, for example, it is a condition of legal immunity that before organising industrial action unions must hold a secret ballot in which all those about to take part in the action are entitled to vote. Provided a majority of those voting supports the proposed action, it is lawful. The EA 1988 goes further by giving union members the right to apply to the courts for an order restraining their union from inducing them to take any kind of industrial action without a properly conducted secret ballot, with majority support.

Under the EA 1988, too, union members have the statutory right not to be unjustifiably disciplined by their union. It specifies the union actions which count as discipline and the conduct for which discipline is justifiable. Previously, union members could be disciplined for working during a strike or other industrial action. Under the present law, union disciplinary action for this is unjustifiable and individuals have the choice whether to work during a dispute or not. The most common examples where individuals are protected against unjustified union discipline include: going to work despite a union call to take strike or other industrial action; crossing a picket line; speaking out against a strike call or other industrial action; and refusing to pay a levy to fund a strike or other industrial action.

The individual rights embodied under current legislation can be enforced by industrial tribunals (ITs), the Certification Officer (CO) or the courts, assisted in some cases by a new body the CRTUM. Complaints about unjustifiable discipline by a union, for example, proceed to an IT which makes a declaration. Complaints about union executive elections proceed to the CO or the courts. In court cases, union members can seek the assistance of the CRTUM. All these measures, whilst increasing the legal rights of trade unionists as individuals, diminish the collective freedoms of trade unions as bargaining agents with employers.

Depoliticising Trade Unions and Industrial Relations

The final implicit aim of governmental policy on trade unions over the last 10 years is to depoliticise the unions and industrial relations. The underlying belief is that union political activity, however difficult this is to define in practice, strengthens the power of trade unions and works against the interests of employers and those of the Conservative Party. It also runs counter to the view that if the unions have a role, it is the economic not the political one which should predominate. Depoliticising the unions and industrial relations, in short, could facilitate an ideological change on the part of unions and their members, enabling them to identify more closely with the goals of a dynamic capitalism operating in a competitive enterprise culture. A number of measures has been taken to achieve this aim. These include: making political strikes unlawful; instituting political fund review ballots; requiring balloting arrangements for union elections; privatising parts of the public sector (see Chapter 2); government abstention in settling trade disputes; and excluding the Trades Union Congress (TUC) from public policy making.

The definition of a trade dispute in the Trade Union and Labour Relations Act 1974 (TULRA 1974), as amended by the EA 1982, now requires disputes to 'relate wholly or mainly to' the subjects listed. This change raises doubts about the status of any dispute having mixed motives, including 'political' elements, even though the difficulty of drawing any clear line between political and industrial disputes has been recognised by the courts (*Sherard* v. *AUEW (1973)*). This change in the legal definition of a trade dispute, in seeking to exclude disputes with a political element, could effectively restrict some types of industrial action aimed at improving terms and conditions of employment.

The TUA 1984, as amended by the EA 1988, requires unions with political funds, which are normally used to support the Labour Party and to conduct political campaigns, to ballot their members, at least once every 10 years, on whether they wish to continue to spend money on party political matters. Ballots must be by post and are subject to independent scrutiny. Also the Secretary of State has powers to specify by statutory orders any bodies which may act as independent scrutineers. If review ballots are not held, the authority to spend money on political objects lapses.

The other set of balloting arrangements which appears to be aimed at depoliticising the unions is that relating to elections to union executives, accompanied by provisions requiring unions to keep accurate registers of their members' names and addresses. Besides stipulating strict balloting arrangements, the law provides candidates with the right to prepare their own election addresses and have them distributed at no cost to themselves. The thinking behind these arrangements is that these legal rules should result in more moderate and representative candidates being elected as union office holders.

Privatising substantial parts of the public sector (see Chapter 2), and requiring public sector organisations to contract out certain of their services such as cleaning and catering (see Chapter 12), has transferred a large number of workers out of public employment. This means that government is no longer their employer, directly or indirectly, and cannot be called upon to increase public expenditure to finance their pay rises. Privatised organisations, such as the power, water and energy industries, are now required to have regard to market and strict financial considerations when responding to pay and conditions claims, thus depoliticising the process of wage bargaining.

Since 1979, successive governments have decisively rejected any positive role in industrial peacekeeping. All of them have been strongly disposed against government ministers having a role in intervening in intractable disputes, as mediators of last resort, as had been the practice ever since the late nineteenth century. Trade disputes, the government believes, even in the public sector and no matter how bitter, should be seen to be left to the direct employers and the trade unions to resolve between themselves. By this view, the outcomes will be determined by managements standing firm and by relying upon market forces to generate financially prudent solutions and a sense of economic reality amongst the workforces and their union leaders.

Successive governments have also excluded the TUC from economic and industrial policy-making. This is in direct contrast to the previous practices of the post-war period. There is no direct consultation between government and the TUC as the interest group representing affiliated unions, their members and working people generally. By this view, it is government alone which is responsible for taking political decisions and the marketplace for economic decisions. There is no role for the TUC in either of these decision-taking processes.

Conclusion

This chapter has focused on governmental policy on the relatively narrow area of trade unions, not on the wider area of industrial relations. Nevertheless, in a system of industrial relations traditionally based on 'free' collective bargaining between autonomous employers and independent trade unions, governmental policy on trade unions is clearly aimed at influencing the behaviour of employers, union leaders and union members in their activities as the key actors in the industrial relations system. But to what extent their activities have actually been affected by the new policy initiatives stressing individualism, market forces and the legal regulation of trade unions and trade disputes is yet to be definitively analysed.

In the popular mind, industrial relations in the 1980s were typified by bitter trade disputes in the private sector involving, for example, Times Newspapers and News International at Wapping, the *Stockport Messenger* at Warrington and P and O at Dover. In the public sector, too, popular attention was focused on a succession of sometimes protracted disputes between the employers, and the trade unions. These disputes included coal mining (the NUM dispute 1984–5), steel production, the fire services, the civil service, the railways, school-teaching, local government, and more recently, the ambulance service. Important as these events were for those directly concerned, they were special cases in industrial relations and it is not possible to draw general conclusions for them. To do so is to underestimate the complexities of industrial relations and to overexaggerate the significance of trade disputes as indicators of 'bad' or 'good' industrial relations between employers and trade unions and employers and union members.

To return to the main theme of this chapter, the 1980s have seen a distinct change in emphasis in governmental policy towards trade unions. The policy, though explicitly expressed as aimed at reforming the unions, has in practice been implicitly aimed at restricting them and their activities. The measures outlined in this chapter have to varying degrees been directed at limiting the ability of trade unions to: recruit and retain members; protect members in the workplace; maintain membership solidarity; obtain new recognition agreements from employers; negotiate effectively as wage bargaining agencies; bargain on non-wage issues with employers; take part in effective industrial action; participate in sympathy action; and influence economic and social policy. And, at the time of writing, the process is incomplete, since the government proposes further changes in the law affecting trade unions, no change in economic policy, more privatisation and resisting the European Commission's (EC) draft Community Charter on fundamental social rights (the Social Charter).

It is too early to evaluate to what extent the Conservative governments of the 1980s were successful in achieving their trade union policy aims. But some pointers can be given. First, it is debatable to what extent British unions were weakened in the 1980s. Indeed union membership held up remarkably well during this period, given the relatively hostile economic, political and legal environments facing the unions. According to the Certification Officer, there were 10.5m trade union members in Britain at the beginning of 1988, compared with 13.2m in 1979 (CO, 1989, p. 42 and 1981, p. 51). Whilst this was a substantial fall in union membership, it did not represent a disastrous collapse. Further, in the private sector at least, union wage bargaining was generally able to maintain, if not increase, money wage incomes in line with price rises and productivity increases. It was public sector employees who largely bore the brunt of a crude wages policy, constrained by cash limits and cutbacks in real levels of public spending in most of the public sector during these years.

Second, it is also questionable whether the extension of individual trade unionists' rights has in fact been implemented at the expense of union solidarity and cohesion. Although inter-union solidarity has been constrained, because of legal bans on sympathy action, the statutory balloting provisions seem to be having the contrary effect on internal union affairs. They appear to be democratising union decision-making, legitimising their collective activities and reinforcing intra-union cohesion in many cases. According to the Advisory Conciliation and Arbitration Service (ACAS) it seems clear that industrial action ballots 'are fast becoming a permanent feature of negotiating processes'; by the end of 1987, 526 such ballots had been taken, with 440 (84 per cent) supporting such action and only 80 (15 per cent) against (ACAS, 1988, p. 11).

Third, other balloting requirements such as those for closed shops, union executives and political fund reviews do not seem to be producing any serious difficulties for the unions. It is likely that at the end of 1986, for example, 'no more than 30,000 employees were covered by formally approved closed shop ballots' (ACAS, 1987, p. 13). Similarly, postal ballots covering elections to union executives and the review of union political funds have proceeded fairly smoothly and largely without incident from the unions' point of view. Substantial majorities have been recorded in favour of retaining union political funds, for instance, not rejecting them. Indeed some unions, largely in the public sector, have instituted political funds for the first time.

What, then, is the future for the government's restrictionist policy towards the unions? It depends partly on the outcome of the General Election in 1991 or 1992. If the Conservatives regain office, then restrictionist policy is likely to continue, not necessarily because it is effective but for ideological reasons. If the Conservatives lose, a different policy framework is likely to emerge, since the Labour Party's policy proposals on trade unions and industrial relations provide a somewhat different emphasis. According to its policy review document, if re-elected to power, Labour plans to 'increase the individual rights of people by creating a Charter for employees which will ensure that all workers are covered by the full range of employment rights'. Labour would also 'increase the collective rights of people at work and redress the balance between employers and trade unions which the Tories have deliberately swung so far in the employers' favour'. The more collectivist philosophy underlying Labour's policy proposals are reflected in its statement that: 'Labour believes that trade unions are the most effective channel through which employees can attain sufficient influence with their employers'. In Labour's view, unions help defuse potential conflicts at work, whilst 'through collective bargaining, unions play a key role in the management of change' (Labour Party, 1989, pp. 21 and 24).

The other challenge to restrictionism with its emphases on individualism, market forces and legal regulation of trade unions is likely to come from the European Community (EC). In Autumn 1989, the EC adopted its draft community charter on fundamental social rights. Its aim is to set out 'the major principles on which the European pattern of labour law and, more generally, the European concept of society and the place of labour in that society are based'. It covers a wide range of issues including: the improvement of living and working conditions; employment and remuneration; the right to freedom and movement in the EC; the right to social protection; the right to vocational training; the right of men and women to equal treatment; and the protection of children, adolescents, the elderly and the disabled. The draft charter also incorporates statements on rights to: freedom of association and collective bargaining; information, consultation and worker participation; and health protection and safety at work (CEC, 1989, pp. 1–4). When and how the draft charter is implemented and applied, therefore, are likely to be crucial factors affecting the continuation or demise of restrictionist trade union policy in Britain during the 1990s.

5

Environmental Policy

JOHN BRADBEER

Introduction

Unlike the other chapters in this volume, the subject matter of Chapter 5 is neither self-evident nor necessarily an important part of government policy. Although there has been an environmental movement in Britain for most of this century, only in the last quarter of a century has it been anything other than a minority interest. As a significant political issue, it has had to await Mrs Thatcher's now famous speech to the Royal Society in September 1988 and the 15 per cent share of the vote obtained by the Green Party in the 1989 European Parliament elections.

The term 'environment' is widely and loosely used. In this chapter, the environment will be considered as fulfilling three broad functions for society and the economy:

1. as supplier of natural resources, such as foodstuffs, minerals and water, usually in the form of market goods;
2. as supplier of services, such as scenery, which are rarely market goods;
3. as assimilator of wastes arising from production and consumption, for which markets rarely exist.

Sometimes the adjectives, 'built' and 'natural' are added to the term 'environment'. The former refers to the man-made milieu of settlements. Planning this environment has become a significant activity and is discussed in this review. The natural environment is often contrasted with the built environment yet it too often betrays evidence of human actions, whether deliberate or inadvertent.

It must be noted that the Department of the Environment (DoE) has wide responsibilities for the built environment and not all of its work will be discussed in this chapter. Equally, environmental policy is the responsibility of other ministeries, such as the Ministry of Agriculture, Food and Fisheries (MAFF) and others have the power to influence the environment, such as the Treasury.

This chapter commences by reviewing the recent history of the environment as a popular and political issue. It then considers aspects of environmental policy under the Thatcher governments and concludes by discussing the environmental agenda and the challenge it poses to the ideology of Thatcherism.

The Environment as a Popular and Political Issue: its Rise, Fall and Resurrection

Many suggest that Rachel Carson's book, *Silent Spring*, published in 1962, marked the birth of the modern environmental movement. It had a major impact in the USA and Europe, and several serious pollution incidents which followed, made environmental issues newsworthy. In the USA, public concern was such that a reluctant President Nixon signed the 1969 National Environmental Policy Act, which remains one of the world's most far-reaching pieces of environmental legislation. Friends of the Earth and Greenpeace were formed during this period which climaxed in 1972 with the publication of *Limits to Growth* and its prediction of an early ecological end of civilisation and stimulated general debate on environmental matters.

The environment seemed to occupy a less prominent position during the next decade. While oil price rises and embargoes underlined the importance of energy to modern industrial societies, the impact of the recession which followed the 1973 oil shock, loomed larger in public perception. With deflationary policies being followed by New Right governments in North America and Europe, unemployment became the major concern. Coupled with the outbreak of the second Cold War and escalation of the nuclear arms race, environmental issues came a poor second to questions of survival.

The mid-1980s saw a major change in priorities and the environment re-emerged as a major issue, often taking politicians by surprise. Global environmental problems replaced nuclear annihilation as the dominant threat to human survival. Depletion of the ozone layer and the attendant threat of radiation and the emission of gaseous pollutants producing acid rain, or worse, warming of the earth (the Greenhouse Effect) became issues of public concern. Also for the wealthier two-thirds of the population, the environment as a source of services to consume has become important.

Two explanations for the rise, fall and revival of the environment as a political issue have been offered. The first is the issue attention cycle proposed by Anthony Downs (1972). He saw environmental concern in the USA as passing through a five-stage cycle:

- *stage 1 the pre-problem stage*: the problem exists and may be severe but the public is unaware, the media uninterested and only interest groups are alarmed;
- *stage 2 alarmed discovery and euphoric enthusiasm*: the problem is suddenly discovered as a result of some particular event; the public call for solutions and politicians promise action;
- *stage 3 realising the cost of significant progress*: this comes slowly and follows disclosures about the sacrifices necessary and the uncertainty of successful technological solutions;
- *stage 4 gradual decline of public interest*: public concern falls either through boredom or rejection of the scale of the changes necessary or the costs involved;
- *stage 5 post-problem stage*; the public forgets about the issue but most original problems remain; a few institutions devoted to the problem may survive but on severely reduced funding.

Downs accurately predicted the relative eclipse of the environmental movement in the later 1970s but the revival of interest a decade later is inconsistent with the model. The second explanation suggests that society since the mid-1960s or so is now fundamentally different from the earlier years of the century. One version of this explanation is the 'post-industrial society', a term coined by Daniel Bell (1973) to describe socio-economic and cultural change producing a classless society and new political agendas, which may favour new issues such as the environment. A second version of this explanation is that of 'New Times', especially as articulated by *Marxism Today*. This suggests that social, economic and cultural changes have occurred and that we now live in a post-Fordist economy and a post-modernist social and cultural formation. New Times are characterised by diversity, uncertainty and individuality and a general bewilderment. Environmental issues can become a focus for individual identity and action in New Times, whilst environmental problems can be regarded as a legacy of the Fordist economy and of discredited modernist social and cultural values.

British general elections since 1979 have been fought on the economic and social aspects of New Times and the environment has been only a minor issue, although the main parties did make some reference to it in 1983 and 1987. In the 1989 European parliamentary elections, it did become a major issue, often being exploited by Labour as part of its attack on a decade of Thatcherism.

Generally, scientific understanding of environmental problems has run ahead of public concern. Global warming through increasing concentrations of carbon dioxide in the atmosphere was recognised by the late 1960s and depletion of stratospheric ozone recognised a few years later. As further research has been done, the scale and complexity of the problems has become apparent and it is clear that increased knowledge has not provided simple and direct answers. Nonetheless, public interest has grown and the environment appears to have avoided the usual fate of issues in the attention cycle. Quite possibly, the full realisation of the scale of problems and the costs of effective environmental policy action has yet to occur. Often in western societies environmental problems have been denied a place on the political agenda and Crenson (1972) coined the term 'unpolitics' to describe how air pollution in American cities was not allowed to be regarded as a problem. The period of unpolitics of the environment in Britain appears to be over but its intractable nature may lead to the environment becoming extra-political and its problems seen as beyond resolution.

Environmental Policy Since 1979

It may be thought that there has been little environmental policy produced in the Thatcher years. Such a view misses both the wider characteristics of policy and the distinctive nature of environmental policy. 'Policy' can be both action and inaction, and each may be carefully calculated for its effect. Equally, policy action can result from a conscious wish to initiate change or to respond to perceived problems or a concession under pressure from other governements and international institutions. Environmental policy may be formulated for its own sake or used as a subordinate issue in a wider argument, as has often seemed to be the case in United Kingdom–EC relations. Environmental policy can be formulated and applied at four distinct geographical scales: local, national, EC and international. As Chapter 12 shows, the autonomy allowed to local government has been much reduced since 1979, but for more than a century, local government has had an important role in environmental policy. Conversely, the importance of the EC in environmental policy has grown significantly and the environment has come to a greater prominence in EC deliberations. The 1970s and 1980s have also seen a growing trend toward international cooperation on environmental issues, especially under the aegis of the United Nations Environmental Programme.

As suggested earlier, for environmental policy the Thatcher years can be divided into two unequal parts. Until her speech to the Royal

Society in September 1988 in which she expressed her concern at global climatic problems, the environment had not been a political priority. Since then, it has risen appreciably in significance and was underlined in the 1989 Cabinet reshuffle when Christopher Patten replaced the unpopular Nicholas Ridley to become the sixth Secretary of State for the Environment in ten years. Even in the low priority accorded the environment in the early 1980s a number of principles can be discerned. The review which follows is selective and examines environmental policy in six areas.

Agriculture, Countryside and Nature Conservation

Many environmentalists would see these as three large and distinct policy areas. The justification for bringing them together is that they formed the heart of the first piece of environmental legislation of the new Conservative government and that the legislation and the subsequent debate about its effectiveness reveal much of the character of recent environmental policy.

The 1981 Wildlife and Countryside Act began life as a fairly technical and broadly bipartisan bill in the closing years of the Labour government. On its reintroduction in the new parliament, it accumulated more sections and, as some commentators saw it, was transformed from a dull bill into a controversial one. Much of the Act is unexceptional, among other things strengthening protection of flora and fauna, introducing Marine Nature Reserves and giving the Countryside Commission new status. Controversy surrounds its treatment of the relationship between agriculture and landscape and wildlife conservation. Protected areas such as National Parks and Sites of Special Scientific Interest (SSSIs) have come under pressure from changing agricultural practices. The Act sought to temper this conflict by a complex but voluntary system of notification by landowners of their intentions to the conservation bodies, which were supposed to respond by offering management agreements to protect the valued sites. The Act allowed landowners to demand compensation for entering into management agreements, based on future profits foregone by not damaging the sites. The National Parks authorities and the Nature Conservancy Council were to be given no new funds for compensation payments. As most actions which threatened landscape or habitat would attract grant-aid from MAFF, whose budget was vastly larger than those for conservation, environmentalists were incensed at this part of the act.

Tests of principle were not long in coming. Especially prominent were arguments over draining wetlands such as Halvergate Marshes in Broadlands and West Sedgemoor in Somerset. In both cases compromises were finally agreed, involving extra funding and ad hoc solutions, not strictly within the terms of the Act but preserving the voluntary principle. Elsewhere and less publicised, landscapes and habitats were destroyed by agricultural intensification. Agriculture has increasingly been criticised from two sources. Environmentalists have attacked modern farming practices for transforming the countryside (the theft of the countryside in Marion Shoard's phrase (1989)), destroying habitats and polluting the environment with farm wastes and agrochemicals. They have found allies in government, as reform of the Common Agricultural Policy (CAP) has become a key issue between Britain and the EC. The costs of payments under CAP and of storing the food surpluses it generates have caused a gradual reform of the policy. Quotas to limit production have been introduced and a policy of set-aside (payments to take land out of production) adopted. Perhaps one-third of the farmland of England and Wales would be set aside, if intensive farming is maintained elsewhere. This could be the poorer agricultural land, which often has higher amenity, landscape and nature conservation value than the now intensively farmed lowlands. However, agriculture does have a management role in the countryside and set-aside land given over to golf courses will have little conservation value. The government has been reluctant to see a less intensive and more ecologically harmonious agriculture as a solution to over-production.

In 1984 MAFF conceded the principle of grant-aiding farming in Less Favoured Areas (LFAs) (essentially the hill farms of the north and west) for farming in ways which protect the environment. In 1985 an EC regulation under the CAP established Environmentally Sensitive Areas (ESAs). These are to be especially aided to support farming which is compatible with and enhances environmental conservation. Twelve such ESAs have been designated in Britain. Nonetheless, agriculture is still given favourable treatment and regarded as production, not conservation orientated.

Although Nicholas Ridley's plans to privatise National Nature Reserves have been dropped, his scheme to split the Nature Conservancy Council and merge its Scottish and Welsh operations with the Countryside Commissions there, is to proceed. This will bring nature conservation in those countries firmly under Scottish and Welsh Office control and is intended to weaken the conservation case against agricultural development.

The Planning System

Central to environmental policy at the local level for more than forty years has been the planning system. As a frequent justification for land-use planning is market failure, the planning system has come under close scrutiny from a government committed to rolling back the powers of the state, cutting bureaucracy and asserting the primacy of the market. Although the planning system has survived, it has been weakened in a number of ways. The 1980 Local Government, Planning and Land Act began the process of making planning less comprehensive and rigorous. This was taken further with the creation of Simplified Planning Zones (SPZs) under the 1986 Housing and Planning Act. In these zones, many of the existing planning regulations do not apply. The present planning system sees Structure Plans, strategic statements, prepared by County Councils, and Local Plans and planning decisions taken by District Councils. Structure planning is under review and its abolition would end county involvement in planning and leave planning as a locally based case review process.

The Secretary of State has considerable powers under the Town and Country Planning Acts, as he can issue instructions to planning authorities and acts as the final arbiter in cases of appeal against planning decisions. In both roles Secretaries of State have been active, and they have swung the balance further in favour of developers.

A continuing problem for the planning system has been the public inquiry into very large and complex projects such as coalfields, power stations and the Channel Tunnel. Major public inquiries have been held into the Vale of Belvoir coalfield and the Sizewell B and Hinkley Point C nuclear power stations. Objectors have argued that the need for such developments should be as much a part of the inquiry as the siting. Government has grudgingly conceded this but the scale, legal formality and costs of representation at inquiries has placed voluntary opposition groups at a major disadvantage. Public confidence is lacking in a system which is seen as so heavily weighted in favour of government.

One possible improvement would be the use of environmental-impact-assessment (e-i-a) as developed in the USA since the 1960s. The EC argues that this is so and issued a Directive to this effect in 1985. Until then, the British government had set its face against e-i-a, notwithstanding advocacy of e-i-a from the planning profession and its use by the oil industry in British planning applications. Britain now has e-i-a, but very narrowly interpreted and with limited scope for application. In the case of the Channel Tunnel, government encouraged the consortium to obtain a private act of parliament, thus avoiding any planning inquiry.

Pollution

Waste generation is an unavoidable product of economic activity. Structural economic change, such as the loss of old and polluting manufacturing capacity in the 1980s can reduce pollution. However, other factors are important and UK pollution has increased, particularly that of water, and increases in motor vehicles have offset reductions in air pollution from other sources. The government receives advice on pollution from the Royal Commission on Environmental Pollution, which escaped the early purge of quangos in 1979–80. The Royal Commission has long advocated an integrated approach to pollution control and in particular, the merger of the Hazardous Waste and Air Pollution Inspectorates. In 1987 the DoE abandoned its resistance to the merger and created a unified Pollution Inspectorate. However with about 200 staff to monitor many processes at numerous plants and sites, enforcement of existing legislation remains difficult. A similar situation exists for water quality control. From 1989 this became the responsibilty of the National Rivers Authority but it too has a small staff, with each of its inspectors having an average of 500 square kilometres to patrol.

Until the early 1980s, the Regional Water Authorities had made considerable progress in cleansing fresh water in England and Wales, in particular tackling the under-investment in sewage treatment works. However the financial disciplines imposed by the Treasury on the public sector soon manifested themselves in declining water quality standards. Whilst some of the grossest river pollution has been eliminated, classically in the Thames, many other formerly clean rivers are now moderately polluted, particularly from agricultural sources. Prosecutions for pollution are increasing but fines remain small. The Secretary of State has powers to waive sewage discharge standards and in the run-up to water privatisation gave short-term waivers for almost one sixth of the sewage treatment works.

The EC has been particularly active on water quality. It has set standards for drinking water and failure to meet these in parts of East Anglia and in Scotland, has led the EC to refer Britain to the European Court. Britain's initial response to the directive had been to seek lengthy extensions to the time limits for compliance, and its failure to enact EC standards led to the prosecution. The costs of meeting the directive have been estimated at £1.4bn. A second EC directive to prove costly and embarrassing is that on bathing water, issued in 1976. Britain responded most negatively, denying any proven link between sewage discharge and health risks to bathers and then only designating 27 bathing beaches (Luxembourg designated 2 beaches!). Public concern gradually forced a change in attitude and Britain now has over 350 designated bathing beaches. Nonetheless, a major programme costing over £200m is needed to bring 54 up to EC standards. In most cases, the solution adopted has been to build longer sea outfalls but to continue to discharge raw sewage. The EC is now actively considering a new directive to forbid this.

Energy

Although the government has avoided any formal and comprehensive energy policy, several principles have emerged. The very avoidance of a formal national energy policy is a clear indication of the importance given to market forces in the energy economy. Sectoral decisions have given a clear perspective to energy policy. Budgets of energy conservation bodies were cut and justified as the fact that energy saving was rational behaviour for industrial and domestic consumers and needed no promotion. Likewise, attempts to influence energy consumption by fiscal policy have been resisted, and in consequence, falling energy prices in real terms have slowed the energy conservation process. However in the 1989 Budget, the tax differential between leaded and unleaded petrol was increased, and unleaded petrol, previously about 1 per cent of all sales rose to 25 per cent within months. The energy saving potential of public transport is considerable, but public transport has had a very low priority in public spending plans.

A major element in energy policy has been the reduction in Britain's dependence on domestically produced coal. This has taken two forms. First, British Coal has been streamlined and pits closed, concentrating production on the low cost fields of Yorkshire and the East Midlands. Paradoxically, this has increased Britain's reliance on high sulphur coals and has hindered attempts to cut sulphur dioxide emissions. Secondly, Mrs Thatcher especially has been an enthusiastic advocate of nuclear power. Britain's unhappy technical and economic experience with nuclear power since the 1970s prompted the decision to base a new nuclear power programme on an American design. Nuclear safety issues have grown in importance, especially since the Chernobyl accident in 1986. The location of new nuclear power stations, nuclear waste reprocessing plants and waste disposal sites as well as the decommisioning of obsolete plants have become tendentious issues.

Privatization and the Environment

Although there have been few proposals to privatise environmental services or regulation, environmental issues have contributed to the two major delays which the privatisation process has experienced. In 1985 a Green Paper announced the intention to privatise the water industry and in 1986 a White Paper gave details of a transfer of the existing Regional Water Authorities (RWAs) to the private sector.

Environmentalists and industrialists objected to the scheme whereby RWAs would remain water quality regulators of themselves and other water users. The government had hoped for the bill's quick passage before the General Election and withdrew it. When the second Green Paper appeared in 1987, the regulatory functions of the RWAs had been removed and given to a new National Rivers Authority. This was duly enacted in the 1989 Water Act.

Electricity privatisation was postponed late in 1989 because of technical arguments over pricing after privatisation. The roots of these lie in the vast costs of power stations and how they should be shared and the uncertainties and risks of decommisioning nuclear power stations after closure. The government had already withdrawn some obsolescent nuclear power stations from privatisation.

For both privatisations (and see Chapter 2 for a wider discussion), the government has had to reconcile its belief in the greater efficiency and cheapness of private enterprise and its abhorrence of regulation with the costs of meeting environmental standards. For water, a 'green dowry' of £4bn was given, effectively eliminating debt from the industry. However, meeting EC water standards could add 25–30 per cent to consumer charges in the near future. For electricity, the government imposed an obligation on the industry to meet 20 per cent of demand from non-fossil fuel sources. This could include hydro-electricity and environmentally benign sources such as solar or wind energy, but in the short-medium term, it necessitates nuclear energy. Such extra costs can be passed direct to consumers under special pricing arrangements.

Global Atmospheric Issues

A report from Britain's UN Ambassador on global warming is credited with triggering Mrs Thatcher's concern for environmental matters. Britain's attitude to atmospheric pollution problems has been mixed. The problem of acid rain has been recognised for more than two decades. Burning fossil fuels and some industrial processes release sulphur dioxide and oxides of nitrogen into the air. Winds carry them long distances and they fall as acid rain or snow. In the 1960s new power stations were built with extended smoke stacks in the belief that gases would disperse in the atmosphere and cause no further problem. Forest die-back and the acidification of lakes in Scandinavia and West Germany showed that acid rain was a real problem. Britain denied that its power stations played any part and argued that no-one fully understood the complex geochemistry of atmospheric and environmental interactions. Later, when agreements were sought to reduce sulphur dioxide emissions, Britain refused to join the '30 per cent club' to cut emissions by one-third. It was claimed that by switching to low sulphur oil from the North Sea, Britain had already made a major reduction in emissions and that no further action was needed.

Depletion of the stratospheric ozone layer and the attendant threat to human health was realised in the 1970s and the complex atmospheric chemistry of chlorofluorocarbons (CFCs) was later understood. World action to curb production and release of CFCs followed in the 1980s. Britain, while accepting these, has been less sympathetic to technology transfers to Third World countries to help them avoid further contributing to ozone depletion. The major environmental issue for many is global warming, the so-called Greenhouse Effect. Many gases naturally present in the atmosphere in only small amounts trap solar radiation reflected from the earth's surface. Carbon dioxide is the main greenhouse gas and its concentration has increased markedly since the 1950s. Methane and CFCs are less abundant but even more powerful greenhouse gases. It is estimated that global temperatures could rise by an average of 4° by the middle of the next century and lead to general increases in sea-level. The major sources of carbon dioxide are fossil fuel burning and deforestation. Dealing with the Greenhouse Effect has hardly begun and will require major international efforts.

Discussion of Policies Adopted

The environment poses major problems for human survival and in the shorter-term perspectives of politics, it poses a challenge to British traditions of policy-making and to the ideology of Thatcherism. Environmental characteristics are such that problems are difficult to address. They are complex and impinge on almost all other policy areas; they are rapidly changing and may suddenly appear; and they are no respecters of national boundaries. Growing public awareness and concern for the environment makes policy formulation more critical.

In Britain the political and administrative system has placed great emphasis on gradualism and an incremental approach to policy. Problems are dealt with as they arise and in a piecemeal fashion and for the environment, this often succeeds only in displacing them. More than others, environmental problems require large-scale and radical solutions. The legislative process is complex and Parliament can deal only with four or five major bills per session and each department may only get two major Acts passed in a Parliament. Given the size of DoE's responsibilities, it is hardly surprising that the Environmental Protection Act 1990 will be only the second purely environmental legislation of the Thatcher governments.

British political culture also places stress on confidentiality and attaches lesser importance to public participation in policy-making. Given the rise in environmental interest, many feel that this is a significant challenge to the system. Traditionally, also, government has tended to coopt certain pressure and interest groups and exclude others from the policy process. Thus agricultural policy-making has been open to groups like the National Farmers' Union but relatively closed to environmental pressure groups.

Environmental policy in Britain has usually favoured an approach emphasising ambient environmental quality. Practically, this has meant accepting discharges of wastes of exploitation of the environment to a level at which the environment changes unacceptably. Thus, so long as discharge or exploitation rates are low, there is no need to be concerned nor to introduce regulation. Natural biophysical and biochemical processes and the natural dilution, absorption or regenerative capacities of the environment maintain its quality. The American approach, followed increasingly by the EC, emphasises emission standards for waste discharges. All discharges, irrespective of volume or location must meet certain minimum standards and environmental quality is maintained by regulating all discharges. Related to this contrast, is the debate between Best Practicable Means and Best Available Practice. Britain favours the former, arguing that standards of effluent discharge and therefore the quality of pollution control technology do not need to be as high for a single waste discharge on a large river as on a small one or where there are other discharges. The latter approach insists that the best control technology currently available should be used to reduce pollution potential of all wasters, wherever discharged. It is the Best Practicable environmental option which is to be recognised in the 1990 Environmental Protection Act and its operation will prove complex in practice.

Many commentators have suggested that Mrs Thatcher has given a very significant hostage to fortune by her public espousal of environmental issues. There are several reasons why this should be so and most challenge directly the ideology of Thatcherism.

Markets

Many environmental problems are caused by market failure. For some functions, like landscape quality, there are no markets and nor is it easy to see how there ever could be. For other functions, notably water and air, pollution shows that markets have not worked as producers have found it easy to externalise pollution costs and impose them involuntarily on society. For a government committed to market forces to acknowledge a major area where markets do not exist or function most imperfectly, the environment is a major challenge.

Individualism and Voluntarism

Individual consumer sovereignty fails hopelessly in the face of many environmental problems. There is nothing a whole country, let alone an individual consumer, can do which will have any significant impact on global warming. Only global-scale, concerted action (including mutual assistance and ultimate sanctions) will suffice. Maintaining river water quality requires all users to cooperate and one careless or wanton act can nullify years of effort. The environment is clearly a public good which requires public regulation. Since 1979, the rhetoric has been that of freedom of choice and of an end to regulation. Protecting the environment is not easily reconcilable with this and experience has shown its limitations.

Sovereignty

The environment is no respecter of national boundaries, yet a narrowly interpreted British interest has been evident since 1979. Global environmental problems will require major collaborative programmes between North and South and acknowledgment of supra-national authority. In the EC, environmental matters have assumed critical importance with the harmonisation of the Single Market. Britain may insist that with its robust environment it does not need to meet EC standards, but others may argue that low environmental standards give Britain a reputation of the 'dirty man of Europe' and an unfair competitive advantage.

Science and the Technical Fix

Some argue that environmental problems are susceptible to careful scientific analysis, which will yield clear and unequivocal answers. Then, a few new regulations, perhaps minor alterations in fiscal policy or investment in new technology will solve the problem. Belief that all problems have technological answers is the 'technical fix'. In practice, science has shown how complex environmental problems are and has yielded few simple answers. Administrative solutions often fail to work (the water industry is being reorganised on average every decade) and major technological projects exacerbate problems. Thus environmental problems may require deep-seated and fundamental social, economic and political changes. Certainly, the belief that economic growth and environmental protection are entirely compatible will be carefully revised.

Such profound changes go to the heart of the ideology of Thatcherism. Battle lines will be drawn up on the environment. It is possible to see the environment as another good to be bought and sold, or as something to be acquired as a status symbol or positional good. Environmental responsibility could be presented as being the duty of the individual (penalties for litter dropping or dog fouling) and individuals may displace unwanted environmental change (the NIMBY – not in my backyard – approach). The 1990 Environmental Protection Act well illustrates these tensions with its mixture of individualism on litter penalties, regulatory adjustment on local waste disposal while allowing for the privatisation of actual disposal and enhanced powers for the Pollution Inspectorate, without greater resources to enforce them.

In the medium term, Christopher Patten has expressed his wish to follow the recommendations of the Pearce Report (1989). David Pearce is a well known British environmental economist and was commissioned by the government to write a report on environmental policy. In it, Pearce made what are the traditional recommendations of environmental economists; in particular arguing that government make the polluter must pay principle the basis of policy. This should take the form either of competitive bidding for rights to discharge pollutants or of formal taxation of discharges. The former offers polluters the option of investing in pollution control or of bidding for licences to discharge. The latter option, which Pearce favours, would compel all polluters to bear the costs of their actions. A system of fiscal incentives to invest in pollution control could also be coupled to it.

Although such measures could be reconciled with market priorities, it would be only at the cost of recognising basic market imperfections and accepting a significantly wider role for government in regulation. Furthermore, the impact of such pollution taxation would be considerable. A carbon tax, such as has been suggested to curb carbon dioxide emissions would not only bear on industry and commerce, but also on households, either directly through raised petrol prices, for instance, but also indirectly through increased prices for goods and services.

Commodification and individualisation of the environment are perfectly compatible with Thatcherism but will contribute little to human survival. The real agenda will be to work out a strategy for sustainable and equitable occupation of the planet by all its peoples. To fulfill this awesome responsibility, fundamental cultural and social as well as economic changes will be required, for the status quo is simply environmentally unsustainable.

6

A War on Crime?
Law and Order Policies
in the 1980s

STEPHEN P. SAVAGE

Intoduction

Prior to the 1979 General Election 'law and order' policy, the means by which governments seek to control crime and maintain public order through enforcement of the criminal law, exhibited many of the features of the consensus politics of the post-war period. Indeed, so broad was the agreement over policy in this area (with the exception perhaps of support for or opposition to the reintroduction of capital punishment), that in many respects law and order was hardly a 'political' issue in the sense of falling along distinct party-political lines. This is not to say that law and order policy itself remained static during the period (Ryan, 1983), rather that the major developments which did take place did so within a broad framework of political consensus.

This environment changed markedly in the campaign for the 1979 Election. That law and order was high on the Conservatives' agenda was made abundantly clear when Thatcher declared that 'the demand in the country will be for two things: less tax and more law and order' (28 March 1979). Rising crime, public disorder, political protest and industrial unrest were all merged to form an image of a society under seige from the forces of lawlessness. Blame was attached variously to the trade unions and union law, 'permissive' education, the failure of both Labour and Conservative governments to direct adequate resources to the police and the penal system, and, not least, inadequacies within the criminal justice system itself. The latter covered a range of additional issues, including the 'welfarist' and 'treatment' approaches to juvenile crime favoured by liberal professionals, such as social workers and probation officers, and implemented in part in legislation during the 1970s. Such strategies were based on the assumption that most offenders were victims of social deprivation, who would benefit by improvements in their social and family environments rather than increased punishment. To Thatcher and her followers, this had meant the decline of the deterrence factor in the penal system, and almost implied 'excusing' the criminal rather than punishing him. Part of the Conservative electoral platform therefore was the pledge to 'get tough' on offenders through changes in sentencing law. It also sought to address other features of the criminal justice system, including providing 'adequate' powers to the police and the creation of more prison places so that the penal systen had the capacity to respond to this 'war on crime'.

It is against this backcloth that Conservative policy on law and order emerged. This chapter seeks to outline the major features of that policy as it developed throughout the 1980s, and to consider the central features of more recent policy and their likely role in future law and order policy. It is divided into two main sections, the first covering policy developments from 1979 to the mid-1980s, the second dealing with initiatives in the second half of the decade and into the 1990s. It will be seen that, particularly as the 1980s has progressed, the early approaches to crime control have been modified significantly in the direction of what many (including a number on the political right) consider to be 'liberal' in emphasis. The concern with final parts of the chapter is with the extent to which such moves constitute a contradiction in the politics of the Thatcher governments. As will be seen, the conclusion is that even such apparently 'liberal' policies can be reconciled with the ideology of the right, particularly with notions of 'individualism' and 'self-responsibility'.

Law and Order Policy – 1979–85

There is no denying that the pre-election commitments on law and order were translated into action from the earliest days of the 1979 Thatcher government. Both in terms of the provision of resources and in terms of legislative reform, the government was quick to move on what they saw as a priority issue for the new administration.

While many other areas of public expenditure were subjected to a restrictive if not reductionist policy in the early 1980s, the law and order budget was allowed something of a privileged existence. One of the first acts of the 1979 government was to introduce substantial increases in police pay, honouring a pre-election pledge to implement in full the recommendations of the Edmund Davies Committee, set up by the previous Labour government. Funding was also made available, as it has on occasions since, for increases in the police establishment, producing what by 1985 had become an 8 per cent increase in police personnel. This is alongside a parallel increase in the resources which have been made available for expenditure on police equipment, particularly for public order policing. The government also made provision for an expansion in the court system, and set in motion a major programme of prison building which would, it hoped, abolish prison overcrowding and thus reduce pressures on the courts as well as on the administration of the prisons themselves. Overall expenditure on law and order has, as a consequence, increased in excess of 40 per cent in real terms since 1979. Despite the fact that the Home Office has since insisted that all of the services involved seek to make the most efficient use of their resources (particularly the police, on whom the great bulk of the budget in spent), there is certainly some truth in Margaret Thatcher's claim that 'Never, ever, have you heard me say we will economise on law and order' (10 August 1985).

Resources, however, tell only part of the story. It is in the field of changes in the law that the most controversial elements of the Thatcher record on law and order lie. The first stage in this direction was the passing of the Criminal Justice Act 1982, which implemented many of the proposals of the 1980 White Paper *Young Offenders* (Cm. 8045). This signalled a marked shift from the 'welfare' approach of earlier governments. The Act established new sentences for the courts in the form of shorter sentences (21 days to 4 months) in detention centres, which were themselves to be tougher and more disciplinarian regimes than their predecessors (the so-called 'Short,Sharp Shock'). It also replaced Borstal training in favour of sentences to a Youth Custody Centre for offenders of 15–21 years of age. Overall, the Act was seen as a victory for the 'law and order lobby', over the preferences of many who actually worked in the penal system, particularly in the area of juvenile justice.

Far more controversial, however, was the passing of the Police and Criminal Evidence Act 1984, possibly the most contentious piece of legislation in the 1980s, and possibly the most contentious ever in the criminal justice area. The Act contained a thorough overhaul of the existing law defining police powers and evidence in criminal trials. It created new national powers of stop and search, redefined powers of arrest (to include the power of arrest on even a trivial offence if the suspect fails to identify himself), and established new laws on police detention and interrogation. Other clauses covered powers to set up roadblocks, search premises and undertake body-searches (Zander, 1986). The law on detention in police custody possibly attracted most attention. It establishes the power of detention for up to 24 hours without charge on a non-serious offence, and for up to 96 hours without charge on a serious offence.

Such clauses were regarded by critics as drastic extensions of police powers at the expense of civil liberties (Christian, 1983). Even senior members of the judiciary were concerned that the Act went too far in granting the police new powers. The debate which surrounded the legislation was a bitter and prolonged one. It is impossible to develop these issues in this context. However, several points can be made in the light of the criticisms made of the Act. Firstly, much of the legislation is drawn directly from the Report of the Royal Commission on Criminal Procedure 1981, which was set up by the previous Labour government, and it is highly likely that had Labour still been in office it too would have followed many of the Commission's proposals. Secondly, the Act is accompanied by an expansive and rigorous Code of Practice governing police conduct (eg. the Code lays down strict rules for lengths of interrogation periods, periodic review of detention, etc.). Thirdly, some commentators have argued that critics of the Act ignore the laxity of the laws regulating police powers prior to the Act, and even go as far as to say that in many respects the Act actually reduces police powers (Reiner, 1985). Finally, one should note that, largely as a result of the Report, the police have now lost the power to decide on prosecutions. The Prosecution of Offenders Act 1985 took the responsibility for the prosecution process out of the hands of the police, and created an independent Crown Prosecution Service. Talk of a massive 'extension' of police powers in these respects is problematic to say the least. Other pieces of legislation during the first half of the decade to note include the Public Order Act of 1986, which laid down restrictions on marches and demonstrations, and the Sporting Events (Control of Alcohol, etc.) Act, which dealt with restrictions on alcohol to combat violence and disorder amongst football spectators.

As regards policing, however, developments beyond actual legislation had attracted critical attention during the first half of the 1980s. Early in the first Thatcher administration, major disturbances occurred in many of Britain's innercities, such as Brixton in London, St Pauls in Bristol, and Toxteth in Liverpool. They involved clashes between the police and particularly black youth. (Similar occurrences were to take place in the mid-1980s in Tottenham in London and Handsworth in Birmingham). Whatever other causes involved, it became clear, most notably in the Scarman Report released in 1982, that at least a part of the problem lay in poor relations between the police and the black community, and that, at least as far as Scarman was concerned, these were to an extent the result of bad policing and an element of racism in the force. Scarman set out a number of proposals for changes in police methods, training and consultation with the community, many of which were since implemented in policing policies.

The second development of major significance was the policing of the miners' strike in 1984–5. Massive police operations were involved in policing the mass pickets at the various coalfields in Nottingham, South Wales and South Yorkshire and other areas, which raised serious doubts about the role of the police in industrial disputes. On the one hand, criticisms were made of police tactics employed to control the picket, which involved mounted police and baton charges, some of which were, so it seemed, derived from methods developed in the Hong Kong riot police squads. On the other hand, concern was expressed over the centralised control of the movement of police officers from forces around the country to the coalfields, which smacked of a neo-national police force, possibly under the direct influence of the Thatcher government, which had set itself out to defeat the National Union of Mineworkers (NUM).

Both sets of events helped fuel the debate over the issue of police accountability, which raged throughout the early to mid-1980s. Some of the subsequent developments in law and order policy took some of the sting out of that issue.

Law and Order policy Since 1985

More recent government policy on crime control, much of which will set out the stall for policy into the 1990s, can be grouped under two main headings. On the one hand is the legislative reform which followed the government's 1986 White Paper *Criminal Justice: Plans for Legislation* (Cm. 9658), and which spawned two Acts of Parliament, The Criminal Justice Acts of 1987 and 1988. On the other hand there is a more diverse range of policies and strategies which we can label 'Crime Control and the Community' – this includes the government's 1990 White Paper *Crime, Justice and Protecting the Public* (Cm. 965), which amongst other things sets out the government's plans for a new form of punishment 'in the community' and a range of other developments which locate the task of crime control increasingly within community networks. As will be seen, these developments raise interesting questions about the relationship of contemporary law and order policy to traditional right wing notions of crime and the means to reduce it.

Criminal Justice Acts 1987 and 1988

Despite the rate of change in the criminal justice field in the first half of the 1980s, the government has insisted that much remains to be done. Apart from rationalising and streamlining the criminal justice system, it has sought to confront head-on some of the traditional features of British court procedure. In particular, it has made no pretence about its determination to sweep away what it considers to be obstacles to the conviction and appropriate punishment of the guilty. Amongst other objectives, it is against this backcloth that we can situate the Criminal Justice Acts of 1987 and 1988.

Both pieces of legislation (separated only because of the interruption of the 1987 General Election), stemmed from the 1986 White Paper *Criminal Justice: Plans for Legislation.* This was introduced as a set of proposals which would continue the work of the other pieces of legislation referred to above, expressing the government's 'full support to the police, the courts and the prison and probation services'. The White Paper set out its main objectives:

> To ensure that the courts have an adequate range of powers to enable them to punish the most serious offenders with the right measure of severity and to enable less serious offenders to be dealt with effectively in the community.

> To ensure that the court system and its related services operate as efficiently and as effectively as possible.

> To increase the effectiveness of the international fight against crime by improved arrangements for extradition.

> To improve the provision which is made for victims.

The legislation which followed, after protracted parliamentary debate, was extremely complex and wide-reaching. All I shall attempt to do is to outline in broad terms the major features of the Acts, and pick up on one or two particularly contentious and indicative aspects of the reforms (for a discussion see Morton, 1988).

The Criminal Justice Act 1987

The Criminal Justice Act 1987 was concerned exclusively with serious fraud. It was influenced heavily by the recommendations of the Roskill Committee on Fraud Trials, set up in response to public concern about the effectiveness of methods of combating serious commercial crime. The Act established the Serious Fraud Office under the supervision of the Attorney General, laid down conditions for committal proceedings and pre-trial hearings, and introduced a new offence of 'conspriracy to defraud'. In general, the reforms were aimed at modernising criminal procedure in the light of the increasing complexity of this form of criminal activity.

Criminal Justice Act 1988

It was left to the Criminal Justice Act 1988 to deal with the vast bulk of legislation thrown up by the White paper. In that regard, a number of major legal reforms were introduced:

- *Extradition*: The Act set out new extradition procedures, i.e. the procedures enabling a state to gain the return of someone accused of or convicted of committing an offence in its own territory from another state. It sought to do away with rules holding in the UK which, according to foreign governments, were unduly restrictive. It abolished the requirement that, before a person could be extradited to another country, the requesting country establish in UK courts a prima facie case against him or her. This was justified on the grounds that it brought the UK into line with the European Convention on Extradition.
- *Evidence in trials*: The Act introduced new rules by which evidence in criminal trials could be given; this changed the position in two major respects. Firstly, it dramatically extended the right of courts to accept 'documentary evidence' (evidence not given in person but on documents submitted to the court). This was largely in response to the recommendations of the Roskill Report (1986) and its concern about the complexity of evidence in certain, particularly fraud, trials. Critics argued that this reduced the rights of the defence to cross-examine witnesses and lowered the standards of proof in such cases. Secondly, provision was made for the use of video-links, whereby children under the age of 14 could give evidence to the court in certain cases of alleged sexual offences, without actually being present in the courtroom. This was in response to growing concern about the traumas suffered by children when giving evidence in open court in such cases, and the belief that this had led to many unjustified acquittals.
- *Over-lenient sentences*: An established tradition of British criminal law is the right of appeal against sentences which are deemed too severe. It has been the government's contention that an equivalent procedure must be available in cases where the sentence is deemed too lenient, and media attention to certain notorious sentences passed, particularly in rape trials, had fuelled this belief. The Act introduced a mechanism whereby the Attorney General could refer such cases to the Court of Appeal which may, if it so decides, increase the sentence. This effectively strengthens the hand of the prosecution in the sentencing process. This new power has already been put into operation in a number of criminal cases.

- *Transfer of court business*: The Act continued a trend established in the 1970s of shifting certain offences (theft of a motor vehicle and criminal damage below a value of £2,000) from being triable by a jury in the Crown Court to being summary offences, triable only in a Magistrates' Court. The justification for this is to relieve pressure from the Crown Court system, which is bursting at the seams, but critics say it effectively reduces even further the right to trial by jury and thus the right to a fair and rigorous trial.

- *Increased maximum sentences*: New sentencing ranges are introduced, increasing maximum sentences for firearms offences, cruelty to children, and corruption.

- *Confiscation of the proceeds of crime*: New powers are created to allow the courts to confiscate the proceeds of organised crime so that the offender cannot enjoy the fruits of his offence after serving his sentence.

- *Criminal compensation*: The Act carries further the trend for greater provision for the victims of crime, by creating an obligation on sentencers to make compensation orders for victims of assault to be paid by the offender. It reduces the discretion available to judges and magistrates on whether to make such orders, and now requires them to give reasons for not doing so.

- *Jury trial*: The Act abolishes the defence's right to peremptory challenge of jurors (whereby up to three jurors could be expelled from sitting on the panel without the defence having to give any reason – normally based on the simple appearance of the juror). No change, however, is made to the power of the prosecution to ask a juror to 'stand by for the Crown', effectively the same as a challenge. The maximum age of eligibility for jury service is increased from 65 to 70 years of age.

- *Young offenders*: In an attempt to ensure that more young offenders are given non-custodial sentences, the Act limits the powers of the courts to pass custodial sentences. It makes obligations on the court to find alternative orders.

Together with a range of miscellaneous reforms (e.g. the creation of a new offence of possessing an indecent photograph of a child), these are the main features of the 1988 Act. Overall, the reforms highlight a number of features of the government's approach, not just to criminal justice but public policy as a whole. Firstly, they are influenced by the desire to make economies. The transfer of business to a Magistrates' Court (far cheaper than jury trial) and the pursuit of non-custodial penalties as an alternative to the expense of keeping offenders in institutions, are expressions of this. Secondly, there is clear evidence of a continued attempt to strengthen the hand of the forces of law-enforcement. Changes in the rules of evidence, the new appeal against over-lenient sentences, and the abolition of the peremptory challenge, all enhance the powers of the prosecution at the expense of the defence. Thirdly, we can see an illustration of a notable feature of the Thatcher governments: the extent to which policy is 'event-led'. Certainly the last two reforms cited were directly influenced by the furore over particular criminal cases; in the case of the new right of appeal by a number of notorious rape cases; in the case of changes in the jury system by famous acquittals in prosecutions brought by the government itself – the Cyprus Spy case and the Clive Ponting trial.

We can now turn to the second feature of contemporary law and order policy as it has emerged since the mid-1980s: crime control in the community.

Crime Control in the Community

'Community-based' approaches to crime control have been a central feature of liberal and progressive strategies on penal policy from the 1960s onwards. They were based on the assumption that the best means to reduce crime, particularly juvenile crime, is to 'treat' the offender in the community rather than punish them in prisons and other custodial establishments. Expressions of this philosophy were the development of Intermediate Treatment (supervision of the offender in a community setting), and the Community Service Order (an alternative to custody involving an order to serve a specified number of hours on community work, such as repairing damaged fencing). It was precisely such 'welfarist' approaches, which rested heavily on the involvement of social workers and probation officers in the penal process, which the Conservative Party of the late 1970s attacked for 'going soft' on crime, and as such for allowing crime to increase rather than decline.

It is something of a paradox, therefore, to find the same party warmly embracing the notion of community-based approaches to crime as the 1980s progressed, for this is certainly what has happened. Alongside its more predictable attempts to strengthen police powers and the prosecution process, it has pursued a range of strategies which have involved mobilising the community in the fight against crime. They have taken a variety of forms, and to a great extent are interdependent:

1. *Community policing*: The Home Office has given strong encouragement to all police forces to adopt or expand community policing. By this they mean policing based on close contact with

the community, consultation with the community about policing matters, more officers on foot-patrol, close links between the police and other agencies such as social services and schools, and so on. While the initial thrust for this came from the Scarman Report in the wake of the inner-city riots of 1980 and 81, the enthusiasm with which the government has endorsed the concept indicates a deeper motive.

2. *Crime prevention*: The government has given its concerted support, backed by resourses, to a massive campaign on crime prevention. It has set up a Ministerial Group on Crime Prevention, bringing together no less than 11 government departments to coordinate national initiatives in the area, and in 1987 set up 'Crime Concern', a national organisation 'to promote the best practices in local crime prevention' (Conservative Election Manifesto, 1987). The basis to the campaign is the belief, long advocated by criminologists inside and outside of the Home Office, that the best means to reduce crime is to limit the opportunities for crime in the first place – better security, better building design so that potential targets for crime are in public view, etc. Furthermore, it was felt that the backbone to an effective crime prevention programme is community awareness and involvement in mutual protection.As John Patten, a Minister of State at the Home Office has said:

> Individual responsibility for one's own property and responsibility towards the wider community are both important in reducing the opportunities for crime (*Guardian*, 9 April 1988)

A striking expression of the campaign has been the national explosion of Neighbourhood Watch schemes, in which local residents, with the help of the police, organise themselves to protect their area from crime or the threat of crime. Research has yet to show convincingly that such schemes actually work – they can simply displace crimes to other areas – but there is no doubting the scale of these developments, with over 70,000 Watches nation-wide.

3. *Punishment in the community*: The answer to the problems of dealing with the offender also lies, it seems, in the community, at least for the less serious offender and particularly the young offender. To the surprise of many, and to the distaste of the more traditional law'n'order lobby, the government in July 1988 published a Green Paper on *Punishment, Custody and the Community*.The document was designed to raise a number of new perspectives on the thorny issue of how best to deal with offenders outside of the easy option of custody.

The Green Paper is at pains to make it clear that its pursuit of alternatives to custody should not be seen as supporting a 'softly softly' approach to crime. It is insistent that what is at issue is punishment in the community, real restrictions on the offender's freedom of action, and not some weak-kneed alternative to punishment. Its central thesis is that the community is, for most sorts of offender, a far more appropriate place for punishment than the prison or the youth custody centre. This view is based on the government's acceptance of a virtual truism in criminological thought: punishing people through custody, while appropriate in certain cases, is more likely to worsen the offender's chances of committing further offences after release. Indeed, in what may be seen as a remarkable indictment on its own policy of the 'Short, Sharp Shock', the Green Paper states that 'Even a short period in custody is quite likely to confirm them as criminals, particularly if they acquire new criminal skills from more sophisticated offenders'.

However, it is concerned that existing alternatives to custody are not tough enough either to win the confidence of sentencers (who then pass custodial sentences), or to actually succeed in altering the young offender's attitudes to life.

Its basic proposals are:

- Custody should be reserved for very serious, particularly violent, offences.
- A new sentence of 'supervision and restriction order' which would enable the courts to make requirements of the offender which might include: compensation to the victim; community service; residence at a hostel or other approved place; prescribed activities at a day centre of elsewhere; curfew or house arrest; tracking of the offenders whereabouts. The new order would therefore include many existing powers but also some novel features. The Green Paper also raises the possibility, in relation to tracking, of using electronic tagging, of the sort in operation in parts of the USA, to monitor the movements of offenders, perhaps to make sure they stay at home in the evening. The task of running tagging schemes could, it says, be undertaken by private companies. The new order is offered as an alternative to custody, mainly for offenders guilty of property crimes (theft and burglary), who are at present being imprisoned.

The proposals were to reappear, virtually unscathed from criticism by such bodies as the National Association of Probation Officers, in the 1990 White Paper *Crime, Justice and Protecting the Public* (Cm. 965). This document stressed even further the view that imprisonment may worsen, rather than reduce, the chances of offenders committing crimes once the punishment is over, and spelt out in more detail the philosophy behind punishment in the community.

Many aspects of the government's current proposals have been welcomed by other parties – such as the plan to base fines on the ability to pay (they will be based, as they are in countries like Sweden, on a portion of the offender's daily income), and the broader objective of finding alternatives to prison through non-custodial penalties. Indeed, many commentators have dubbed the White Paper a 'liberal' document. However, the plans for a supervision and restriction order, and the proposals for its operation as previously outlined, have come under attack. To the traditional right it is seen as yet another 'soft option' which will fail to deter criminals from committing further crimes. From the opposite side, concern is mounting that the new order may, paradoxically, have the effect of increasing rather than decreasing the numbers of offenders who end up in custody. This has happened with other non-custodial penalties in the past (for example, the Community Service Order); sentencers will often pass such sentences for very minor offences or for offenders with little previous record, when they should really be used only where a prison or youth custody sentence could be considered (i.e. for the more serious offenders). Should the offender then commit another offence, or break the conditions of the order, they may then receive a custodial sentence. The overall effect may very well be an increase in the numbers in custody see (NAPO, 1988). Linked to this is the danger that orders for tracking or tagging may be used disproportionately on young black offenders, given that elements of racism have been seen to be pervasive in the criminal justice system (NAPO, 1988).

A point I wish to raise is whether the White Paper,and the other community-based approaches referred to above, are some sort of break from the traditional ideas of the right. On face value, the enhanced role of the community in crime control seems more at home with the politics of the opposition parties than a Thatcher Administration. Yet in a very real sense these developments and proposals are quite consistent with other areas of policy. The common thread is individual responsibility: responsibility for one's own property (crime prevention); responsibility towards the wider community (Neighbourhood Watch); responsibility for the consequences of one's criminal actions (being forced to make compensation to victims, learning the consequences of one's actions by experiencing strict limitations on one's freedom), and so on. A fairly consistent line can be drawn between the drift towards the use of the community and rolling back the state, as John Patten has made clear:

Scepticism about what can be achieved by the State acting alone, has rightly become established in perceptions of economic policy; a similar realisation is needed in dealing with crime (*Guardian*, 9 April 1988).

When added to that other great concern of the government, the reduction in public expenditure and the scope for that in community alternatives, perhaps the strategy is not inconsistent after all. As we have seen, there is even scope for the introduction of private sector involvement in the running of the schemes, increasingly a feature of the Home Office's thinking on law and order policy. We have already witnessed serious attempts to allow private companies to participate in prison building, catering and certain court services. The Green Paper *Private Sector Involvement in the Remand System* (1988) sets out quite explicitly the potential role of the privately owned and/or managed institutions in the pre-trial phase. This is completely consistent with the government's approach to other areas of policy and with the views of the radical right, as other chapters in this book demonstrate. Another sense in which the proposals are consistent with, rather than contrary to, the principles of the Right is the developing critique of the prison as a form of 'nanny state', for as the White Paper puts it, 'Prison is a society which requires virtually no sense of personal responsibility'.

Conclusion

The government's more recent record on law and order policy is no less complex than at other stages of its period in office. Indeed, it has succeeded in embracing policies favoured by the opposition parties, such as the reduction in the prison population, crime prevention programmes, non-custodial penalties, and so on, and dressed them in its own distinctive clothes. Yet in doing this it has been forced to admit that its earlier strategy largely based on more police powers and more resources, has been generally ineffective in crime reduction. Crime rates have increased by around 40 per cent since 1979, and the prison population continues to climb, to reach a figure now in excess of 50,000. We shall no doubt see crime rates begin to slow down over the next few years, a trend already just apparent in burglary offences. But this will have more to with the decline in the numbers of young people in the population, than with the effectiveness of the government's policy, although no doubt we shall be told otherwise.

Further policies lie in waiting. We shall almost certainly see changes in the right to silence, whereby the suspect can refuse to comment on the charges made against him without that prejudicing his case. In line with the scheme already applied to Northern Ireland, the courts will soon be able to draw negative conclusions about suspects who refuse to speak or make statements. This is seen by many as a major shift in the balance between the prosecution and defence in favour of the former. The Home Office have also made it clear that they would like to see even more cases shifted from trial by jury to Magistrates' Courts, and this could apply to many cases of alleged theft. The Home Office is also considering reformulating the Police Codes of Practice referred to above, in what will most likely be a reduction of suspects' rights.

Such reforms will fuel the debate about the extent to which the government has allowed civil liberties to be whittled away during its period of office. Its own case has been based on the assumption that much needed to be done in terms of police powers and court procedure to win the war against crime. Until that war shows real signs of success, that case will remain a difficult one to maintain.

7

Health Policy

IAN KENDALL and GRAHAM MOON

A significant feature of the operation of the National Health Service (NHS) throughout its history has been the relationship between the perceived need to contain the costs of the service within what the politicians have seen as 'reasonable bounds' and the goals of efficiency and equity that form the crucial part of the explicit rationale for introducing the service. Efficiency was taken to imply 'rational planning' and 'effective management' of health care resources. Equity implied the perhaps utopian goals of equal access according to need and irrespective of ability to pay.

It can be argued that, prior to the NHS, the organisation and allocation of health care was both inefficient and inequitable. With the establishment of the service in 1948, governments had to grapple with the difficulties of balancing the goals of efficiency and equity within a context where the easy assumption of some reformers – that better health care would make for a healthier nation and so reduce the cost of service provision – proved to be the precise obverse of reality. As early as 1953 it was felt necessary to establish a committee of enquiry to consider the voracious appetite of the NHS for resources. The tasks of this committee established an enduring feature of the policy agenda for the NHS – concern about its 'present and prospective cost', how to limit 'the burden on the Exchequer' through the 'effective control and efficient use of . . . Exchequer funds' and at the same time 'providing for the maintenance of an adequate service' (Ministry of Health, 1956).

Once cost containment assumed centre stage, the aspirations of some of the Service's founders were neglected. Capital programmes were severely constrained with very limited investment in new hospital building and health centres throughout the 1950s. There was no plan for hospital development until 1962, and the variations evident in the local authority community care plans, published in 1963, seemed to indicate an absence of any coherent health service planning. Meanwhile resources were distributed primarily on the basis of historic cost budgeting. All areas may have been doing better, but many of the geographical disparities inherited by the service in 1948 remained intact.

Another factor inhibiting the efficient planning and management of the Service was its administrative structure. Widely seen as an essentially political compromise between government and professional interests, it involved a separation of hospital, family practitioner and other community health services. This led to a growing interest in the potential for internal restructuring and a series of documents produced by the 1964–70 Labour and 1970–4 Conservative governments led to a major reorganisation in 1974. The goals of the reorganisers were only imperfectly realised. Within the NHS, the family practitioner services retained a degree of autonomy incompatible with a unified service. Meanwhile the parallel restructurings of local government and the personal social services created a pattern of professional, administrative and budgetary divisions that were to remain a stumbling block to realising the growing commitment to community care, and which were to be the subject of critical comment by the Audit Commission and the Griffiths Report in the 1980s (see Chapter 10). It was also argued that administrative restructuring was being used to resolve problems that were essentially economic and technological; governments were seeking to address problems of resourcing and costing by the imposition of what they hoped would be more effective structures.

At least the planning system was in place in the reorganised NHS. Long-standing issues associated with inequality and the priorities of the Service were made a central feature of health policy by the 1974–9 Labour government which sought to remedy geographical disparities in resource allocation and redirect investment towards the so-called 'Cinderella areas' of mental health, mental handicap, community care and the care of elderly people. But the planning system and its associated priorities were introduced in 1976, the same year as the IMF cuts were imposed on public expenditure in the UK. It was not an auspicious moment to attempt a more active pursuit of some of the original goals of the NHS. Within three years, a Conservative government was elected (1979) and it seemed likely that public expenditure would be the focus of considerable attention.

This rest of this chapter will examine the responses of successive Thatcher governments to the goals of efficiency and equity. Central to this examination is a key question: how has a government with such an explicit commitment to the reduction of public expenditure responded to the resource demands of the NHS, demands which all commentators agree will continue to expand due to demographic trends, rising expectations and medical advances?

The following section reviews the major policy initiatives affecting the NHS which have been introduced between 1979 and 1989. These developments culminated in the announcement that a review of the operation and finance of the NHS was to be conducted in 1988. The process of this review and its outcome is summarised and its key proposals explored. Attention then shifts to the public and professional responses to the review proposals. These responses indicate the extent of the difficulties involved in undertaking a major reform of what remains a popular institution involving professional groups held in general esteem by the public. The chapter concludes by setting the changes made over the past ten years within a broader context.

Ten Years of Conservative Health Policy

The finances of the British NHS rely more significantly on general taxation than do those systems operating elsewhere in the European Community (EC) where social insurance contributions and direct charges to consumers are more common. With the election of the first Thatcher government in 1979 there were early indications that the new administration was reviewing ideas for shifting the basis of health care finance to one centred on either the European social insurance model or, more radically, the private insurance model used in the USA.

The new government may have had radical aspirations but, in the event, neither of the above alternatives was pursued. Political expediency dictated a recognition of the considerable popular support enjoyed by the NHS, while economic expediency reflected the growing claims that, with a tax-based NHS, Britain was actually benefiting from a service that, in comparison with other nations, remained relatively cheap. In addition the basic principles of the Service received a resounding official endorsement in 1979 with the publication of the report of a Royal Commission on the NHS. The Commission and its associated research reports were also critical of the 1974 reorganisation, recommending a slower and more reflective approach to any future organisational change. They warned against the imposition of uniform solutions upon such a large organisation.

If this left the government seemingly committed to maintaining the NHS, it did not eliminate room for manoeuvre. The previous Labour government's attempts to limit pay beds in NHS hospitals and control private hospital development were both abandoned. Supportive comments were made regarding private hospitals and nursing homes as alternatives to the NHS. The latter were to receive dramatically increased indirect support via the social security budget during the mid-1980s (see Chapter 10). Within the Service there were significant increases in dental and prescription charges and steps were taken to reduce significantly the role of the NHS in the provision of opthalmic services.

Commitments to remedy inequalities in resource allocation to regions and to priority areas such as psychiatry and geriatrics were continued. There was however a prolonged wait for the White Paper on services for elderly people which had been ordered by the previous Labour government; when it appeared it contained no commitments to increases in expenditure, a clear statement that the meeting of need depended upon national economic performance, and an implication that the advancement of community care would rely less on public provision and more on the community itself (DHSS, 1981).

Policies to ameliorate the wider class based scenarios regarding inequality, outlined in the Black Report (1979), were rejected on grounds of cost (DHSS, 1979a). Eight years later a similar rejection befell an updated analysis and explanation of class inequalities in health and health care. Poverty was not accepted as a root cause of ill-health, rather the government, particularly through the pronouncements of one of its junior health ministers, preferred to emphasise personal responsibility for health and the need to adopt appropriately responsible lifestyles.

Although themes of fairness and equity may not have been entirely absent from the Conservatives' health policy agenda they were therefore not prominent. If the Service was to continue in a recognisable form, then the overriding concern with cost containment might best be served by a renewed emphasis on efficiency. Initially this theme was promoted by the traditional means of a further organisational restructuring of the service. This was unsurprising given the considerable body of criticism that had been directed at the 1974 reorganisation. That structure was widely characterised as a top-heavy bureaucracy and some simplification had been supported by the Royal Commission. The result was the abandonment of any attempt to maintain a geographical relationship between local government and health authorities and the adoption of a simpler structure based on districts and regions. The document outlining these proposals indicated that the government was additionally interested in managerial reform within the Service (DHSS, 1979b). At this stage it seemed that this reform was to be left to the health authorities themselves to take forward.

The new administrative structure came into effect in 1982, with subsequent confirmation that the Family Practitioner Committees (FPCs) would be reconstituted as separate health authorities in their own right. It was a strange conclusion to a process of administrative restructuring that began in the early 1960s and which, at one point in time, aspired to unify the health and personal social services in a unitary system of local government.

Before the health authorities had fully completed reorganisation, the government commissioned and wholeheartedly supported a report recommending internal managerial arrangements radically different from those previously prevailing. General managers with extensive powers were to be appointed to head up regional and district health authorities. In the past such suggestions had been rejected or significantly modified in recognition of what were seen as the distinctive qualities required to run a profession-based service like the NHS. Similar reservations were expressed on this occasion by professional groups, health authorities, and the House of Commons Social Services Committee; this was associated in many instances by requests for pilot schemes to evaluate the costs and benefits of the new approach. Such reservations and requests were ignored and the new general managers were appointed at great speed. The government may have abandoned any notion of significantly diminishing a major social policy programme of public expenditure on health care, but it appeared to have a growing commitment to displacing the traditional modes of public service administration and professionalism by a form of private sector managerialism. This faith in private sector management was also exemplified by attempts to encourage the contracting-out of ancillary services such as catering.

Government policies towards the NHS were therefore assuming a pattern recognisable in some other public policy programmes. Although the broad parameters of government health service responsibilities remained unchanged some, possibly increasing, relief on the problem of costs (to the tax payer) was to be gained from expansion in the private sector and increased charges. The potential role of the voluntary and informal sectors was also highlighted, particularly in the area of community care. Cost containment was to be achieved by refusing to enter into major new policy commitments such as those advocated by the Black Report or those which might have been anticipated to arise from the White Paper on services for elderly people. In addition, there was to be a more rigorous application of cash limits. Health authorities were required to produce efficiency savings through, for example, cash limited drug budgets, generic prescribing and resource management. Finally, the system of administration and management was changed, not so much through the type of restructuring undertaken in 1982, but through the application of 'private sector efficiency' by 'contracting-out' services and the bringing in of a system of management modelled on the private sector.

In terms of the original aims of the NHS the emphasis seemed to be largely on efficiency. But it was also a particular form of efficiency. The traditional ideal of 'rational' coherent planning to meet needs seemed to be displaced by a new ideal of 'strong' managerial control to remain within cash limits.

The government may have claimed that this focus on efficiency was designed to benefit the consumer, but the latter seemed increasingly sceptical of the outcome. The view gained ground that the government's cash limits were leading to 'real cuts' in services. The results in some cases appeared actually to be inefficiencies: consultants apparently told not to work in order to prevent their unit overspending. The needs-led approach, for which there was certainly widespread support, seemed to be clearly at risk when hospitals were closing special units for seriously ill children. The mounting public concern in the latter half of 1987 promoted the establishment of a major review of the Service and its delivery. This occurred within eight months of a general election in which the Conservative Party's manifesto had contained no indication that a such review might be undertaken; indeed the announcement of the 'Prime Ministerial Review' came within a fortnight of John Moore (Secretary of State for Social Services) dismissing rumours that any such action was intended.

The National Health Service Review

The Review Process

Organisations such as the Adam Smith Institute (ASI), the Institute for Economic Affairs (IEA), the Conservative Political Centre (CPC), and the Centre for Policy Studies (CPS) have become increasingly influential under the Thatcher governments as sources of radical ideas for change (see Chapter 1). Predictably the Review provided an opportunity for them to advance their vision of how health care in the UK should be organised and financed (Paton, 1988).

The ASI and the IEA were the more radical of these right-wing 'think tanks'. They advocated a much greater involvement in health care by the private sector. Individuals would receive health care vouchers redeemable for care in either the NHS or the private sector. The value of these vouchers would equate to a state contribution to health care; extra cover would involve private health insurance on which tax relief would be payable.

The CPC and the CPS outlined ideas requiring less fundamental reform: internal markets, and income generation initiatives. Internal markets would, at the very least involve local health authorities in buying and selling services from and to each other. More significantly they would also involve the separation of the act of 'purchasing' health care from that of 'providing' it; health authorities would assume the former role but might relinquish the latter to other organisations. The latter would involve health care providers in raising income without depending on taxes or grants, for example by providing pay beds or, as the CPC urged, by raising money from the private sector. The CPS was particularly associated with the arguments for the separation of financing arrangements for provision from those for purchase of health care. There was, they argued, no reason why the organisation controlling the provision of hospitals should, of necessity, also be the organisation which managed their use. The functions could be separated to facilitate greater private sector involvement. Both the CPS and the CPC favoured state health insurance, one variant of which would be an enhanced version of the present system of national health insurance, whereby individuals would pay a identified sum, earmarked for health care, into a state run insurance scheme.

The Independent Hospitals Association, the body linking private hospitals, adopted a position similar to the ASI and IEA. They favoured a mixed system for financing provision and purchase, the integration of the private and NHS sectors by an internal market system with health care managers purchasing services from either sector subject to cash limits imposed by central government assessments of local need. Private insurance schemes, such as those run by Private Patients Plan (PPP) or the British United Provident Association (BUPA) were seen as a facility limited to certain people.

The central tenets of these organisations can be summarised as choice, efficiency and privatism. These goals were entirely commensurate with the government's philosophy but were not without drawbacks. Most importantly they gave little attention to the problems of people unable to afford to compete. For those able to compete the reality of consumer choice in health care also remained problematic. Lessons to be learnt from similar systems in other countries were neglected; many of the proposals would require considerable and expensive management support. The costs of such support might not be borne by the state but they would certainly be borne by the consumer.

The professional organisations representing people involved in the NHS were naturally keen to make their views known to the Review. These views tended to reflect the diverse interests of the organisations concerned and it is not possible to identify a consensus view common to all NHS staff bodies. The nature of these differences was most clearly evident in the submissions of the Institute of Health Service Management (IHSM) representing the NHS managers – the equivalents of local government officers – and the National Association of Health Authorities (NAHA) representing Health Authority members – the equivalent of local councillors.

The two bodies were in broad agreement on two issues: first, that the NHS is a success story and, second, that it should continue to be funded from general taxation (at present the NHS draws some 86 per cent of its finance from this source). They disagreed over the governance of the Service and over attitudes to the private sector. The IHSM adopted attitudes which were much closer to those of the radical right. It advocated experiments with internal markets, private insurance as a top-up mechanism, separating the finance of provision from purchase and management by local boards of experienced, appointed personnel. The last point was the most contentious. The IHSM argued that the existing health authorities, with their mixture of local government councillors and professional representatives, were ineffective, providing neither control nor public accountability; it would be more sensible, they argued, to appoint experienced managers to a board rather than lay persons lacking the required background. The NAHA was, not unsurprisingly, opposed to this view. They recommended the maintenance of the status quo and equated management with bureaucracy and ineffectiveness. In their view, health authorities as presently constituted provided a much needed public input into the running of the NHS.

The basic position of the Labour Party in relation to the Review was one of principled but anxious support for what it saw as a monument to the achievements of the post-war Attlee government. This position tended to result in a somewhat defensive response coupled with rather predictable suggestions. Among these were proposals for a national inventory of hospital buildings, better measurement of health care need, elected health authorities and cash injections. Opposition to private care and contract funding was constant.

Following the appointment of Robin Cook as Shadow Health Minister issues of choice, quality and efficiency began to be addressed with a central theme of democracy in health care (Cook, 1988). Among the key proposals in the Labour 'alternative review' were: pay linked to service quality (e.g. waiting list lengths), parliamentary rather than governmental scrutiny of health authority appointments, the abolition of Regional Health Authorities (RHAs), integration of Family Practitioner Authorities (FPAs) (administering family doctor, dentist, optician and pharmacy services) with District Health Authorities (DHAs), a Health Technology Commission to review the use of drugs and high technology in caring for people, and a Health Quality Inspectorate. It would appear that the Labour Party position shifted to one of promoting changes that would enable the NHS to compete robustly and fairly with the private sector.

A reasonable guide to the consensus of political, professional and public opinion regarding change in the NHS was provided by reports of the House of Commons Social Services Committee. No less than three such reports were produced while the Review was in progress. Of the 140 submissions to the Committee received by April 1988, 75 were in favour of maintaining the existing tax financed health service. In *The Future of the NHS* the Committee recommended: no basic change in funding, limited experimentation with internal markets, private and NHS care to be seen as 'complementary', the amalgamation of the administration of District Health Authorities and the Family Practitioner Services, and a reappraisal of the utility of the regional tier of administration.

In summary the submissions to the Review were therefore concerned with how the money to run a health care service should be raised, and who should be responsible for its distribution and administration. As far as raising money was concerned there were few advocates of radical change towards such systems as direct charging to the consumer for services received. More common was advocacy for mixed approaches to funding and the facilitation of consumer choice. Considerations of the administration and dissemination of monies focused attention on the distinction between the present system, which was criticised as overly dependent on local factors and the decisions of providers, and alternative systems which, it was again asserted, would give greater choice to the consumer of health care.

A further issue which concerned many submissions to the Review was the continuing debate about the administrative structure of the NHS. Yet again attention focused on the number and function of administrative tiers within the Service: how responsibilities should be divided between Regional and District Health Authorities and how the differing strands within and beyond the NHS could be integrated.

The year which it took for the NHS Review to be produced provided ample time for rumours to develop and circulate regarding the likely content of the eventual document (Timmins, 1988). The initial presumption was that the Review would be a root-and-branch reorientation of the NHS in accordance with the more radical tenets of Thatcherism. But the creation of the Department of Health from the old Department of Health and Social Security (DHSS) and the change of responsibility for the NHS from John Moore to Kenneth Clarke, suggested a move away from this radicalism towards the assurance of political acceptability.

It was initially predicted that the Autumn Conservative Party Conference would see the actual publication of the Review. In the event nurses' pay claimed the attention of the Conference. The subsequent clamour over clinical regrading for nurses, the inevitable consequence of the pay award, soured any political gain and, to an extent, deepened the financial crisis facing the Service. The November Queen's Speech contained nothing to suggest imminent publication of a Review replete with solutions and by early December it was becoming increasingly obvious that the expected White Paper would appear on the first anniversary of the initial announcement of the Review.

It might have been expected that, as a consequence of the length of the Review process, there would be a growing awareness of the contents of the final report. In the month preceding actual publication rumours suggested that the prime minister was seeking to re-establish radical elements in the final document. This was indeed the case. The Labour Party leaked drafts of the Review document immediately prior to publication and the leaked material was largely accurate with regard to the final contents of the Review.

The NHS White Paper – Working for Patients (1989)

The NHS Review (Cm 555) was published on 31 January 1989 and billed by the prime minister as the most far reaching reform of the NHS in its forty-year history (DOH, 1989a). It appeared strongly influenced by some of the ideas emanating from the radical right and, as such, was held to coincide closely with the prime minister's own view of the future shape of health care services.

The Review team had comprised, in addition to the prime minister, Kenneth Clarke and David Mellor for the Department of Health, John Major for the Treasury, Malcolm Rifkind representing Scotland, and Peter Walker as Secretary of State for Wales. After the publication of the White Paper this relatively small ad hoc Cabinet Committee undertook the considerable task of selling their proposals to the public and the professional organisations via a series of nation-wide television link-ups costing £1.25 m.

The key recommendation of the White Paper concerned the development of internal markets separating purchaser and provider functions with money following patients. This was to be brought about through encouragement for the creation of NHS Hospital Trusts to run the 320 larger hospital independently of health authorities, the latter operating in a purchasing role. General practitioner services were to be brought into the internal market through direct allocation of budgets, on a voluntary basis to larger general practices to enable the buying of hospital services. The operation of this market was recognised to be heavily dependent upon information provision and, accordingly, it was additionally indicated that there would be an enhancement of computerisation and resource management initiatives.

In organisational terms the Review recommended the replacement of the existing resource allocation system with one based on population weighted for age and the relative cost of providing services. It also proposed local governance of the NHS through management boards with no local authority representation and a restructuring of the

Department of Health into a NHS Policy Board and a NHS Management Executive taking, respectively, strategic and day-to-day decisions. The separate Family Practitioner Authorities would become more managerially oriented and, for the first time, subject to overall control by Regional Health Authorities.

It was, perhaps, most predictable that the government would additionally advocate closer co-operation with the private sector. Treasury opposition had to be overcome to introduce this measure which was manifested in the relatively limited suggestion that tax relief should be paid on private medical insurance for elderly people.

A series of ten working papers were issued subsequent to the publication of the White Paper. The reception accorded to them was mixed. They have filled in some of the detail absent from the White Paper; for example it became apparent that the proposed autonomous Trusts could take responsibility for both groupings of smaller hospitals and community-based NHS services. Similarly smaller practices would be allowed to co-operate over budget holding. Even with the working papers however the government's proposals continued to be criticised as much for an absence of practical detail as for the political position they appeared to represent.

Responses and Developments

A lack of detail coupled with a set of proposals which were more radical than had been anticipated contributed to a reception for the Review that was broadly negative. Both issues fuelled concerns about the long-term future of the Service including suspicions that the Review presaged a wholesale privatisation exercise. The concept of the 'opted-out' hospital was portrayed as a precursor to the selling-off of the heritage of the NHS, although it has obvious parallels with the position of teaching hospitals in the pre-1974 NHS. Reservations also focused on the introduction of a cash-limited internal market in a Service which had traditionally been concerned to banish financial considerations from patient care.

The British Medical Association (BMA), which had once fought hard against the NHS being established, were at the forefront of this reaction. They stated trenchant opposition through a costly campaign, claiming that concerns with costs might override needs for treatment. They rejected moves to involve managers in appointing consultants, warned of the dangers of fragmenting the NHS, and condemned general practitioner budgets and hospital trusts. Even those broadly sympathetic to the idea of internal markets doubted that general practitioners possessed the necessary management skills to run their 'businesses' in the projected new manner; they also decried the short timescale for the introduction of the new ideas and urged the need for small-scale piloting – a view shared by Alan Enthoven, the North American health economist who had initially popularised the approach. These doubts were given added impetus by the coincidence of the White Paper and negotiations over a new contract for general practitioners involving substantially changed conditions of service which many linked to the requirements of budget-holding.

Other concerns generally expressed were that the creation of hospital Trusts, with a strong economic basis to their existence, might specialise in areas of greatest economic gain rather than those appropriate to the needs of local communities. Linked with this was the limited definition of core services provided by the White Paper: it focused strongly on acute care and gave only limited recognition to paediatric and maternity care. This limitation was held to lead to some perverse economic incentives: hospital Trusts might tend to discharge patients to the community before it would otherwise be appropriate, and budget-holding general practitioners would have an incentive to get their patients admitted to hospitals as emergencies rather than straightforward referrals.

Furthermore, there were doubts over the reality of consumer choice within the White Paper framework. While hospitals were offered the choice of becoming self-governing and general practitioners were offered the choice of becoming budget-holders, it was unclear whether consumer choices would actually increase in any real sense. In fact, by changing the organisation and management of the system, it might be argued that the consumer would become subject to greater constraints regarding understanding how to obtain health care. Fears were particularly expressed that people with costly problems of ill-health might find themselves being treated by reference to the size of a general practitioner's budget, and the accessibility of specialist hospital care, rather than by reference to their real care needs.

If the sensitivity of the proposed new system to the needs of the individual consumer was open to question, so too was its broader responsiveness to the community at large. The Association of Community Health Councils was not alone in deploring the disappearance of local authority representation from the smaller, management-oriented health authorities. This change was presented as a distancing of the service from the input of its actual users.

There was general surprise that the White Paper contained no mention of community care despite rumours that it would and despite the centrality of community care in current health policy. The long-awaited response to the Griffiths Report on Community Care appeared some ten months after the publication of the White Paper

(DOH, 1989b, Cm. 555). Its title *Caring for People* evoked clear resonances with *Working for Patients* and in content there were also marked parallels, notably in the promotion of a contract basis for service delivery and in clarity of presentation but absence of detail. Further parallels concerned arguments over the need for pilot projects and a limited timescale. The accommodation and implementation of the two sets of proposals will clearly be interlinked and pose a difficult task for both health and local authorities during the early 1990s. 1991 in particular is a major target date. In that year self-governing Trusts come into being. Following the publication of the White Paper some 200 expressions of interest were made. In November 1989 71 proposals were given permission for development into detailed plans. Most unusually, given the original focus on hospitals as the base unit for self-governance, the 71 included the entire provider element in eight Health Authorities and two ambulance authorities. The plans for general practitioner's budget-holding and the general introduction of the purchaser – provider distinction are also proceeding despite a concerted campaign by the BMA and substantial public misquiet – both of which have provided a major boost to the Labour Party as the defender of the NHS.

Conclusion

The firm orientation of health policy towards a mode of cash-limited, manager-led efficiency that has taken place under the Thatcher governments and that culminated in *Working for Patients* raises three central issues. First, the medical profession, not some would argue without self-interest, have sought to protect the NHS from change. Their success or otherwise in this task, both to date and in the future unrolling of the Review proposals, has implications for some traditional views of their power and autonomy. Second, if the present proposals are carried out they will also need to be effective; they will need to work for patients. If they do not, given the popularity of the NHS, the reaction may well have a significant influence on the political future of the present administration. Finally, the government needs to clarify its long-term intentions regarding the NHS. Although the official line is that 'We have never had the slightest intention of privatising the health services' many critics remain sceptical.

That a 'short, swift Review' took a year to complete indicates that the government was unable to identify an easy solution to the relationship between equity, efficiency and cost containment once it had ruled out the radical alternative of abandoning the concept of a predominantly tax-financed health service available on a 'universal' basis to all UK citizens. Paradoxically the very presence of the Review actually encouraged reform in line with the apparent long-term agenda of the Thatcher governments regarding health care. Co-operation between public and private sectors became a reality and the idea that money would follow patients gained widespread acceptance. It might even be argued that the political and economic costs of publishing the Review could actually have been avoided whilst still achieving many of the desired goals.

The major problem for the government lies in its strategy of achieving these goals through an emphasis on consumer choice and the operation of the market. This strategy may heighten sensitivity to and expectations of service quality in a way that makes cost containment even more difficult in the future. Concern has also been expressed about inefficiencies and escalating costs associated with a possible multiplicity of purchasers and providers competing in the internal market of an increasingly fragmented NHS. Indeed, if the result is to move the NHS too far away from its traditional modes of working, the UK might experience the sort of explosion in health care costs that has occurred in countries with more market-based health care systems and which the NHS has relatively successful in avoiding in its first 40 years of operation.

The government's response to the Black Report did not raise expectations of a more equitable health service. It would of course be ironic that a government which has placed such great emphasis on its concern with cost containment and value for money should bequeath not just a less equitable but also a less efficient and more expensive health service to its successors.

8

Housing Policy in the Thatcher Years

ROB ATKINSON and PAUL DURDEN

Introduction – Housing Policy Pre-1979

The years 1945–1970 saw considerable progress in tackling the housing problems of England and Wales, with major programmes of council house building, slum clearance and improvement being undertaken by both Labour and Conservative governments. This progress was documented in the Labour government's 1977 Green Paper – *Housing Policy: A Consultative Document* – which argued that the acceleration of an existing trend in housing provision, dating from the mid- to late 1960s, away from council building towards the improvement of older dwellings would secure a better balance between the needs of different sections of the community and so be more cost-effective.

The Green Paper also pointed to the un-met needs of groups such as the elderly, the handicapped, single-parent families, etc. and suggested that local authorities should devise strategies to meet those needs by coordinating their own housing activities with those of the private sector.

From about the mid- 1960s both political parties agreed upon the superiority of owner-occupation as a housing tenure and this in part accounts for the shift in funds away from council building to the renovation of owner-occupied dwellings. Governments of both parties believed that owner-occupation should be made more accessible to families on modest incomes and that this development would reduce the demand for new council building, particularly when council tenants bought a private dwelling and released their council house for re-letting.

The Green Paper favoured a residual role for council housing, i. e. it should be a safety net available only to those unable to provide for themselves. This policy stance was justified by the apparent improvement in the housing situation and by reference to the economic crisis of 1976 and subsequent pressure from the IMF which led to a reduction in public expenditure in general and housing expenditure in particular.

These developments were opposed by some sections of the Labour Party and by Shelter who pointed out that the Green Paper had noted the existence of local housing shortages and the growing incidence of serious disrepair. When the local housing shortages were added together there was a deficit of some 0.5m dwellings rather than the crude surplus declared by the Green Paper. These shortages were likely to get worse rather than better given the reduction in council building which took place in the later 1970s.

Linked to the above problem was the quality of the housing stock, despite real improvements in the amenities available (e.g. hot and cold water, indoor w/c) since 1945; by the 1970s more and more owners (public and private) were allowing their dwellings to slip into serious disrepair. This was particularly the case in the private rented sector, but evidence of increased disrepair in the council and owner-occupied sectors was also beginning to emerge. Almost all private rented dwellings were built before 1914, as was a significant proportion of owner-occupied dwellings. Such older dwellings were most likely to need significant levels of expenditure on renovation.

Despite the introduction of area improvement programmes (e.g. General Improvement Areas and Housing Action Areas) to provide grants to improve these properties there appeared to be the real possibility that many could deteriorate into slums in the future.

Another major development was the 1977 Homeless Persons Act, which by broadening the definition of 'homelessness' increased the apparent size of the problem and greatly increased the problems confronting local authorities. In essence households are considered to be homeless if they lack a dwelling or are unable to live there for certain reasons, e.g. the risk of violence. Once such a household establishes that it is in a designated 'Priority Need' group the local authority is legally bound to find it accommodation. Permanent accommodation need be provided only if the household is involuntarily homeless and can demonstrate a local connection. However, with the decline in council building many local authorities were forced to make extensive use of bed and breakfast accommodation.

The final important development of the 1970s was the increased role given to the Housing Association movement, a move favoured by all shades of political opinion. Housing Associations are non-profit-making bodies registered and supervised by the government sponsored Housing Corporation (a QUANGO, see Chapter 1), devoted to the provision of rented housing for low income households. Favourable financial arrangements meant that Housing Associations were able to run at a loss (since the passing of the Housing Act, 1988, Associations have had to set market rents on all new lets).

Housing Associations were also widely preferred because it was believed that they offered more sensitive and competent management of their dwellings and tenants than did local authorities, leading to a higher level of tenant satisfaction than was common among council tenants.

Housing Associations enjoyed the approval of both major parties in the 1970s and thus received a more favourable capital allocation, allowing them to continue to build and renovate properties while councils were experiencing dramatic cutbacks. It was hoped that the Housing Associations could compensate for the dramatic decline in the private rented sector and that their expansion would, partially offset the decline in council house building.

It can be seen that during the 1970s there were four major developments in the field of housing policy: (1) owner-occupation was confirmed as the major tenure; (2) council housing began to take on a residual role; (3) the decline of the private rented sector continued and even accelerated; (4) the expansion of the housing association movement.

Housing Policy Since 1979

The housing policy of the Thatcher governments has had four explicit objectives and at least one implicit objective (see Cm 214 for more details):

1. *To encourage owner-occupation*: For most Conservatives owner-occupation is seen as a good in itself, as the 'natural' tenure. Owner-occupation was seen to encourage personal and civic responsibility, required personal financial commitment and thus reduced state expenditure and involvement. However, it should be noted that, for the Exchequer, revenue lost through tax relief on mortgage interest payments may well exceed the saving on housing subsidies otherwise paid.

2. *To minimise local authority housing provision*: Many Conservatives have an ideological distaste for anything other than residual housing provision by local authorities. Conservatives also emphasised council tenants' lack of rights, 'insensitive' manage-

ment of tenants, a bad record of maintenance and inflexible allocation rules which acted as a deterrent to labour mobility. Finally, council housing was thought a Labour Party electoral stronghold.

3. *To revitalise the private rented sector*: As already noted the private sector had declined dramatically since 1945, from just over 50 per cent in 1945 to just under 10 per cent in 1980. Conservatives, while acknowledging the role of slum clearance, the rise of council housing and owner-occupation as factors causing this decline, believed that rent control and excessive security of tenure had played major roles in that decline.

4. *To target resources more accurately on the most acute problems, thus alleviating the most pressing housing problems and obtaining better value for money.*

The implicit object is to gain political advantage. Given the common belief that home owners tend to vote Conservative and council tenants to vote Labour it was assumed that the encouragement of owner-occupation and the rundown of council housing would benefit the Conservatives.

This amounts to a belief that housing is essentially a consumer good, best provided for most people by the market and that the role of public agencies should be limited to facilitating people's participation in the market. While this view is largely derived from the ideology of Thatcherism, support for the view that the state should reduce its involvement in the provision of low rental dwellings could be derived from the Labour government's 1977 Housing Green Paper.

The housing situation in 1979 gave considerable cause for concern. Local authorities were under-financed and often unable to meet even their statutory responsibilities. There was no sign of a revival in the private rented sector nor were Housing Associations able to expand their activities to fill in these gaps in provision. Only owner-occupation continued to flourish and as a result it was increasingly seen as the answer to many of the country's housing problems.

Local Authority Housing

1980 Housing Act

The Thatcher government's first attempt to address the 'problems' of council housing was the 1980 Housing Act which gave local authority tenants security of tenure, encouraged more 'sensible' management and also gave tenants the 'right to buy' their dwellings at a discount and with a local authority mortgage if required. Most tenants of three to four years standing were entitled to purchase their dwellings at a discount of 33 per cent, increasing by 1 per cent for each additional year of residence to a maximum of 50 per cent subject to various conditions. These terms were improved by legislation in 1984 and 1986 to give a maximum discount of 60 per cent after 30 years' residence and giving residents in flats a 70 per cent discount after 15 years' residence.

As the figures in Table 8.1 show, there was a massive increase in the sale of council houses from 1980 onwards, prior to this sales had numbered a few thousand a year.

TABLE 8.1 *Sales of Dwellings owned by Local Authorities and New Towns in the UK: 1980 – (in 000s)*

Year	Local Authorities	Housing Associations	New Towns	Total
1980	83.7	n.a.	n.a.	83.7
1981	105.8	7.5	5.0	118.3
1982	209.7	18.2	5.8	233.7
1983	143.3	17.3	5.9	166.5
1984	112.5	12.6	4.7	129.8
1985	101.2	9.3	3.6	114.1
1986	97.0	8.0	3.7	108.7
1987	113.1	7.2	4.9	125.2
1988	172.8	8.5	7.2	188.9

Note: n.a. = not available.

The vast majority of sales in this period were of houses, rather than of flats and maisonettes which accounted for about 30 per cent of council properties. Although a high proportion of the better quality council housing has been sold there has also been strong demand for poorer quality dwellings when available at substantial discounts.

Needless to say the 1980 Act has been politically contentious. The government argued that in the short to medium term local authorities would gain financially from sales through repayment of capital debt and reduced management and maintenance costs, even though they are free to utilise only a limited proportion of their income from sales. Such a view assumes that councils will not undertake any substantial building programmes in the near future.

Critics of the Act argue that council dwellings should be retained for those in greatest need and that sales have reduced the availability of dwellings for the homeless and thus increased housing stress.

Thus while the sale of council properties may have improved the quality of life for many people, it entails the redistribution of public wealth to better off tenants rather than to those most in need. Such sales have also had the added benefit, from the government's point of view, of transferring the costs of maintenance, repairs, etc. from the public to the private sector and thus reducing public expenditure. Despite cutbacks in central funding for council housing and the sale of stock the government remained concerned about the size of the public sector and sought further ways to reduce it. The 1986 Audit Commission study *Managing the Crisis in Council Housing* provided support for some of the government's views.

1986 Housing and Planning Act

The next step was taken in the Housing and Planning Act, 1986. This Act allowed councils to transfer their stock to other landlords (e.g. Housing Associations, private landlords). There was no requirement that tenants be balloted on any proposed transfer although most councils using the Act have felt obliged to do so. Such a transfer may be advantageous to councils as it releases capital for use elsewhere, but it does involve a loss in tenants' rights unless the transfer is to a Housing Association.

It has been argued that one of the intentions behind the Act was to push tenants into purchasing their dwellings as an alternative to being transferred to another landlord, where they might lose some of their rights and have to pay higher rents. Paradoxically some Labour authorities are interested in voluntary transfer to a 'satellite' Housing Association because it reduces tenants' rights, particularly the Right to Buy, thus minimising the loss of 'public' housing.

1988 Housing Act

Further moves to break up the council sector were signalled in the 1987 White Paper(Cm 214) and the 1988 Act which followed; Cm 214 argued that it is the intention of government that while local authorities will continue to play a major role in meeting local housing needs:

> there will no longer be the same presumption that the local authority itself should take direct action to meet new or increasing demands. The future role of local authorities will essentially be a strategic one identifying housing needs and demands . . . maximising the use of private finance, and encouraging the new interest in the revival of the independent rented sector. (Cm 214, p. 14).

Although the White Paper acknowledges that many councils provide a good service to tenants it still insists that too many estates are badly managed.

A remedy offered to dissatisfied tenants in the 1988 Act is the 'Tenants Choice' provision, which not only allows council tenants to choose to transfer to other landlords but also to initiate the transfer process. Tenants may choose to transfer to commercial landlords or Housing Associations, in which case they must be approved (by the Housing Corporation), or to set up a tenants' cooperative. While the Act gives tenants more choice it also allows approved landlords to bid for almost any local authority dwelling. If tenants wish to stop such a take-over they need to mobilise 50.1 per cent of those affected as those who do not vote will be considered to have voted in favour of transfer. Thus the scales are weighted in favour of such transfers. However, Clause 93 of the Act does make provision for those who do not wish to transfer to remain within the public sector.

The Housing Corporation plays a key role in the transfer process as it must approve any prospective bidders for council dwellings and this should reduce the risk of landlords abusing the process. In fact only registered Housing Associations are likely to be approved.

Clearly the government believe that many local authority tenants wish to move out of the public sector. But who will take them on? Most Housing Associations, even if willing, lack the management expertise to absorb more than 0.5m dwellings over the next few years. However, this problem would be reduced if councils were to establish 'satellite' associations to which they could transfer housing department staff. The establishment of tenants' cooperatives would be even more problematical as this would require tenants to devote a great deal of time as well as the acquisition of management skills.

The situation is further complicated by the Local Government and Housing Act 1989, which stops councils using rates to subsidise rents; this is likely to produce a substantial increase in rents, thus encouraging more people either to buy or transfer out of the council sector.

Housing Action Trusts (HATs)

The 1988 Act also provides for the establishment of HATs, with a life of five to seven years, on certain rundown council estates. The Secretary of State at the Department of Environment will take over responsibility from the council, transfer it to the HAT who will then renovate the estate and pass it onto an approved landlord (either public or private). To achieve this HATs are given considerable statutory powers and receive relatively favourable financial treatment compared to local authorities.

To date progress has been slow, with many local authorities and tenants proving hostile and stubborn opposition. Opposition to HATs has been such that the £90m initially set aside for the programme in 1990–91 was reduced in the autumn 1989 Public Expenditure White Paper to £45m.

The Privately Rented Sector

As already noted one of the key housing aims of the government was to revive the privately rented sector and one of its first moves in this direction was contained in the Housing Act 1980, which effectively abolished the long-term security of tenure enjoyed by tenants in controlled tenancies. The legislation allowed new lettings to become regulated tenancies which reduced security of tenure, making it easier for landlords to regain possession of their properties. Furthermore two new types of tenancy were introduced – assured and shorthold – with rents largely determined by the market. They functioned as follows:

> 'assured tenancies' for new or substantially renovated dwellings to be let by approved landlords at freely negotiated rents for a specified period, with full security of tenure subject to compliance with the terms of tenancy, with provision for re-negotiation on expiry and referral to the County Court in the event of disagreement between landlord and tenant;
>
> 'shorthold tenancies' for a specified period of between one and five years which guarantee the landlords possession on expiry, but given either party the right to seek registration (by Rent Officers) of an appropriate 'fair rent'.

Government hoped that these developments would lead to an influx of capital investment and persuade more owners to offer their properties for rent thus reviving the private rented market.

Ironically, there was (and is) no guarantee that the rents people could afford to pay, even with the help of housing benefit, would be sufficient to make investment in rental property an attractive investment except at the top end of the market and in dwellings for multiple occupation. There is little evidence that the 1980 Act has revitalised the privately rented market to a significant extent.

Further attempts to revitalise this tenure were signalled in the 1987 White Paper(Cm 214) and the Housing Act 1988. In both these documents the privately rented sector is referred to as the 'Independent Rented Sector', a term not widely used. The use of this term would suggest that government is attempting not only to revive the tenure numerically but also ideologically and politically by dropping its previous title and associated 'stigma' of poor housing conditions, 'greedy' landlords, etc.

However, the 1987 White Paper is forced to acknowledge that despite six years of attempts to revive the sector:

there is now very little private investment in providing new rented housing. And when landlords obtain vacant possession of dwellings at the end of tenancies they often prefer to sell outright into owner-occupation rather relet. Owners who do not want to sell their property sometimes keep their houses vacant rather than let to a tenant because of the inadequate returns, and the difficulty of regaining possession when they need it. Many of the remaining private landlords also have difficulty in finding sufficient resources to keep their property in good repair. (Cm 214, p.9).

As far as the government is concerned this unsatisfactory state of affairs has largely come about as a result of statutory restrictions on landlords' freedom of action regarding rents and security of tenure. Yet there is clearly a demand for this type of accommodation, as Lord Caithness, speaking for the government in the House of Lords, noted:

> There is a substantial demand for good quality private rented accommodation. Landlords will not come forward to meet the demand unless rented property becomes once again an attractive investment proposition. (*Hansard*, House of Lords, Col. 1343, 24 October 1988).

Thus the answer is to remove these restrictions on landlords, a contentious assumption from which major provisions of the 1988 Act originate.

Building upon the provisions of the 1980 Housing Act, particularly 'assured tenancies' and 'shorthold tenancies' which are to be extended to all new lettings, the 1988 Act once again attempts to revive the privately rented sector. The regulations surrounding 'assured tenancies' have been relaxed, making it easier for landlords to establish and renew them. For 'shorthold tenancies' rents will be set largely with regard to market levels and their minimum length reduced from a year to six months. Where a landlord is resident on the premises most of the existing controls over new letting are removed. Clearly these changes are designed to 'free-up' the private rented market.

However, these measures also provide a considerable incentive to landlords to be rid of existing tenancies covered by the Rent Acts so that dwellings can be re-let at higher rents. To protect such tenants from harassment the government intends to create a new offence where the landlord harasses the tenant knowing that his actions are likely to lead the tenant to leave the home. Clearly the spectre of 'Rachmanism' still haunts the Conservatives from their last attempt, in the late 1950s, to reintroduce a free market into the private rented sector.

Criticisms of the government's intentions for the privately rented sector focus on both their underlying justification and on their practicality.

1. Deregulation is aimed primarily at easing the shortage of dwellings
    for rental in areas where jobs are to be found. However, a survey of
    rented housing in London carried out in 1983–4 (GLC, 1986)
    found that less than two-thirds of all households were protected by
    the Rent Acts and that less than one-third of all new lettings were
    protected. Despite the apparent ease with which existing
    regulations could be evaded there was little evidence of any
    increase in the supply of dwellings for rent. Those tenancies which
    were protected were typically towards the bottom of the price
    range and occupied by households of modest means.

    Given this, it seems unlikely that deregulation would increase the
    availability of accommodation for such households unless rent
    increases of a magnitude sufficient to attract new investment could
    be achieved. If this were to occur the rents of such dwellings would
    be well beyond the finances of such individuals, unless Housing
    Benefit were raised to an unprecedented level (for more detail see
    Whitehead and Kleinman, 1987).

    If rents do rise to a level acceptable to potential landlords and if
    housing benefit is raised to allow lower income households to
    afford the new rents and so take advantage of the improved supply
    of dwellings there will, in practice, be a massive shift of public
    subsidy to private landlords which the public may not support.
    Aware of this problem the government has made clear its intention
    not to increase housing benefit in line with rising rents; but this
    could be counter-productive, in that denied a profitable market
    return landlords will not increase the supply of dwellings for low
    income households. This could lead to more provision for the
    higher income groups and an increased risk of homelessness for the
    poor. For local authorities anxious to minimise homelessness it
    could mean being obliged to cover the difference between rent
    levels eligible for housing benefit and those necessary to increase
    the supply of dwellings, assuming that local authorities have the
    finance available.

2. The government has said that it wants to create 'a better balance
    between the needs of tenants and landlords', but its proposals
    radically reduce the rights of private tenants without giving a
    plausible assessment of the likely benefits in terms of increased
    provision. As the Institute of Housing has noted:

    > Deregulation in itself will not bring about a significant expansion in
    > supply while potentially leading to a deterioration in the conditions of
    > those tenants already in the sector (Institute of Housing ,1987).

Conclusions

The opposition parties view the 1988 Act with varying degrees of scepticism. The Liberal Democrats are basically sympathetic to the intentions of the Act, but are concerned about what they see as its undemocratic elements (e.g. HATs and the arrangement for the disposal of local authority housing stock), and doubt that some aspects are workable. Labour sees the Act as an attack on local democracy and substantially irrelevant to those in greatest need if not actually harmful to them.

Given this, how can the housing policies of the Thatcher governments be assessed? The Institute of Housing has posed a number of questions concerning objectives somewhat broader than those of the 1987 White Paper and the 1988 Act:

1. will the government's policies succeed in providing sufficient dwellings to meet need in those parts of the country where housing is in short supply?
2. will they lead to a better quality of new housing and improved standards of maintenance for existing housing?
3. will they lead to better standards of management for rented housing?
4. will they give consumers of housing more power and choice? (Institute of Housing, 1987).

In answer to the first question the Institute of Housing argues that the government's intended reliance on private funding for 'social housing' is unwise. It is true that the assured tenant Business Expansion Schemes (BES) have attracted a flood of money from those seeking an Income Tax- and Capital Gains Tax-free investment, but in terms of revenue lost to the Exchequer this is a costly approach, as is most private investment in dwellings for rental when compared with public borrowing. As the National Federation of Housing Associations has pointed out, expensive finance makes it difficult to provide decent dwellings which people on low incomes can afford unless housing benefit is paid at a generous rate, and there is no reason to expect this from the government. Nor can one be sure that privately financed rental dwellings will be provided in the areas of greatest need. Such comments from two authoritative and supposedly non-political bodies strengthen the scepticism of the opposition political parties about the main thrust of Conservative housing policy and especially about the Housing Act 1988.

With reference to the second question, whether the new Act will serve to improve the quality of housing depends on a number of factors. First, on the willingness and ability of local authorities and Housing Associations to commit resources to the renovation of their housing stock when they may lose it through the Right to Buy provisions or through the designation of a HAT. Second, on the effectiveness of HATs (and none have yet been put into practice). Third, on the willingness of owner-occupiers to carry out renovation in the context of a financial regime less favourable to renovation.

The Institute of Housing thinks that in regard to renovation local authorities are likely to respond positively to the new Act, if they have the means to do so and are convinced that there will be real gains to the community. However, it is highly questionable whether the finance necessary will be available to local authorities. Indeed the Autumn 1989 Public Expenditure White Paper suggests that by 1992–3, for the first time ever, central government support for Housing Associations will be greater than the amounts spent by local authorities; there thus seems little likelihood of councils playing a major role in this arena.

In the case of management the government believes that competition in the supply of low income dwellings will produce better, more responsive, management. It is undeniable that some local authorities have a poor record in this area and that some Housing Associations have proved very competent. But the latter has often been true only because Housing Associations tend to be small and their stock less difficult to manage. If Housing Associations and cooperatives are now to manage large blocks of former public sector housing they may well encounter the kinds of problems which have bedevilled some local authorities. As a result there may be no aggregate gain in managerial efficiency, the problem will simply have been displaced and the Housing Association movement discredited.

In the case of private sector landlords the Institute of Housing has pointed out that they are not noted for their sensitive or even efficient management; if they are to assume a larger role in future rigorous supervision of this sector will be essential. Ironically such moves would by no means extricate the state from involvement in the private rental market; its role would become that of a regulator and were abuses demonstrated it would be held responsible.

As regards the fourth issue any increase in consumer choice is to be welcomed, and the Housing Act 1988, *may* achieve that, but the only immediate beneficiaries are those local authority tenants willing to take advantage of the Tenants' Choice provisions. On the other hand new private and Housing Association tenants in assured tenancies will find that the balance of power has moved in favour of their landlords and that for many of these tenants the only new 'freedom' they have is that to become homeless! Thus for existing tenants there is a marginal loss of their rights and no appreciable gains.

No doubt the present government believes that the new Act is in the public interest, but there is ample cause to suspect that the Act was shaped less by detached appraisal of the UK housing problems than by ideology. This has taken the form of a dislike for democratically elected local councils which see things differently, a desire to cut public spending, party-political considerations and wishful thinking. The government has perhaps been pragmatic in its approach to housing issues (especially owner-occupation), but remains far too inclined to equate the good of the country with that of the government.

What can be done to deal with the problems outlined above? To a considerable degree many of the problems we have with housing stem from the willingness of successive governments to subsidise owner-occupation, and hence the relatively well off, more generously than those in greater need. The government's determination to freeze or means test child benefit to achieve value for money, but not to treat tax relief on mortgage interest in the same way, is an example of this attitude.

Apart from ideological and electoral reasons there are few good reasons why public spending should not be redeployed to ensure a higher level of provision of low rental dwellings. Initially this would mean more generous financial support for local authorities and Housing Associations. Financial support could be designed to reach low income tenants, in whatever tenure category, by the replacement of most housing subsidies (including mortgage tax relief) by a general 'tenure neutral' housing benefit (a development analogous to the introduction of child benefit in 1975). Such a benefit could then be combined with other income for tax purposes and be 'clawed back' from the better off, thus avoiding universalism, targeting resources on those most in need and giving better value for money; an approach the Conservatives might be expected to support.

While simply providing more money will not solve the problem, the management practices of many local authorities, for instance, still leave considerable room for improvement: many of the inadequacies of public sector housing (especially poor maintenance) do stem from inadequate financial support. If sufficient money were made available to maintain council dwellings properly there would be far fewer complaints about the quality of local authority management and no need for undemocratic HATs. Similarly if more resources were available to local authorities for new construction targeted on the needs of the elderly, disabled and homeless, some shedding of responsibility for meeting general needs housing would seem more acceptable. What those opposed to the current government's plan fear is a financial situation in which local authorities are not even able to perform the residual 'enabling' housing responsibilities left to them by the Act.

Despite current government orthodoxy there is no reason why local authorities should not provide housing. They are at least accountable to the local electorate, which is more than can be said of their probable successors.

9

Education Policy: Education as a Business?

MALCOLM McVICAR

Introduction

The basic structure of education in Britain during the post-war period was laid down by the 1944 Education Act. This Act, born of the wartime coalition government and closely associated with the name of Rab Butler, then Minister of Education, essentially created a partnership between local authorities and central government in the provision of the State education service. This partnership remained largely intact until the 1980s.

On top of the structure was laid education policy. This, naturally, was not stuck in a time warp of the middle 1940s but changed quite dramatically over the succeeding decades. The system expanded, comprehensive secondary schools were adopted across much of the country and higher education became much more accessible. Until the mid-1970s, however, the dominant beliefs about education were that it was 'a good thing', that it could bring an end to many of the social and economic problems of the country and that much of the direction of the service should be left to the professionals who worked in it.

There was, in fact, a large degree of agreement between the two major parties on education policy, not necessarily in rhetoric but certainly in reality. However, during the 1970s this approximate consensus began to breakdown and the legislation of the 1980s has heralded a very different structure and policy approach to education. It is important to identify the reasons for this breakdown in consensus because they underlie many of the new policies.

During the 1970s there was a growing sense that somehow education has 'failed'. From the right there came an intellectual challenge to the basic assumptions on which contemporary policy was based. Critics claimed that the 'progressive' reforms of the 1960s had failed and that standards had declined. From the left came the claim that the education system was reinforcing the social divisions in society rather than eroding them and that in spite of all the theoretically progressive reforms, the state education service remained dominated by middle class norms and values which failed to serve the needs of working class children.

The Labour prime minister, James Callaghan, highlighted these concerns with the education system in a famous speech delivered at Ruskin College, Oxford in 1976, which many critics have claimed marked the beginning of the 'Great Debate' on education. He asked four key questions of the Department of Education and Science (DES):

- Were children leaving primary school with an adequate level of literacy and numeracy?
- Did the secondary school curriculum meet the needs of the majority of children and, in particular, did it prepare people for the world of work?
- How adequate was the system of public examinations?
- How adequate was the educational system for the majority of youngsters who did not go on to higher education?

The response of the DES was that there were serious problems in all four areas and that, in particular, the education system should be more responsive to the economic needs of society. This emphasis on instrumentalism – or the belief that the education system should be aimed primarily at meeting the economy's needs for trained manpower rather than on developing individuals' diverse potentials – has come to dominate education policy.

This growing concern with instrumentalism accompanied the serious and prolonged economic crisis of the mid-1970s. The impact of this crisis on the nature and direction of British politics has been discussed elsewhere (see Chapter 2, p. 28). It is, however, important to stress that some of the blame for the poor performance of the economy was attached to the educational system. Far from leading to a secure, high technology base for the British economy, it was argued, the massive expansion of education had coincided with the collapse of that economy. At a time of rapidly growing unemployment, when it would have seemed reasonable to expect more emphasis on the contribution which education could make to individuals surviving outside the labour market, much greater emphasis was placed on vocationalism.

The economic crisis also required a revival of the profitability of the private sector. This was to be achieved in two ways. First, a reduction in the level of taxation and hence cuts in some areas of public expenditure and, second, the transfer to the private sector of profitable parts of the public sector. This strengthening of the private sector also needed to be underpinned by a reinforcement of cultural norms and values. Education was thought to have a crucial role to play in creating these supports, a role which it had not played effectively in the past.

Thus, by the time of the 1979 General Election education was firmly on the political agenda. This does not mean that you would find anything very sophisticated or comprehensive in the Party Manifestos. For the details of the agenda items you have to look at policy outputs.

The Emergent 1980s

There have been three major pieces of education legislation since 1979: The Acts of 1980, 1986 and 1988. Until the 1988 Education Reform Act the education policy of the Conservative Administrations could be described as incrementalist. There was not a comprehensive, co-ordinated and planned blueprint for education policy sitting on the new Secretary of State's desk on 4 May 1979. Rather, it was a mixture of individual decisions, shifts in resources and legislation, some of which were shifts in resources and legislation, some of which were contradictory but which basically moved in the same direction. Although reached by incrementalist steps, that policy direction was radically different to the previous status quo. These steps may be grouped together as a number of themes.

Cuts in Public Expenditure

Until the late 1980s the government wanted to cut public expenditure and thus to reduce the overall burden of taxation on the economy. Since it was committed to an expansion of some programmes, such as defence and law and order, and since some were too difficult politically to cut, such as health, the burden of the cuts has fallen disproportionately on some of the social programmes. Public spending on education fell by 10 per cent in real terms between 1979 and 1986. It rose by 4 per cent in real terms from 1987 to 1989. The magnitude of these cuts has caused great problems for the state education system.

Weakening the Power of Local Government

Those local councils which have responsibility for education are called local education authorities (LEAs). During the whole of the 1980s the powers and independence of local government have been weakened and this has certainly affected LEAs. It is a basic fact of life that retrenchment in public spending reduces the power and freedom of action of the bodies responsible for that spending.

Alongside these expenditure reductions went greater 'earmarking' of central government funds, thus reducing LEAs' freedom to order their own priorities. For example, staff development funding was largely made specific to centrally-determined priorities. The strengthening of governing bodies and of parental power, explained below, may also be interpreted as weakening the position of LEAs in the service. However, the major reduction in LEA powers did not come until the 1988 Act.

Vocationalism

At the beginning of the 1980s it was feared that the DES might be too slow to respond to the need to change direction in education policy. It was particularly thought that the DES was too closely identified with the major educational pressure groups – the LEAs and the teaching unions. Thus, a number of new initiatives were launched through the Manpower Services Commission (MSC), now called the Training Commission (TC). With a growing number of young unemployed the government brought in a series of training programmes, notably the Youth Opportunities Programme (YOP) and its successor, the Youth Training Scheme (YTS). These were highly contentious, with some claiming that they were genuine training schemes designed to remedy the defects of the schools and others claiming that they were simply devices to keep the numbers registered as unemployed down. They were, however, financed outside the main education budget and, in time, became an important part of non-advanced further education funding. With the funding, however, went a clear concept of a contract to deliver specific services. This weakened the power of the colleges and the teachers and strengthened the power of the MSC. In the late 1980s the TC turned its attention to the curriculum in higher education through the 'Enterprise Scheme'. By offering relatively small additional sums of money to colleges whose budgets had been seriously eroded, the TC was attempting to shift the emphasis in the higher education curriculum towards more vocationally related training, personal transferable skills and an enterprise culture.

The DES responded to the development of a 'competitor' in education policy by launching its own initiatives in vocational education. The most important of these was the Technical and Vocational Education Initiative (TVEI). This was intended to influence the whole school curriculum although its main focus was the lower two-thirds of the 14–18 ability group.

All of these initiatives had the clear aim of giving people the skills and attitudes they would need for the work place. They show clearly the strong emphasis being given to vocationalism in contemporary education policy.

Parental Choice

One of the major themes in the Conservative Party's Election Manifestos in 1979 and 1983 was strengthening parental choice. Many critics believed that the professional teachers and educational administrators, who had vested interests in maintaining the status quo, had become too powerful in the 1960s and 1970s and had furthered their 'progressive' ideologies against the wishes of the parents. One way to counteract their influence was to strengthen the power of the consumers of the service – or at least their parents.

One way to improve 'choice', always a difficult concept in a state education system, was to help parents opt out of that system and into the private sector. In the 1980 Education (no. 2) Act the government introduced the Assisted Places Scheme. This was a system of means-tested benefits designed to allow a relatively small number of parents who otherwise could not afford it to send their children to private schools. Lack of funding meant that the Scheme has never made the impact which its advocates hoped for but this did little to weaken its contentiousness. At a time of cutbacks in funding for the public sector, it was clearly an indication of little confidence for that sector by brining in a scheme to help parents opt out.

Parental choice within the state sector was to be strengthened by giving parents greater power over the selection of the schools to which their children could go. Since the full, free market could not operate in the sector it was necessary to create as many of the mechanisms of the market as possible. It was claimed that parents living in an area knew which were the 'good' schools and which were the 'bad' ones. Schools' reputations might be based on examination results, the behaviour of staff and pupils or other factors. If more parents could send their children to their first choice of 'good' schools, then enrolments would drop at the 'poor' schools and – faced with a threat to their survival – the staff at the poorer schools would make strenuous efforts to improve their performance or, in the last analysis, face closure.

There was a fear, however, that the LEAs were preventing this modified market working by fixing enrolment targets so as to ensure reasonable recruitment levels for both good and bad schools. To circumvent this the 1980 Act required LEAs to set a 'standard number' of pupil places related to their enrolments in 1979–80. Enrolment targets below this number required the approval of the DES.

LEAs were then obliged to make arrangements for parents to prioritise the schools they wanted their children to attend and had a duty to comply with these preferences unless it would prejudice the provision of efficient education. Further to strengthen the position of parents, LEAs were required to establish local appeals committees to hear grievances over school allocations.

A more radical development was announced by Kenneth Baker, then Secretary of State, to the Conservative Party Conference in the Autumn of 1986. He announced the introduction of a pilot scheme to set up City Technology Colleges (CTCs). These were to be outside the LEA provision, were to have part of their foundation costs met by industry or other sponsors and were to receive their running costs directly from the DES. Although they were to offer free education, they were to be selective in recruiting pupils, were to operate a longer school day with a clear obligation to undertake homework and had a strong emphasis on technology. They were confined to urban areas and initially there were to be up to 20 of them.

There are a number of policy issues inherent in this development. These include the involvement of industry and commerce in the provision of state education, the emphasis on technology and the creation of an elite sector in the nation's schools. Critics argued that this was a backdoor way of reintroducing grammar schools.

Strengthening Management

Another theme present during this period was the strengthening of management and the accompanying weakening of the power of the professionals and their trade unions. The term 'management' was not used very much in the education system in the 1960s and 1970s but during the 1980s not only was it used increasingly but it also became closely associated with techniques which derived largely from the private sector. The general assumption at the beginning of the decade was that the public services were inefficient and ineffective, with amateurish managements impotent in the face of organised labour and 'featherbedded' from the harsh realities of life by generous public spending. As the emphasis on efficiency, effectiveness and value for money increased, so the role of management was progressively strengthened.

The power of the teaching unions had probably been grossly overestimated in 1980 anyway, but there were demonstrations of collective action in the pay disputes of the mid-1980s. However, in the Teachers' Pay and Conditions Act 1987, the government scrapped the existing negotiating machinery, (usually referred to as the Burnham Committee), and imposed a new salary system and conditions of employment. Thus, effectively, collective negotiation was abolished in the education service by government decree. In addition to this, there were threats of replacing nationally agreed wages and conditions with a return to local arrangements, a move which would gravely weaken the teaching unions.

Strengthening Governing Bodies

Part of the government's strategy has been to strengthen the power of school and college governing bodies, both as a counter to teacher and LEA power and as a vehicle for enhancing parent power. The 1986 Education Act in particular extended the responsibilities of governors into some areas of the curriculum, including sex education, discipline and staff appointments. The Act reduced the number of LEA nominees on governing bodies in an attempt to weaken what was seen as the grip of party politics on those bodies and extended their power by giving them responsibility for oversight of the curriculum and for the general conduct of the school. The theory was that if governing bodies could be made more important and made accountable to the parents this would enhance parent power. Accordingly, each year there are to be meetings of all the parents with the governors at which the latter would report. Governing bodies and LEAs were also required to produce a policy statement describing each school's curriculum, again to inform parents on what was happening in the schools.

The Education Reform Act 1988

The themes identified above were not linked together in one set of decisions or legislative acts, rather they were found in a whole collection of decisions, legislation and policies. Individually, few were seen as radical and far-reaching but taken together they constitute a very considerable movement from the status quo in 1979. However, all of the developments were to pale into insignificance when compared to the 1988 Education Reform Act. This was launched under the leadership of the Secretary of State, Kenneth Baker, and was the most important single development since 1944. It contained a set of very radical proposals which were intended to transform the education service in England and Wales.

The extent of the Act is outlined below, but it is worth asking first why the government thought it was possible in 1988 to propose radical legislation in this area of social policy when they had clearly shied away from it earlier. Clearly by 1986–7 the old partnership between the DES, the LEAs and the professionals had broken down. The LEAs were much weaker than they had been ten years earlier and the feebleness of the unions had been demonstrated during the successive industrial relations problems. The DES was very clearly in a much stronger position relative to these other groups than at any other time in the post-war period.

The personality of the minister is also important. It is quite possible that previous ministers had always had the potential power to initiate such far-reaching reforms but had not used that power either because of a wish to take the majority of the system with them or because education had a low policy priority for governments. Baker had none of these constraints. The reform of education had had a high place in the 1987 Manifesto and Baker did not feel that he had to take the LEAs and the unions with him – they could do as they were told. He was also keen to improve his standing in the Cabinet and the Conservative Party and a reputation as a dynamic man who achieved radical shifts in policy would do him no harm in furthering his personal, political ambitions.

There were also those who supported these reforms. This support came not only from the right wing think-tanks, which provided much of the policy preparation or the groundwork for the reforms, but also from some elements in the DES and from some in the sector, such as the Polytechnic directors, who thought that they and their institutions would benefit.

Thus, the scope for radical action was facilitated by a coming together of a number of factors. This facilitation did not mean, of course, that there was no opposition to the proposals. Indeed, there was a coalescence of groups resolutely opposed to the Bill and this opposition was well voiced in Parliament. However, with a secure majority in the Commons the legislation was always assured of a safe – if rocky – passage. The Act covered the three main stages of state educational provision: schools, further education and higher education. We will deal with each in turn.

Schools

The changes which related to the schools took further the themes which were identified in section 2 and introduced a new reform, the national curriculum.

The National Curriculum   The UK had a tradition of devolving responsibility for designing and implementing the school curriculum to LEAs and headteachers. Apart from a requirement to provide religious education, the 1944 Act had not specified the inclusion of any subjects in the curriculum. This was thought to be an important area for local professional autonomy and a characteristic of the partnership approach to education. However, the Secretary of State claimed that this was one of the reasons why British school children were performing less well than their European counterparts and that in order to improve the education system the country needed both a national curriculum and a method of assessing whether it was being delivered effectively.

The national curriculum is to be both broad and balanced and is to cover schooling up to the age of 16. It consists of a core curriculum comprising English, mathematics and science, (and Welsh for Welsh speaking schools), and seven other *foundation* subjects: history, geography, technology, music, art, physical education and a modern language (for 11 to 16 year olds). Welsh was to be an additional foundation subject for pupils in non-Welsh speaking schools in Wales. The amount of time to be devoted to the national curriculum has not yet been specified for all levels of education but is supposed to be no less than 70 per cent of the total curriculum for 14–16 year olds.

In addition to the national curriculum, religious education is to be provided in all schools and for all pupils above nursery level. This is to comprise religious education as such, to an agreed syllabus, and a daily act of collective worship. The syllabus should reflect the dominance of the Christian religion in the UK, without being denominational.

The Act established a National Curriculum Council and a Welsh Curriculum Council, (NCC/WCC), to keep the national curriculum under review and to advise the DES. Although recommended, the national curriculum is not compulsory for CTCs.

There are substantial reserve powers allocated to the Secretary of State, which do not require further legislative enactment. These clearly strengthen central government power over the education system.

Attainment Targets and Testing Establishing a national curriculum would, of course, be meaningless unless there were ways of monitoring its implementation but also the government had a strong commitment to testing as an integral part of the educational process.

The Act established four *key stages* at 7, 11, 14 and 16. At each of these stages pupils are to be assessed according to attainment targets set by advisory, subject working groups. The attainment targets set out national standards in each subject area at each key stage, so that pupils, parents and teachers can assess individual, class and school progress. The subject working groups determine the basic content of what is to be taught at each level but, in theory, there is still scope for the professional judgement of teachers on the details of content and the method of teaching.

The assessment methods are intended to be uniform nationally and not under the control of teachers or LEAs, although they do involve some teacher assessment. To monitor the assessment system the Act established a School Examinations and Assessment Council (SEAC). This is separate from arrangements for GCSE and GCE A level examinations.

Parental Choice   The rights which parents enjoyed under earlier legislation have been strengthened by the 1988 Act. If the level of demand from parents merits it, secondary schools must enrol up to their standard number and LEAs can no longer use the excuse of efficient service delivery as a way of moderating parent demand. Governing bodies and LEAs must also set out the criteria of selection which they will use if demand exceeds the number of places available and there must be an appeals system available to aggrieved parents. The threat of market forces to 'bad/unpopular' schools is thus reinforced.

In addition to the CTCs permitted under the 1986 Act, the DES was now empowered to enter into arrangements with non-state bodies to set up City Colleges for the Technology of the Arts. These were to concentrate on the application of modern technology to the performing arts, and the idea has been likened to the Fame School in New York.

Weakening Local Government   Although it was not in the 1987 Conservative Party Manifesto and was not in the initial draft of the Bill, the Act abolished the Inner London Education Authority (ILEA) with effect from 1 April 1990 and allocated its functions to the inner-London boroughs and the City of London Corporation. It had been argued consistently since 1870 that the geographical concentration of a large population in the inner London area required an integrated education service which spanned the boundaries thought suitable for other local government services. When the London County Council (LCC) was abolished in 1963 as part of the reform of London local government its functions were transferred to a unifunctional authority, ILEA.

Although faced with some formidable educational problems, often against a background of severe urban deprivation, ILEA was thought by most professional educators to be an excellent LEA and credited with some outstanding authority-wide specialist provision. The integrated nature of the service and the specialist provision are at risk from the 1988 Act.

The transfer of functions will also bring to the fore the severe financial problems faced by ILEA. For many years the authority had spent more than the official government targets allowed and had, accordingly, been penalised by the withdrawal of government grants.

Simply transferring the existing level of provision to the boroughs would have caused them great difficulties and would have forced some of them into 'overspend'. The government has therefore provided additional, transitional funding and a four-year period in which they have to bring spending down. Recognition of the great difficulties in achieving this transfer of responsibilities and assets is implicit in the requirement on the receiving authorities to present plans for service provision to the DES and for a high level of DES involvement in the early years of service provision. However, the combination of taking on new functions from a breaking-up of ILEA and the imposed rationalisation of the service will pose many problems for the boroughs.

There could be no clearer evidence of the subordinate position of local authorities to central government in the UK than the abolition of ILEA. However, although perhaps less dramatically, the Act also weakened further the powers of LEAs outside London.

Perhaps the most radical proposal for schools outside London was to allow them to opt out of LEA control altogether. The Act created a new category of 'grant maintained schools', directly financed by the DES. All secondary schools and primary/middle schools with over 300 pupils are eligible for this status. If a sufficient number of parents are interested, then a ballot of all parents has to be held. If a majority of the parents, (or a majority of those voting in a second ballot if the first had a turnout of less than 50 per cent), support it, then a school can achieve grant maintained status. Responsibility for running the school then transfers to a new governing body, where the majority of governors are 'independent' and appointed by the DES. Once a school has opted out, it can never opt back in again, even though the parents who initially voted for it may well have severed all connections with the school.

For the rest of the schools within an authority, the previous themes of strengthening governing bodies and management and weakening local government are combined. The concept of accountable and responsible management underlies the provisions for the local financial management of schools. In order to make headteachers responsible managers, they had to be given control over as much of their school budgets as possible. Before 1990 heads in most maintained schools had only ever controlled a small capitation allowance for educational support. The budgets for staff, caretaking, cleaning, maintenance, etc. had all been held by the LEA. From April 1990 heads and governing bodies of all schools with over 200 pupils are responsible for all expenditure except capital and certain collective services.

This meant that the level of responsibility of heads and governors increased very significantly, with many teachers claiming that they had neither the inclination nor the training to be managers of what in some cases were quite substantial operations. The LEAs are obliged to transfer resources to the schools according to published formulae. This had led to a range of problems. For example, if the formula used takes average staff salaries as a base, then this disadvantages those schools with older staff who generally have more salary increments than younger staff. Many of these problems have yet to be resolved.

LEAs may well be left in very difficult positions. For example, under the Act the LEAs remain the legal employers of the teachers in maintained schools, yet the governing bodies have the power of hire and fire *from their school*. LEAs presumably have to find places for any teachers 'fired' by governing bodies or endorse their dismissal procedures.

The role of the LEAs in the provision of the education service has been reduced significantly. In theory, their new role includes, in addition to providing certain common services, strategic, rather than detailed, management, setting overall budgets and monitoring performance. There would seem to be certain parallels with the government's proposals on health service reform here. It would seem that LEAs like District Health Authorities, could become buyers of services from independent providers, who may be in the private or the public sector rather than the providers of an educational *service* themselves.

Further Education

The Act extends some of the proposals for schools into further education. The most important development in the 1988 Act was the removal of public sector higher education (PSHE) from the local authority sector altogether and its transfer to 80 independent corporate bodies. The emphasis was clearly on taking the major public sector providers out of the LEA sector. However, this still left a large number of colleges with some higher education and all the further education colleges in the LEA system.

Further education colleges have much greater autonomy from the LEA since 1 April 1990. Like the schools, they enjoy a devolved budget for the vast majority of functions and the governing bodies now have power to 'hire and fire' staff. LEAs must produce every year a plan for the provision of further education in its area and show the principles which it uses for the devolution of resources.

Higher Education

Higher education in Britain is usually divided into the public sector and the university sector. These terms are no longer appropriate for both sectors obtain more than 80 per cent of their funding from the state, but this binary division does relate to the level of resourcing and arguably the different cultures of the two types of institution.

The creation of a totally new, independent public sector had long been departmental policy at the DES but the strength of the local authorities had always prevented this development. However, the same factors which permitted radical reforms of the schools also facilitated these reforms.

In charge of each new higher education corporation is a new governing body, whose membership is heavily slanted towards industry and commerce. This reflects the departmental view that the polytechnics and colleges should be much more vocationally oriented than the universities. The governing body will appoint chief executives of the new corporation, posts previously referred to as principals or directors, and the emphasis is again clearly on a private sector management model.

To allocate government funding to the new sector the Act established a new Polytechnics and Colleges Funding Council, (PCFC), which replaced the former National Advisory Body. The changes in the university sector were less dramatic, but the existing University Grants Committee (UGC) was abolished and replaced by a University Funding Council (UFC), with a similar brief to the PCFC. The emphasis on representation from industry and commerce in these Councils indicates the strong drive towards vocationalism in higher education which is clearly part of government policy.

More significant than the structural changes in higher education are the developments in the methods of funding both institutions and students. The major initiatives have so far been in the public sector and are basically an attempt to introduce an element of competitive tendering into the funding of higher education. In 1990–1 colleges were guaranteed a base-line funding approximating to 95 per cent of their 1989–90 levels. They then submitted bids for student numbers above this level at prices determined by the institutions. PCFC, then, in theory, selected the lowest bids compatible with quality, and thus were able to expand the numbers of students by more than the increase in funding. It is too early to tell if this scheme will be modified or to assess its success, but the clear possibility exists of extending it to more than the present level. This would be, effectively, competitive tendering.

The government has also stressed its wish for higher education institutions to become less dependent on the state and to develop alternative sources of funding. Since the potential sources of such funding are limited, this will mean either that colleges increasingly enter the market place as providers of services previously provided by industry or commerce or become more closely allied with meeting the immediate needs of the private sector.

The government had adopted a curiously contradictory policy on expanding the higher education system. The number of public pronouncements on the topic indicates a genuine commitment to increasing the numbers of students in higher education, especially since many other advanced economies have much higher participation rates. However, it is also committed to introducing a student loan scheme and reducing the value of grants, measures which will inevitably discourage large numbers of people from entering the system.

Conclusion

Where does all this take us in overall educational policy? How you interpret these policies depends upon the ideological or policy position which you view them from. It is perfectly possible to see all these reforms as genuine attempts to increase the effectiveness and efficiency of the educational service, to make it more responsive to the needs of the consumers – pupils, students, parents and employers. Weakening the power of bureaucratic local authorities and strong professional groups who may have placed their own interests above those of the consumers sounds a very democratic and worthy aim.

However, it is possible to argue that the reforms introduced over the last 10 years represent an unprecedented centralisation of power into the hands of the DES and the government. The formidable powers of the Secretary of State over teachers' pay, the national curriculum and its assessment, opting out, etc. are all indicative of this centralisation. It could even be that the ability of schools to opt out of the LEA sector will allow the DES to have its 'own' schools – the forerunner of a truly *national* service?

It is also quite reasonable to interpret these reforms as moving inexorably down the path of transforming the state education service into a two-tier system, in which most provision is made through a privatised system with a residual, very much second class service for those unable to pay. The reforms which have occurred so far would facilitate the privatisation of the state education service. Given what has happened in other parts of the state sector, who can doubt that the will here may also exist?

10

'A Caring Community?' Personal Social Services Policy in the 1980s

NEIL EVANS

> It is no good having a bleeding heart if you haven't got the money to pay for it (Patrick Jenkin, Secretary of State for Social Services, 1979).

Introduction

This chapter will focus on those aspects of welfare known as the personal social services, i.e. services provided by local authority social services departments (SSDs)for:

- elderly people;
- children and their families;
- people with mental or physical handicaps;
- children and young people who have broken the law;
- people recovering from mental illness.

The emphasis will be on two policy issues which have been particularly significant in the 1980s:

- the development of community care;
- the protection of children at risk of abuse.

SSDs were unlikely to escape the cold blast of critical attention from the newly elected Conservative government of 1979. A government committed to challenging the state provision of services and espousing a belief that such provision saps the desire of individuals to help each other through voluntary or charitable endeavour, was unlikely to allow the SSDs to expand unchecked. Services prior to 1971 had been provided within small low budget Departments. With amalgamation under the 'Seebohm restructuring' of 1971 and the local government reorganisation of 1974 SSDs became spenders second only to education departments, with expenditure increasing by 68 per cent between 1968–73.

SSDs had some success in staving off cuts in the later 1970s, claiming the need to expand to meet the needs of the increasing numbers of elderly people revealed by demographic trends. As health authorities reduced the provision of hospital beds for people with handicaps and recovering from mental illness, alternatives were needed. 'Community care' was the name given to policies designed to replace hospital care and expectations grew that SSDs should be responsible for such policies. But as larger more visible departments they became increasingly subject to scrutiny. The Inquiry in 1972 into the death of Maria Colwell was to be the forerunner of a series of investigations into the deaths of children in circumstances which questioned the policies and practices of departments charged with protecting children. Ironically social workers were also criticised for being too intrusive, and inflicting on their clients particular sets of values which were seen to be anti-family and which had the effect of keeping disadvantaged people in, rather than freeing them from, dependency on the state.

The expanding role of state provision of welfare in the three decades following the Second World War was seen, by the right, not only as a drain on the 'wealth-creating' sectors of the economy but an obstacle to the proper exercise of freedom and choice on the part of individuals and families. In an interview soon after taking office in 1979 the Secretary of State for Social Services, Patrick Jenkin, expressed the view that

> many people have seen the risk of creating dependency both individual and collectively through systems of support which have not been built on the basis of community care but on the basis of 'we will take your problem off you' (1979).

Social workers, it was argued, far from solving problems, had a vested interest in their continuance. To rein in the 'welfare bureaucrats' was identified as a major precondition for the re-establishment of the family as the primary site of caring.

The Barclay Committee set up in 1980 to clarify the roles and tasks of social workers was assumed by these professionals to be a barely veiled exercise in demonstrating that most tasks currently undertaken by social workers could be taken on by volunteers and voluntary organisations. Jenkin, again, in 1979:

we very much welcome and encourage the move towards growth in voluntary effort, and the movement of the volunteer bodies into all areas of the Social Services. Indeed many of the voluntary bodies can bring great expertise, skill and experience to some of the most difficult areas in social services.

In fact the complete absence of government action on the Committee's recommendations in its Report of 1982 reflects its unwelcome message that

> There are many things being done by social workers which it would be to the detriment of clients to have left undone and if social workers did not do them many of them would not be done (Barclay, 1982).

Nevertheless the Committee acknowledged that

> the bulk of social care is provided, not by the statutory or voluntary social services agencies but by ordinary people . . . . who may be linked into informal caring networks in their communities . . . [and that] . . . if social work policy and practice were directed more to the support and strengthening of informal networks, to caring for the carers, and less to the rescue of casualties when networks fail, it is likely that the need for such referrals would be reduced (Barclay, 1982).

This was an early recognition of the notion of the 'mixed economy of welfare', with care provided by a combination of informal carers, the voluntary and private sectors and, social services, which was to form the basis of the much awaited White Paper *Caring for People* (Cm 849) in the Autumn of 1989. The economic advantages of such a system were attractive indeed. In the face of a 'rising tide' of elderly people, and a significant level of continuing public support for welfare services, the government, committed to reducing local authority expenditure (see Chapter 12), considered the refashioning of the mix of service providers as an urgent priority.

For the right, scarce resources can best be utilised by targeting those in greatest need and achieving savings through the competition which would flow from the expansion of the private sector. Unfortunately the traditional clients of social services, elderly people, children and people with disabilities, are characterised by a low level of income and thus few opportunities for profitable initiatives on the part of the private sector. Exhorting people to provide for themselves through savings and insurance, or developing voucher schemes for services, were attractive, but offered little in the short term.

The massive expansion of private residential care in the early 1980s was, in the event, financed from the public purse, albeit from central government, through increased social security payments, rather than from local authority SSD budgets. The challenge to social workers was not limited to economic competition from the private and voluntary sectors. In fact a new lease of life to organisations such as the National Society for the Prevention of Cruelty to Children (NSPCC) might well be expected to furnish opportunities for social workers. Certainly the burgeoning private residential sector was a source of potentially lucrative business opportunities for disaffected NHS and SSD staff. Perhaps more significant to plummeting morale amongst social workers during the 1980s was the questioning of their role. The right, echoing an earlier critique of the profession advanced by the left, challenged social work to justify its claim to special 'expertise' in the resolution of individual problems. While the child abuse tragedies appeared to continue unabated, social workers could be portrayed in the media and the eyes of some politicians, as at best ineffectual and, at worst, positively contributing to the collapse of the moral fabric of society. Specifically social workers were charged with undermining traditional family values and, in the case of treatment of persons convicted of crime, with excusing offenders rather than supporting their victims. To be identified as a part of the problem rather than part of the solution was a bitter pill to swallow.

Policy Since 1979

Community Care

The wealth of pronouncements on the virtues of community care from politicians over the past thirty years has been matched only by the plethora of cautionary tales by academic commentators. How seductive but imprecise is the notion of 'community'? How far does the rhetoric of care in the community match the reality of policy developments on the ground? Such questions were as frequent in the 1970s as they are at the end of a decade of Conservative administrations. The White Paper *Caring for People* (Cm 849), published in the Autumn of 1989, is the government's attempt to provide a clear policy of community care.

The term 'community care' was first used in the report of the Royal Commission on law related to Mental Illness and Mental Deficiency in 1957 which led to the 1959 Mental Health Act. The development of a new family of drugs allowed some people with chronic mental health problems to be sustained outside a hospital setting with periodic long-acting injections. The work of psychologists and sociologists which revealed the damaging characteristics of large closed institutions was matched by the evidence that generally people preferred to remain in their own homes and provided the basis for community care policies.

While the needs and rights of patients faced with discharge into the community after long periods in hospital have justifiably excited public concern the reductions in rates of admission of people who previously would have formed new generations of long-stay patients has been a slow but persistent characteristic of policies in the 1970s and 1980s.

By 1979 the incoming Conservative government was faced with growing evidence of the inadequacies of current policies and the potentially explosive growth in demand created by the increasing numbers of very elderly people projected for the final two decades of the century. The inertia built in to the budgeting systems of the NHS and local authorities appeared to render them incapable of responding to the needs of people now in the community rather than in hospital. Joint funding and joint planning initiatives on the part of District Health Authorities and SSDs in the late 1970s were encouraging innovative, but small-scale, new developments. Government funding restrictions brought local authority capital building schemes to a virtual standstill. For social services chiefs faced with 'no-growth' or declining revenue budgets the 50 per cent of total expenditure which has been devoted to residential care appeared as a natural target. While the expenditure of as much money on the 2 per cent of elderly people in residential care as on the 98 per cent living in the community might appear to be a good example of 'targeting those in greatest need' there was growing evidence that not all those in residential care had needs markedly different from others who remained in their own homes.

The consensus around the virtues of community care has become increasingly strained during the 1980s. Professionals in both the health service and social services have challenged the notion that community care is cheaper than residential care. If a high quality of service, sensitive to individual needs, is provided it is likely to be more expensive than maintaining large poorly staffed hospital wards. Small but vocal professional groups argued that hospitals provided 'asylum' for vulnerable, dependant people who would be a risk in what often appeared to be a hostile rather than caring community. The resistance of local people to the creation of a hostel or group home in their neighbourhood was cited as evidence that long-stay patients would be discharged in the blinkered pursuit of a policy of community care rather than to meet their particular needs. The spectre was raised of large numbers of destitute psychiatric ex-patients inhabiting a twilight world of homelessness, corrupt landlords and prison cells. With a declining stock of cheap rented housing and changes in social security and housing benefit to the disadvantage of people under 25, opportunities for 'self-reliance' would be no more than pious hopes of policy-makers. While the fear was that the voices of the lonely, isolated ex-patients of long-stay hospitals would not be heard, the concerns of the carers of elderly and disabled people were becoming increasingly evident. Would care *by* the community replace care *in* the community with minimal health and social services support for carers? While the government might applaud the selflessness of families and neighbours what practical expression would this find? The government, it was claimed, particularly by feminist writers, sought a return to 'Victorian' values of family life to cajole women into undertaking unpaid, or poorly paid, caring and domestic tasks.

Demographic Change

The demographic changes which Britain shares with the rest of Western Europe were slow to enter the consciousness of politicians and policy-makers. While numbers of elderly people have been increasing in both absolute terms, and as a proportion of the total population, since the 1950s the policy implications of this had received only rudimentary attention in the 1960s and 1970s. In the UK the percentage of the population aged 65 and over rose from 10.7 in 1950 to 14.9 in 1980 (OECD, 1988). The OECD projected that the UK total of 5.4m people aged 65 in 1950 will have almost doubled to 10.6m in 2050.

Rarely are such demographic changes seen as anything other than a problem, i.e. the 'burden' which will be imposed on future generations by a lumpen mass of unproductive elderly people. With young people entering employment later the imagery has been of a declining rump of economically active people sustaining dependants at either end of the age range. The most immediate manifestation of this view was the government's attempt to abolish the State Earnings Related Pension Scheme (SERPS) and its success in reducing its scope in the social security reforms of 1986 (see Chapter 11). That increased longevity of the population might be viewed as a success of public health policies and of improved diet, housing, nutrition as well as medical and nursing care which reduced infant mortality rates would indeed be optimistic. Rather, negative stereotypes of old age as a period of decline and marginal usefulness to society have been reinforced.

The Audit Commission Report *Making a Reality of Community Care –* **1986**

> Every year, some £6 billion is spent from public funds providing long-term care and support for elderly, mentally or physically handicapped people . . . About 1.5 million adults in England and Wales receive some form of care (Audit Commission, 1986).

The 1986 Audit Commission Report identified an important conflict between the government's stated policy objective of extending community care and the consequences of the growing numbers of elderly people in private residential care funded largely by social security payments. Given the projected increase of 37 per cent in numbers of very elderly people between 1986-96, alternatives to expensive residential care would be required. The Commission urged that

> a rationalization of Funding policies must be undertaken . . . so that present policy conflicts are resolved, . . . a more rational organisational structure must be established . . . [and] . . . the organizational structures of the different agencies need to be aligned and greater managerial authority delegated to the local level.

The Commission emphasised the role of local managers in control of budgets and free to purchase services from 'whichever public or private agency seems appropriate'. While the notion of a mixed economy of care was firmly supported, the Report avoided identifying which agency, the NHS or the local authority, should assume the firm and clear managerial responsibility required. The Commission recommended that a 'high level review of the current situation should be set in train [and] . . . the one option that is not tenable is to do nothing about present financial, organisational and staffing arrangements'.

In an Occasional Paper (no. 4, 1987) spawned by the wider review of community care, the Audit Commission produced a significant contribution to the development of needs-led services for people with learning difficulties. With no brief to suggest any increase in expenditure the Commission has used the opportunity of arguing that existing resources could be better used to support progressive developments in the services for people with learning difficulties. The concept of consumer choice was given expression in the Commission's recognition of a different attitude towards people with a mental handicap, recognising them as full and valued citizens who have as much right as anyone to an ordinary life in the community.

The Griffiths Report – 1988

The choice of Roy Griffiths to produce recommendations for the future of community care reflects a pervasive characteristic of the Thatcher government's approach to policy-making in the personal social services, as in the public sector more generally. Out go Royal Commissions and large Committees of Inquiry reflecting a broad range of relevant (or, it is argued, vested) interests. Rejected are the processes of undertaking research or seeking formal evidence. Favoured is the model of an individual or small group charged with formulating specific recommendations within the context of firmly established, if not always explicit, parameters. In this case Griffiths based his review on the 1986 report of the Audit Commission, discussed above, and the report of The House of Commons social services Committee on *Community Care with special reference to adult mentally ill and mentally handicapped people.*

Griffiths in March 1988 summed up the sense of confusion and lack of direction in community care policies in two telling phrases; the first referred to a feeling in many SSDs that

the Israelites faced with the requirement to make bricks without straw had a comparatively routine and possible task [and a sense that] community care is a poor relation, everybody's distant relative but no-body's baby.

The Report reaffirmed a shift in focus for SSDs, who should act

as the designers, organisers and purchasers of non-health care services, and not primarily as direct providers, making maximum possible use of voluntary and private sector bodies to widen consumer choice, stimulate innovation and encourage efficiency.

They should ensure that 'the needs of individuals within the specified groups are identified, packages of care are devised and services co-ordinated and where appropriate a specific care manager assigned'. While Griffiths held back from a specific recommendation that SSDs become the 'lead' authorities responsible for planning and implementing community care policies this indeed was the inevitable consequence of his proposals, unpalatable though this was to a government content to strip local authorities of functions rather than to add to them. For Griffiths the proposals for 'a Minister clearly and publicly identified as responsible for community care' and social services funded by a ring-fenced specific grant followed naturally from his belief that policy should be matched by resources.

It is widely assumed that the deafening ministerial silence which greeted the low-key publication of the Griffiths report on the day after Chancellor Nigel Lawson's Budget of 1988 reflected reluctance to endorse the pivotal role accorded to SSDs by Griffiths. We had to wait until November 1989 for the government to commit itself to specific proposals, which appeared in the 1989 White Paper *Caring for People.*

The White Paper *Caring for People*: Community Care in the Next Decade and Beyond

The White Paper follows closely the Griffiths proposals. The main provisions are:

● Local authorities will be required to produce three-year plans, updated annually, for the development of community care within their areas.

● Local authorities will be responsible for 'assessing individual need, designing care arrangements and securing their delivery within available resources'.

● Levels of income support and housing benefit will be the same whether someone lives in their own home or in residential care.

● From 1991 there will be a phased transfer of social security funds to local authorities, who will take responsibility for people in private and voluntary homes. Such funds will not be available for residents in homes run by SSDs.

● A new specific grant to local authorities, via Regional Health Authorities, will be designed to ensure that a care programme is in place for all seriously mentally ill people who are discharged from hospital.

A central role is accorded to 'case management' which should include:- (DoH/DSS, 1989, p. 211).

● identification of people in need;
● assessment of care needs;
● planning and securing of delivery of care;
● monitoring the quality of care provided;
● review of client needs.

The care manager will generally come from the SSD but will be expected to work closely with health services staff to ensure that both 'social care' and 'health care' needs are met. To secure the delivery of care care managers must 'make use wherever possible of services from voluntary, "not for profit" organisations and private providers insofar as this represents a cost effective care choice'. Local authorities will be expected to make their plans public, to provide systems for appeal and complaints and to monitor and evaluate the quality of services. For their part local authorities will be subject to the scrutiny of the social services Inspectorate. Central government will thus satisfy itself that local authorities 'have plans in line with national objectives', and that performance targets embodied within the plans are in fact met.

The government has rejected the unpalatable Griffiths proposals for a Minister of Community Care and for a specific grant to local authorities to meet their new responsibilities. Crucially absent from government pronouncements have been statements about the level of resources available to extend consumer choice, to develop domiciliary services and to support carers. In fact the White Paper suggests that increases in expenditure in real terms since 1979 have been sufficient to keep pace with demographic changes. Implicit in the proposals is a view that with social security expenditure on non-statutory residential and nursing home care increasing from £10 m in 1979 to over £1,000 m in 1988–9, a redistribution will sustain community care developments in the 1990s. Ironically a White Paper seeking more rigorous planning, budgeting and evaluating of services has signally failed to cost its own proposals.

Child Abuse and the Children Act 1989

One of the few references to children to be found in the White Paper *Caring for People* pointed out that in England many of the 27,000 social workers 'are involved primarily in child care services'. The high priority accorded to child care work reflects the evidence during the 1980s of a level of child abuse, particularly child sexual abuse, dramatically higher than had previously been thought. The intense pressure on SSDs, subject to Inquiries into deaths of children in their areas, for example Jasmine Beckford, has contributed to the desire to provide a rapid and rigorous response to allegations that children are at risk. This priority could be achieved only at the expense of other SSD provision. The president of the Association of Directors of Social Services commented in June 1989 that

> we are responding to what we and the public regard as high priority work at the expense of the legitimate expectations of others in need of our services.

For example in *Caring for People* the government calculated that only 3 per cent of social services expenditure was devoted to mental health services. While the right sought a re-affirmation of traditional family values the Conservative administrations since 1979 have struggled to provide a policy response to the increasingly evident, but uncomfortable, fact that the home might be an extremely dangerous place for some family members. For much of the 1980s the government response to media clamour for action was to point to the child care law review which followed the Select Committee for Social Services Report on children in care (the Short Report) in 1984.

The culmination of the review is the 1989 Children Act which, while seeking a radical change in the relationship between parents, or carers, and social workers, can scarcely be said to establish policies unique to Thatcherism.

Child care policy is embroiled with the complex task of resolving questions around the nature of the state's responsibility towards children and conflict surrounding notions of parental rights and responsibilities. The 1970s saw the identification of the 'welfare of the child' as the paramount consideration in situations of conflicting interests among family members. Unfortunately the 1980s have not produced a resolution of the lack of certainty about how best the welfare of children be protected and promoted. Social workers have felt attacked, both for efforts to shore up families and when separating children from parents when this has appeared to be the appropriate option. Committees of Inquiry have not provided consistent answers. In 1985 at the end of a 300-page report the Committee of Inquiry into the death of Jasmine Beckford concluded that 'society should sanction, in "high risk" cases, the removal of such children for an appreciable time'. Unfortunately the Committee offered little guidance in the identification of 'high-risk' stating 'we do not define "high-risk", mainly because we think that it is not susceptible of definition'. Nevertheless the unequivocal message to social workers was to be more decisive and more ready to contemplate permanent removal of children from parents. By 1988 the Butler-Sloss Report into 'an unprecedented rise in the diagnosis of child sexual abuse during the months of May and June 1987' in Cleveland concluded that

> Social Services, whilst putting the needs of the child first, must respect the rights of the parents; they also must work if possible with the parents for the benefit of the children. These parents themselves are often in need of help. Inevitably a degree of conflict develops between these objectives.

The government's response to the 1984 Short Report was to set up an inter-departmental working party which published a consultative document *Review of Child Care Law* in September 1985. A White Paper *The Law on Child Care and Family Services* (Cm 62) appeared in January 1987 and formed the basis for the Children Act of 1989. The government established a number of important principles in the White Paper:

- While the state may assist parents 'the prime responsibility for the upbringing of children rests with parents'.
- 'Services to families in need should be arranged in a voluntary partnership with the parents'. As far as possible children in care

should remain in contact with their parents and return home as soon as feasible.

- Only a court should authorise the transfer of a parent's legal rights to the local authority. This should only happen if a child has been harmed or is at risk of being harmed, and 'a court order is the best method of safeguarding the child's interests'.
- The period of removal of a child from parents in an emergency, prior to a full court hearing, should be reduced and be open to challenge by parents.

While the government sought to rationalise the more than twenty routes into local authority care the eventual provisions of the 1989 Act fell short of establishing a family court system. While establishing greater uniformity of practice amongst the different courts which might be concerned with arrangements for the care of children, the government has yet to grasp the nettle of legal vested interests which would be required to set up a single form of family court. A number of other question marks remain over a piece of legislation which has attracted wide support amongst professionals and been virtually ignored by large sections of the media. In particular the issue of resources to implement the changes has, not surprisingly, been one which has led to charges that the government has underestimated both the costs to SSDs and to the legal system. The Association of Metropolitan Authorities claims that the costs of implementing the Act will be more than two and a half times the DoH's estimates. Without adequate resources local authorities will not take up their powers to help children leaving care. The scandal of destitute young people, victims of increasingly restrictive social security provisions and the waning interest of authorities who had previously assumed the role of parent, will remain unchecked.

Overview and Future Trends

There has been an 'increasing, and to my mind unfortunate, trend over the last two decades of governments tending to take more and more of the decisions themselves and letting local authorities be little more than agents of central government. This government has come to the conclusion that we need to reverse that trend (Patrick Jenkin, Secretary of State, 1979).

It would be hard to persuade Directors of Social Services that the 1980s were a decade of decentralisation! With tighter financial constraints through the rate support system, including rate-capping, or, the threat of it, (see Chapter 12), central government has severely limited scope for innovation. Other factors have contributed to the restraint of local autonomy, for example the continuing stream of legislation and welter of circulars and guidance, the burgeoning Audit Commission, an enhanced role for the social services Inspectorate, the rejection of three-year social work training and the Training Support Programme of direct government grants. There is a certain irony in a new decade ushered in by a new Minister of Health, Virginia Bottomley, insisting that the Community Care Bill, due to come into force on 1 April 1991 will enable local authorities to develop services reflecting local needs rather than the prescriptions of an interventionist government.

Social workers in the 1980s have sought to respond to the evidence of continuing disadvantage of significant groups in society, for example the unemployed (particularly the young homeless), single parents, disabled people, growing numbers of AIDS sufferers and black people significantly unrepresented in positions of influence, as much in social services as more widely in society. While notions of empowerment, client access to records and contracts between social workers and service users, have led to worthwhile innovations the pervasive nature and scale of disadvantage has been largely untouched by their best efforts. The effect has been a decade of plummeting morale with consequent problems of staff recruitment and retention. Perhaps optimism is a necessary characteristic of social work as the new decade has witnessed a flood of commentators heralding a brave new world to be ushered in by the Community Care Bill and the Children Act. What then will the 1990s require of social services Departments?

- *Planning*: Planning is back in vogue. Local authorities will be required to prepare three-year plans, rolled forward annually, and devised in consultation with service users and Health Authorities. The social services Inspectorate will monitor the plans and intervene if necessary to ensure relevance and quality. In particular it will encourage local authorities to focus on *outcomes.*
- *Outcomes*: SSDs will need to establish systems of assessment of individual need and manage packages care designed to meet such needs. Integral to this process will be the monitoring of the systems and the evaluation of the outcomes provided for *service users.*
- *Service users*: They will be accorded significantly more influence in the design of packages of care. Complaints procedures, rights of appeal and the ability to change their 'care manager' will enhance their power. Theirs will be a control role in the process of *quality assurance.*
- *Quality assurance*: As SSDs shift in the direction of purchasers of care rather than direct providers social workers will be faced with

the task of ensuring that a range of care providers are maintaining the standards set in the original contracts.

Few commentators minimise the scale of the change faced by SSDs. The 1980s witnessed the major growth of private residential care; the 1990s will see private and voluntary developments in all sectors of care provision. The government's reticence over the financial resources to be made available for the implementation of the Children Act and the Community Care Bill has fuelled fears that social workers, as case managers, will become primarily *rationers* of inadequate resources.

11

Away from the Dependency Culture?
Social Security Policy

FRANCIS McGLONE

The social security system that the Conservative government inherited
in 1979 was a costly and complex scheme almost impenetrable to all
but the expert. It was based on the social insurance scheme proposed in
William Beveridge's Report of 1942. Beveridge had envisaged an
insurance scheme where all those in work would contribute to an
insurance fund, with contributions also coming from employers and
the state, so that in times of need, such as unemployment, sickness or
on retirement, people would be able to claim benefits as of a right.
However, when the scheme was implemented after the Second World
War many of Beveridge's principles were undermined. Insurance
benefits were paid at too low a level and consequently many claimants
were forced to seek additional help from the National Assistance Board
in the form of means-tested benefits. Means testing required a claimant
to undergo an investigation of his or her circumstances. This
investigation of resources and needs was both stigmatising and
degrading and added a large degree of complexity to the social
security system. It also gave considerable power and discretion to
National Assistance Board officers. Beveridge had hoped that means
testing would eventually be reduced to a minimum once the majority of
the population were covered by social insurance.

During the 1960s many solutions were sought to simplify the social
security system and reduce the amount of means testing. The Labour
government introduced earnings related contributions and benefits so
that in return for an increased contribution a higher rate of insurance

benefit would be paid. It was hoped that this would remove many claimants, particularly pensioners, from reliance on means-tested benefits. In 1966 the Labour government renamed national assistance, supplementary benefit and created a new Ministry of Social Security, later renamed the Department of Health and Social Security (DHSS), in the expectation that this would give means testing a new image. Supplementary benefit was to be based more on legal entitlements that discretion. Unfortunately, these hopes were not to be realised, partly due to the increasing numbers of unemployed. With rising unemployment there was also a change in the type of person claiming supplementary benefit, from pensioners to claimants with children. This added a greater degree of complication because of the ever-changing circumstances and needs of unemployed claimants with children compared to pensioner claimants. In the 1970s then there was a dramatic rise in the numbers on supplementary benefit and in the amount of discretionary payments made to cover additional needs. Concern was raised that the whole system was on the verge of collapse. It was in response to this that the DHSS set up an Internal Review in 1976. Out of this Review came a consultative document making various recommendations for reforming the supplementary benefit system. Before these recommendations could be implemented, however, a new Conservative government under Mrs Thatcher came to power.

The Thatcher government lacked any clear and well formulated policies for reforming the social security system, but it was informed by an ideology, derived from the 'New Right' and traditional conservative values, that could act as a guide for future action and as a justification for reform. Moreover, the Thatcher government was committed to cutting public expenditure as part of its monetarist economic strategy (see Chapter 2), and social security was the single largest spending programme of the state. However, implementing this ideology and cutting spending on social security has not proved to be an easy task. Opposition, both inside and outside Parliament, and public opinion has meant that the government has proceeded relatively cautiously, but with successive election victories it is now possible to see a clear movement to break with the past consensus surrounding social security. In the first stage of the government's developing policy towards social security, covering the first two terms in office (1979–87), we see an attempt to implement the ideology, but at the same time to continue with past policies. The main change has been the acceptance by the government of means testing as the basis of the social security system. In the second stage, following the third election victory in 1987, we can now clearly see the government's intention to break completely with past policies on social security.

Short-term Remedies

In the short term the only way that the government could reduce the cost of social security and adapt the scheme to its ideological project was to implement any existing proposals by the DHSS and to rely on a whole series of minor rule changes and amendments to the existing system. The government implemented in 1980 the recommendations set out in the Review of supplementary benefit carried out under the previous Labour government. As the Review had been set up with the constraint that any proposals had to be carried out on a no extra cost basis this meant a transfer of resources between claimants, with 1.75m losing out and 800,000 gaining (Lister, 1989, p. 106). It did mean, however, the end of discretion in the system as the Review had recommended the replacement of discretionary additional payments with clear legal rights. The government did not carry out the proposal that the rate of benefit to the long term unemployed be increased because of concern that this would interfere with work incentives. In addition, the 1980 Social Security Act broke the link between retirement pensions and increases in earnings, leaving it linked to the lower price inflation.

Later legislation saw the government not increasing benefits in line with inflation, actually cutting entitlements and transferring the responsibility for the payment of certain benefits to other bodies. We therefore see the abolition of earnings related supplements on short-term National Insurance contributory benefits, such as unemployment, and sickness benefit. Also, the taxation of unemployment benefit and the restriction of benefit payments to strikers. The overall result of these policies, including the de-indexation of retirement pensions to earnings, was actually to increase the numbers dependent on means tested benefits. To reduce administrative costs the government transferred the responsibility for the first 8 weeks of sickness pay to employers (now 28 weeks). Another method used to reduce administration costs was not to increase the number of DHSS staff in line with the large increase in claims for supplementary benefit due to the rise in unemployment. This was at a time when more resources were being transferred to the detection of fraud and abuse (Ward, 1985, p. 8). Finally we see the introduction of the housing benefit scheme in November 1982 and April 1983.

Housing Benefit

The implementation of the housing benefit scheme presents us with a particularly interesting example of things to come. The problem with the previous means of subsidising the housing costs of people on low incomes was that it could come in one of two ways, depending on whether or not the person was on supplementary benefit. If on supplementary benefit help would come through the DHSS, otherwise it would come from rent and rate rebates paid by the local authority. This was an awkward and clumsy system as the two schemes operated on different principles and this led to anomalies. In many cases people were not aware that they might have been better off claiming the other benefit. Take-up was low and the system aggravated the 'poverty trap' – that is, the tendency for an increase in income to lead to a loss of benefits therefore making the person little or no better off. The solution was to transfer the administration of housing costs for supplementary benefit claimants to local authorities.

Originally known as unified housing benefit, the 'unified' was quickly dropped as it failed to live up to its original objectives of simplification, streamlining and ensuring that claimants received their correct entitlement. This was due to the government stipulating that the scheme be introduced at no extra cost. In addition, the government saw the scheme as a means to cut the number of civil servants. The 'no extra cost' constraint meant that it was not possible to deal with the large number of anomalies that arose, and therefore a whole range of complexities had to be introduced, thus undermining one of the principle aims.

Board and Lodging

The case of the restrictions on people living in rented accommodation with meals provided – board and lodging – was yet another example of confusion and contradiction in government policy objectives. In 1983 the DHSS presented new draft regulations which introduced three tiers of limits on board and lodging: ordinary board and lodging, residential care, and private nursing care. The last two dealt mainly with the elderly. The objectives were to meet the needs of those living in board and lodging while limiting the demand on public spending. It was pointed out by critics that the announced benefit limits were set too low. The government agreed and increased them; however, faced with increasing numbers claiming board and lodging payments and some adverse publicity about abuse by young unemployed people, a freeze on all board and lodging payments was introduced. This was followed by an actual cut and a restriction on unemployed people under 25 which forces them to move from area to area every 2 to 8 weeks or have their benefit cut. The result has been a considerable increase in the number of young homeless people. In fact young peple have proved an easy target for cuts in social security not having the 'deserving' tag attached to them as do pensioners and the disabled. Public opinion surveys have shown that the latter two categories of social security claimants are viewed more sympathetically and more as deserving of help than the unemployed and lone parent families who tend to be seen as poor because of their own personal inadequacies. The social security system itself has been identified as reinforcing these attitudes by its method of paying different levels of benefit to different claimant groups, for example, lower benefits are paid to the unemployed than pensioners.

Overall, then, since 1979 we have seen cuts in social security, restrictions on entitlements together with a deteriorating service delivery from the DHSS. However these various changes aimed at reducing public expenditure did not deal with the underlying problems of the whole social security system: expense, inefficiency and overcomplication. For this the government had formulated its own long term review.

The Green Paper – 1985

In April 1984 the then Secretary of State for Social Security, Norman Fowler, announced 'the most comprehensive review of the social security system for 40 years'. The Review took the form of panels which gathered evidence on various areas of social security. Evidence was taken from the public both in writing and orally, and the conclusions submitted to a central Review team. Many of those wishing to present evidence objected to the limited timescale for submissions and the independence of the Review panel members. They also argued that as the reforms had to be introduced at no extra cost and the adequacy of social security benefit levels was excluded from the terms of reference, the outcome of the Review was a forgone conclusion. From the results of the Review the government published a Green Paper in June 1985 outlining its policy proposals for the reform of social security. The Green Paper was to be followed by a White Paper setting out the proposed legislation before Parliament.

The proposals set out in the Green Paper had four aims: (1) to encourage self-reliance and independence, (2) to be capable of meeting genuine need, (3) to have ease of administration and (4) be consistent with the government's overall policies for the economy. The main reforms were to include:

- The abolition of the State Earnings Related Pension Scheme (SERPS) and its replacement by private pension schemes.

- The replacement of supplementary benefit by a new simplified means tested scheme called income support.
- The establishment of a cash limited social fund to replace lump sum single payments for exceptional needs.
- Family income support to be replaced by a new means-tested benefit called family credit for families on low wages.
- The unification and simplification of the present housing benefit structures.
- The abolition of the death grant and its replacement with a recoverable payment from the social fund for those on a low income.
- The replacement of the maternity grant with a payment from the social fund for those in receipt of income support and family credit.
- Widow's allowance payable for the first 26 weeks of widowhood to be replaced with a 1,000 lump sum payment and the age at which widow's pension is paid raised by 5 years.

National Insurance benefits or health benefits were hardly mentioned therefore undermining the notion that it was the most comprehensive review of the social security system since Beveridge. The government accepted the case for child benefit although a restructuring would be considered. Child benefit is particularly disliked by the Thatcher government because it goes to everyone with children despite their income and is therefore very costly. It is an indication of the political support for child benefit that the government has been unable to abolish it, although the rate at which it is paid has been frozen for several years. The government also announced that it was commissioning a survey on the extent of disability which would report back when the results were known. This seemed rather misplaced coming after the Review and Green Paper, and cast some doubt over the government's stated intention to meet genuine need. Lastly, the government invited comments on the Green Paper's contents. The vast majority of responses proved to be highly critical. A survey carried out by the Child Poverty Action Group (CPAG) of 60 representative groups found only two in overall favour, namely the Institute of Directors and the Monday Club.

Commentators on the Green Paper's proposals found themselves hampered by the absence of important figures on the rates and benefit levels. The government defended this on the grounds that what was important was the new structure and that the benefit rates in April 1988, the proposed date for the implementation, would depend on the rates set in April 1987. A report in the *Guardian* (6 June 1985) claimed that figures did exist but that Norman Fowler had ordered them to be removed as they showed the extent of losers and gainers from the proposed reforms. This was denied but pressure both within and outside Parliament led to the prime minister promising illustrative figures when the White Paper was published.

Criticisms of the Green Paper

Criticism of the Green Paper focused on several key areas. Of particular concern was the abolition of SERPS which had drawn all-party support when it was introduced in 1978. Its aim was to provide an additional pension to those with no employer's pension. They would therefore not need to rely in the future on means-tested benefits. The government's concern was the growing cost due to the projected increase in the number of pensioners into the next century.

Another key area of reform that drew considerable criticism was the replacement of supplementary benefit by income support. The government's stated intention for the basic means-tested benefit was to shift resources to the poorest families with children. Given the no extra cost basis, this meant that there could only be a trade off between different groups of claimants. The claimant group that was to supply these additional resources to poor families was pensioners, as they were identified by the government as now being relatively better off than other groups.

The government's other stated objective was to simplify means testing. Supplementary benefit suffered from overcomplication because it was a mixture of basic rate entitlements and additional payments payable to those with special needs, for example, diets, extra heating, laundry costs, etc. Under the new system of income support these additional payments would be replaced by a flat rate premium payable to different groups: the disabled, families with children, pensioners and lone parents. Lower rates of benefit were to be payable to those under 25 and 18, residual housing costs simplified and help with water rates abolished.

Concern was expressed at the time over the numbers who could potentially lose from the replacement of additional payments with premiums but in the absence of figures any final comment had to wait. Disability Alliance, a pressure group representing the disabled, pointed out that the new scheme created at least seven different ways of qualifying in the disability category with at least five different premiums. This questioned the government's success in simplifying the system. However, most criticism of the new income support scheme was reserved for the new social fund, which was to replace single payments for essential items, such as beds, cookers, items of clothing, etc. These payments had already been severly curtailed by earlier legislation but the new social fund introduced a more discretionary element without a right of appeal to an independent body. This raised fears of a return to a distinction being made between deserving and undeserving poor by the DHSS. The majority of the payments were to be in the form of interest-free loans rather than grants, which meant that claimaints would have to live below the 'official' poverty line for long periods of time while paying off a loan. Comment was again made more difficult without figures for the total amount of the new social fund, and whether or not claimants would be compensated for the loss of single payments.

The government's case for the new social fund was the escalating cost of single payments and the belief that claimants should be able to budget for such expenses within their weekly benefit. A more discretionary fund would give DHSS staff more flexibility to help people in need, including not just those on income support, and the fixed budget for the fund would encourage 'good housekeeping' at local DHSS offices. In fact the government saw the social fund as a means of helping people with exceptional difficulties and this would be only a minority of cases. The grants would generally be for the purposes of 'community care', assisting people coming out of institutions and re-establishing themselves in the community. To help the DHSS make decisions about payments from the social fund the Green Paper expected links to be forged between local authority SSDs, health professionals and the DHSS. The Green Paper contained not only proposals about social security but wider changes in responsibilities. A more flexible system was being proposed, a shift in functions for 'cash & care' to social services and the voluntary sector. The government in effect was questioning the boundaries between social work and the payment of social security benefits.

The reform of housing benefit was partly addressed to the problems surrounding the original scheme. Simplification was the main purpose by aligning housing benefit with the two other means-tested benefits, income support and family credit. This was generally welcomed but controversy surrounded the proposal to make all recipients of housing benefit including those on income support pay 20 per cent of their general rates. This was justified on the grounds of 'local accountability' – that is, that many claimants of housing benefit do not bear the full cost of a rate increase and that this affects their voting in local elections. Concern was expressed that claimants would not be fully compensated for the 20 per cent contribution, particularly in high rated areas. With the introduction of the Community Charge (poll tax) in England and Wales similar rules will apply, with the maximum rebate on the community charge being 80 per cent.

The White Paper – 1985

With the publication of the White Paper in December 1985 few amendments were made. The government did bow to pressure on SERPS and instead of abolition decided to reduce the benefits of the scheme to anyone retiring after 1999. Actual savings will not therefore begin immediately but over the next 50 years. The illustrative figures accompanying the White Paper confirmed the worst fears of government opponents. The government's own figures estimated that nearly 4m would lose out and just over 2m claimants of all means-tested benefits would gain. When the final figures on benefit levels and rates were published in October 1987, the government claimed that there were 1m more winners than losers. These figures were disputed and it was claimed that the government was disguising the true effects of the social security reforms.

Disability Alliance challenged the government's figures on the number of 'sick and disabled' losers as it ignored 1m disabled pensioners who would lose out due to changes in housing benefit and new rules on the maximum limits for savings. Svenson and MacPherson of the Benefits Research Unit at Nottingham University produced figures to show that the real number of losers was nearly 60 per cent of claimants. The difference between the government's and Svenson and MacPherson's figures was due to methods of calculation, whether or not the loss of single payments was included, or the date from which the loss is taken. Also, whether or not transitional protection was added, which meant that the government's figures showed no loss for those on income support on 11 April 1988, the date of implementation of the reforms. This was because the government 'protected' all existing claimants of supplementary benefit from any fall in income on the introduction of the new scheme by freezing their benefit levels. The changes would therefore affect only new claimants after 11 April. The need to introduce transitional protection indicated the extent of the cuts in the new scheme and the realisation of the politically sensitive nature of reducing benefit levels.

Opponents pointed to other evidence of the government's manipulation of figures. The government was accused of deliberately misleading the public over the implementation of family credit. While the change to family credit would increase the disposable income of poor working families, the loss of free school meals and cuts in housing benefit would lead to an overall loss in disposable income and therefore deepen the poverty trap. Another area of dispute was over the government's claim to have roughly equalised the budget for the social fund with that spent on single payments in 1987. This did not take account of earlier restrictions which reduced spending on single payments by £100m and that 70 per cent of the social fund would be in the form of recoverable loans. Finally, there was the missing compensation for the payment of 20 per cent of general rates. It was claimed by the government that compensation of £1.30 per week (£1 for under-25s) was included in the income support rates and that the new income support personal allowances had been fully uprated in line with the Retail Price Index (RPI). As Svenson and MacPherson have argued this is not the case. The government has either compensated claimants for the £1 or £1.30 or inflation-proofed personal allowances, but not both, and this is a further reduction in benefit.

The massive cut in the housing benefit budget of £650m from April 1988 (see Table of Housing Benefit Savings in Esam and Oppenheim, 1988, p. 12) gives an interesting example of government retreat in the face of opposition. No transitional protection was offered to the large number of losers. However following the threat of a backbench revolt by Conservative MPs, who had received numerous complaints from their constituents, the government made amendments to the housing benefit scheme. These included the raising of the capital cut-off limit, which particularly affected pensioners with small 'nest eggs', and transitional protection for certain 'deserving' groups who had lost more than £2.50 per week in housing benefit. The intention of not allowing the payment of housing benefit too far up the income scale or to those with large amounts of capital appeared to fall foul of their own backbenchers' concern with re-election. These amendments will add a considerable level of complication to the housing benefit system.

Impact of Reforms

The reforms to social security in April 1988 have had a major impact on the claimants of means-tested benefits. Reports have been abundant about the extent of losses and people forced onto charity or into debt. The Conservative dominated Social Services Committee report on the April changes show a 10 per cent fall in the number of claimants of income support between February and May 1988, due to a loss of eligibility. The committee also estimates that certain groups of claimants have lost large amounts of benefit. Single young people under 25 have lost up to £8.84 per week, single pensioners £1.68 per week and married pensioners £2.11 per week. The only gainers are couples with children, but even here the amounts are modest, being £2.91 for a couple with two children aged 13 and 16 (*Guardian*, 9 November 1989).

Other reports have highlighted the plight of the young homeless. According to the charity Centrepoint, the number of young people sleeping rough on the streets of London has increased by 50 per cent since 1987 and the number living in squats had nearly trebled, because of the changes in calculating young people's benefit (*Guardian, 26 October 1989*).

The Audit Commission for Local Authorities has recorded that rent arrears among council tenants are up by a third on 1987–8. The Commission have identified the government's policy of reducing housing benefit and increasing council house rents as the reason (*Guardian, 23 November 1989*).

Finally, after a slow start in the first year of its operation, the social fund for 1989–90 is already 40 per cent over budget and the DSS are refusing increasing numbers of applicants for grants and loans (*Guardian, 17 June 1989*). This will not be helped by the virtual freezing of the social fund budget for 1989 and 1990 (*Guardian, 15 November 1989*).

Changes Since April 1988

Changes to the social security scheme have continued unabated since April 1988. From September 1988 most young people aged 16 and 17 have been unable to claim income support. Instead they are expected to take a place on a Youth Training Scheme (YTS) or go without benefit. The government believes that this will act as a deterrent to young people leaving home and living off state benefits. A report by Citizen Advice Bureaux notes that despite government guarantees there is not a place on a YTS scheme for everyone who wants one. The danger is that young people are being left destitute (*Guardian, 16 October 1989*).

On 9 October 1989 the government implemented new regulations to force the unemployed actively to seek work rather than simply be available for work. Now the unemployed must prove that they are looking for work or have their benefit stopped. The government's view is that the unemployed should either seek work or go on a training course. This is linked to the government's Employment Training programme (ET). Although refusal to accept a position on ET will not automatically disqualify a claimant from benefit it will count towards a decision of whether or not the person is seeking work. This appears to be one step short of the government introducing the American system of Workfare where refusal to work leads to a loss of benefits. At present it is not politically acceptable to introduce full-blown Workfare, and instead various backdoor rule changes are being used to obtain the same results. On top of these changes to the unemployed come an increase in the time limits for suspension from unemployment benefit for leaving a job 'voluntarily' from 6 weeks to 13 weeks and now 26 weeks. This is a method to penalise the unemployed for leaving a job without another job to go to, or for being sacked.

Another change in October 1989 was the transfer of responsibility for the payment of board and lodge allowances from the DHSS, renamed the Department of Social Security (DSS), to local authorities. Instead of receiving an allowance from the DSS claimants in board and lodgings now receive housing benefit. According to a report published by a whole range of charities, including the Salvation Army, people will lose up to £20 per week from this change and many will find themselves out on the streets (*Guardian*, 21 September 1989). However, one reform that the government has rectified is the much-criticised time limits on payments to boarders under 25, which forced them to move from area to area.

Assessment of Government Policy

In the first phase of the reform of social security the government's objectives were: simplification, targeting those most in need, the encouragement of self-reliance and personal independence, and finally cutting public spending on social security. The government has failed to a large degree to meet these objectives due to three reasons: contradictions within the objectives themselves, political pressure and inconsistencies with other policies pursued in the economy.

The government has simplified social security in certain areas but because of limitations on public expenditure various complications have had to be introduced. Political pressure to help specific groups has also added complexity and the discretionary social fund is far more difficult to administer than the previous scheme of single payments. Universal benefits, like child benefit, and contributory National Insurance benefits are not only simpler and less costly to administer but also have a far greater take-up rate than means-tested benefits on account of the stigma attached to receiving the latter. The government rejects universal and National Insurance benefits owing to their expense and lack of targeting, but targeting of benefits and discretion necessarily means complication and stigmatisation of recipients. There has been a particular lack of success in targeting the new means-tested benefits on the most needy. Take-up of family credit is only 38 per cent and it is believed that claims for income support are below government expectations (see Esam and Oppenheim, 1989, pp. 49 and 51 for details). On the poverty trap we do see some improvement. No longer does someone lose more than 100 per cent of their benefit but the number caught in the poverty trap has grown (*Guardian*, 9 November 1989). More people than ever are now dependent on means-tested income support. The number in May 1988 was 8.2m (claimant and family), and the increase in the figure since 1979 is far greater than the increase in the last 30 years (Field, 1989, p. 23). A large part of this is directly related to government reforms in social security and the pursuit of economic policies in the early 1980s which led to a large rise in unemployment. Such facts do not fit easily with government talk of a 'benefits culture' or a 'dependency culture' among claimants of social security. The government believes that the payment of certain types of social security encourages people to become dependent on benefit, and lowers their desire to find work or behave in a responsible manner. To date the government has failed to tackle what it sees as the biggest problem of the 'dependency culture', the reliance of lone parents on the state, although it is now talking of introducing legislation vigorously to pursue missing parents for maintenance. Indeed, some measures introduced in April 1988 relating to child care costs and benefit entitlements acted as a disincentive on lone parents to find work. Lastly, the economic objective of cutting public expenditure on social security has proved elusive with a 39 per cent (£13bn) expansion in real terms between 1978–9 and 1987–8. (see *CPAG Poverty Magazine*, Summer 1989, p. 21, for a breakdown of this figure).

The theme of tackling the 'dependency culture' and the 'why work?' syndrome has featured heavily in the government's legislation since 1987. Measures to encourage self-reliance and personal responsibility were included in earlier measures but these have now been taken much further with the virtual introduction of Workfare and the legislation affecting the unemployed, particularly the young. There is concern that further cuts in social security are on the way, given the government's continuing commitment to reducing taxation and trimming public expenditure. Furthermore, at the time of writing the prime minister has failed to give an assurance that child benefit would continue to be paid to all families after the next general election. Advice being given to the government is to reintroduce child tax allowances, pay child benefit to the under-5s only and/or to means test the benefit (*Guardian*, 9 February 1990). We are now entering a new phase in social security policy which is a complete break with the past consensus. The future role of social security in British society will therefore rest on the outcome of the next General Election in 1991 or 1992.

12

Local Government 1979–89: A Decade of Change

SYLVIA HORTON

Over the last decade there has been a significant shift in the balance of power between central and local government. Local government is being transformed from a provider of public services to an enabling agency facilitating, regulating and supporting a wide range of public and private institutions in meeting local needs. This chapter charts the changes that have taken place since 1979 and identifies the ways in which successive Thatcher governments have brought these about.

The Conservative Government's Policies and Local Government

Local government grew in importance during the post-war period as it became the major administrative agency of an expanding welfare state. Responsible for education, housing, personal social services and a whole range of protective and environmental services, it employed nearly 3m people and accounted for one-third of public expenditure by the mid-1970s. Its expenditure was growing at a faster rate than overall public expenditure and consuming an ever larger proportion of GNP; it was also heavily dependent on central government financial support. There was a feeling that its spending was out of control and that this was a major cause of the fiscal crisis of the state.

The Labour government in 1975 made the first attempt to contain local government expenditure and succeeded in curbing it with a two-pronged strategy of cash limits and a reduction in grant support. However when the Conservatives came to power in 1979 local government expenditure still accounted for 28.1 per cent of public expenditure and 12.4 per cent of GNP, with central government providing 60 per cent of local government tax revenue.

Local government was also under attack in the 1970s for its lack of accountability and responsiveness to consumer demand, its wastefulness, inefficiency and poor management. It was accused on the one hand of too much professional autonomy and on the other of overpowerful trade unions willing to exploit their 'essential service' position and hold the public to ransom in industrial disputes. Whilst these arguments came mainly from the right, there were many within the Labour and Liberal Parties who were advocating more decentralisation, democratisation and participation in local government.

When in opposition the Conservatives had been formulating policies to deal with local government. These included reducing its expenditure, increasing its efficiency and making it more accountable to local ratepayers. The 1979 Manifesto also committed the Party to abolishing the rating systems and replacing it with a fairer tax. Its 'New Right' leaning with support for 'a property owning democracy', 'individual responsibility and self-help' and 'consumer choice' implied changes for local government. Equally its ideological commitment to the market and its determination to roll back the state seemed to herald an attack on the near-monopoly position of local authorities as providers of services. But there was no indication what forms this would take. The only clear pointer was that given the new government's monetarist economic strategy and its determination to cut public expenditure local government spending would be attacked.

So in 1979 there was no blueprint for local government as a whole. The government adopted a piecemeal, pragmatic approach, dealing with inherited problems and feeling its way. It developed a range of discrete policies and programmes for housing, education, urban development, social services, planning and transport. It devised others for dealing with local government finance, its internal organisation, competitive tendering and access to information. The overall result amounted to a cumulative assault on almost every activity for which local government was responsible, but it lacked coherence and consistency. Some of the early policies failed to achieve their objectives and were either abandoned or changed. In others there were unforeseen effects and consequences to which the government reacted. This was particularly true in the area of local government finance.

Although during the first two Thatcher Administrations, much of the approach to local government was reactive and incrementalist, almost all the policies can now be seen as fitting into the government's aims: to increase consumer choice and influence; to open up the local government system to the market; to increase the efficiency and effectiveness of local government; and to make local government more accountable to the electorate. By 1987 a more comprehensive programme of reform was evident and the government had a clearer picture of the type of local government system it wanted for the 1990s. With hindsight, a revolution was taking place throughout the 1980s and an era of local government was coming to an end.

The attack on local government made it the centre of politics throughout the 1980s. The government's anti-state ideology brought it into conflict particularly with Labour controlled authorities, still wedded to the idea of the state as an instrument of social justice and determined to resist pressures to dismantle the welfare state system. It also met with strong opposition from Conservative controlled authorities. Whilst many Conservatives welcomed the government's attack on inefficiency and local government monopolies and enthusiastically pursued policies of competitive tendering and contracting out, they often joined with Labour in opposing specific issues. These included, amongst others, the 'poll tax', educational reform, 'green belt' policy and the abolition of London elections in 1985. It was the perceived threat to local democracy however which, as Goldsmith (1985) says, inspired a united front against the Conservatives, and fuelled the 'politicisation' of the whole of the local government system. Nevertheless opposition and resistance did not stop the radical changes in the local government system from taking place, although they may have slowed the process. The Thatcher government used the full panoply of means at its disposal to bring about the changes, including legislation, administrative direction, financial controls and political exhortation.

As in so many other areas of government policy there has been a hidden agenda. Here it can be argued the aims have been to remove the opposition to government policies, to weaken the local power base of the Labour Party, to undermine and destroy public sector unionism and to provide new markets for the private sector.

The Legislation

Legislation has been a very prominent strategy in the government's approach to local government. In contrast to previous governments, which utilised persuasion, negotiation, financial incentives and disseminated information on good practice to bring about change, the Thatcher government has used law on an unprecedented scale.

A significant aspect of the strategy has been the tendency for most of the law to be mandatory rather than permissive. Local authorities have been given powers or duties which they have to exercise, e.g.

competitive tendering. They have had powers removed, e.g. control over Polytechnics. In other instances permissive powers have been converted into mandatory ones, e.g. sale of council houses. In addition central government has increased its own powers to regulate, intervene and direct local government. The overall effect has been greatly to reduce the discretion which local authorities have traditionally had and to increase the power of the centre.

The legislation falls into four main categories. The first relates to local government in general. Twelve major acts have been placed on the statute book most of them mixed in content (see Appendix 1, pp. 254–7). Exceptions are the Local Government Act 1985, which abolished the GLC and the Metropolitan Counties, and the Local Government Act 1986, which prohibits local authority publicity of a party political nature (following the anti-abolition campaign of the GLC).

Almost all of this legislation relates to local government finance directly or indirectly. The Local Government, Planning and Land Act 1980, in addition to abolishing hundreds of detailed regulations, establishing Enterprise Zones (EZs) and Urban Development Corporations, (UDCs), constituted the first attack on local government finance. It replaced the old rate support grant with a new block grant based upon grant related expenditure to be determined by the government. This was subsequently followed by legislation giving the government further powers to impose penalties on overspenders and to abolish supplementary rates (Local Government Finance Act, LGFA, 1982), to impose rate capping (Rates Act 1984), and finally to abolish the rates and radically to change the system of local government finance (LGFA 1988).

The Local Government Act 1988 compels local councils to put refuse collection, street cleaning, catering, cleaning of buildings, grounds maintenance and vehicle maintenance out to tender. This Act also requires local authorities not 'to act in a manner . . . restricting, distorting or preventing competition' and to review all of their activities to ensure that they are not anti-competitive.

The second category of legislation relates to housing. Six main acts have introduced the 'right to buy' and a statutory charter for tenants (Housing Act, HA, 1980) extended these rights (HAs 1984, 86, 88), deregulated private rented accommodation (HA 1988) and transformed the means of government funding of housing (HA 1988) (see Chapter 8). The third category of legislation is education where there have been six Education Acts (1979, 1980, 1981, 1984, 1986 and 1988) (see Chapter 9). The fourth category is miscellaneous and covers transport, social services, planning, urban development, environmental protection and public health. The general thrust here has been to force local authorities to open themselves up to competition, to collaborate with the private sector and to change their primary role from a provider of services to a facilitator.

Within the British constitution, local authorities are creations of ordinary law with neither a legal right to exist or general powers. They can exercise powers only specifically granted to them and are totally subordinate to Parliament. This is in contrast to the USA and Europe where local government is protected in the country's constitution and also has a general competence. However in the past conventions and procedures ensured that local authorities played a prominent role in the policy-making and legislative process. They were consulted about government policy proposals and given the opportunity to present their recommendations or objections before final decisions were taken. Major changes of a constitutional nature had always been preceded by Public Inquiries or Royal Commissions to ensure that an independent review and wide public debate occurred.

The Thatcher government has tended to depart from this pattern preferring to inform rather than consult with local government. This exclusionary approach has resulted in continuous confrontation with local government with campaigns against legislation conducted both inside and outside of Parliament. Central government has demonstrated its power, however, as only one piece of legislation has been withdrawn (Local Government Planning Bill 1979) and very few have changed in spite of hundreds of amendments and strong opposition from Conservative backbenchers on many occasions.

A further effect of the aggressive use of law has been the 'juridification of central–local relationships' (Loughlin, 1986, p. 193). The courts, notoriously ill-equipped to deal with disputes between public bodies, have been brought into the arena of central–local conflict. In general where local authorities have challenged the central government, they have lost. Where they have won, central government has either changed the law or placed itself beyond judicial review. The courts, whilst generally upholding the legal rights of central government to direct or penalise local government, have not always however considered it politically or morally wise.

Changes in Local Government Finance

When the Conservatives took office in 1979, they intended to reduce local public expenditure and to restructure it. The problem was that local government spending was not directly under central control. The previous Labour government had 'persuaded' local government, by a process of consultation, exhortation and cash limits, to reduce expenditure with some limited success, but the initial efforts of the first Thatcher administration to do the same resulted in the target set for 1979–80 being overspent by £300m. They therefore resorted to legislation and direct control to achieve their objectives.

Finance well illustrates the reactive nature of much of the Thatcher government's approach to local government. Its first step was to replace the old Rate Support Grant with a New Block Grant based upon the government's own assessments of standard rates of expenditure rather than local authorities' decisions about what to spend. In addition it introduced new controls over capital expenditure with cash limited expenditure ceilings and blocked allocations. The controls over capital expenditure were relatively successful in getting investment down by 60 per cent between 1979 and 1983. However revenue expenditure proved more of a problem.

In response to the unwillingness of some local authorities to curb their spending, the government tried to force it down by introducing targets, thresholds and related penalties for exceeding either (LGFA 1982). But as Travers (1986) points out, because authorities chose to incur the penalties and raise the rates, this strategy failed. Between 1981 and 1984 £713m of penalties were imposed. The next reaction was to abolish the right of local authorities to raise supplementary rates and precepts and to set up the Audit Commission to oversee local authority finances.

The constant changes of rules relating to the block grant created a situation of total uncertainty for local authorities in which financial planning was impossible. There were no fewer than 11 changes in the financial system during the first two Thatcher Administrations. Local authorities therefore resorted to devices to protect themselves from anticipated cutbacks in the future and to maintain existing services without dramatic falls in standards. These devices included raising more revenue from the rates. Domestic rates rose by 27 per cent in 1980–1, 19.4 per cent in 1981–2; 15.4 per cent in 1982–3 and 7.3 per cent in 1983–4. In addition local authorities resorted to capitalising revenue expenditure and using funds from trading and special accounts.

From 1983 onwards, with local government spending still rising faster than government plans, the government transferred its attack to the rates and to the biggest overspenders who happened to be the Metropolitan Counties, particularly the GLC. The Rates Act 1984 gave the Secretary of State for the Environment power to rate-cap individual authorities or all authorities across the board. Rate-capping was first used in 1985 and involved 18 authorities (see Appendix 2, p. 266). Although 17 of the 18 initially resisted, their campaign collapsed under the threat of surcharge and the expulsion of councillors from political office.

Rate-capped authorities complied with rate-capping after 1985 but most continued, along with other local authorities, to resort to 'creative accounting' to counterbalance their loss of rate as well as grant income. In addition to the capitalising of current expenditure more imaginative methods such as lease and lease back, the rescheduling of debt and dealings in the money market were used. These were dangerous short-term solutions which were to have damaging long-term consequences for some local authorities but in a time of such uncertainty, local authorities tended to think short term. The government reacted again by outlawing such schemes (LGA 1986, LGA 1987) and keeping up the pressure of rate-capping. This did have the effect of reducing rates generally, since it affected the thinking of councils which were not actually capped but which might be if they increased their expenditure.

The major attack on overspending authorities however came with the abolition of the GLC and the six Metropolitan County Councils in 1985. These had accounted for nearly 70 per cent of the overspend. After the abolition the government capped the successor joint boards and so extended their direct control.

It was the impact of a revaluation of the rate base of properties in Scotland in 1985 which led the government to consider their most radical change in local government finance. The first Thatcher Administration, committed to the reform of the rating system, had reviewed the rates in 1981, but failed to agree on an alternative. The Scottish rate crisis led it to examine the issue again and in January 1986 the government published a second Green Paper – *Paying for Local Government* (Cmnd 9714). This proposed a 'poll tax' which the government had rejected in 1981 because it would have imposed a higher relative tax burden on low income households, would be difficult to enforce and would tax the right to vote. In spite of strong opposition, legislation to abolish the rates in Scotland was passed before the 1987 Election and in England and Wales in July 1988. The Acts replaced the domestic rate with a community charge (CC) on adult residents; introduced a national non-domestic rate (NNDR) for business and a new central government revenue support grant (RSG).

The CC is paid by all adults except certain excluded groups (homeless, long-stay hospital patients, prisoners, etc.). People on low incomes are entitled to rebates of up to 80 per cent and some help is available for those on income support. Registration and payment of the charge is compulsory with fines of £50 in the first instance and £200 each subsequent instance for refusal to comply. The NNDR replaces the old business rate and is set by the central government. It is collected locally, pooled centrally and redistributed to local authorities in proportion to their adult population. The new grant is fixed in total by central government and distributed on the basis of estimates of standard expenditure for each category of local government service. The grant is then paid to each authority on a *per capita* basis in relation to a 'needs' assessment.

As with every other government financial policy the 'poll tax' met with strong resistance. There were campaigns to persuade people not to register or pay the tax. These had limited success on registration mainly because of the fines imposed and the high profile they actually gave to the new system. By January 1990 over 90 per cent had registered in England and Wales, similar to the level in Scotland at the same time the previous year. What is not yet clear at the time of writing is how many will refuse to pay the tax. More than 20,000 people in Scotland had made no payment nine months after the tax had been introduced.

The government's rationale for the new system is that it will be fairer and ensure more democratic accountability and control of local authorities. All those who enjoy the services of local authorities will now be contributing to them and the government assume that the 38m electors paying CC will exercise their vote to control local spending. These claims to fairness and democratic control can be challenged. The poll tax will not be fair as it is unrelated to income or ability to pay. It remains to be seen whether participation in local elections will rise as a result of the new tax. But even if it does it may make little difference to local government expenditure since 75 per cent will be financed by central government. Local government spending is much more likely therefore to be responsive to changes in the NNDR and RSG than electoral turnout and ultimately central government can set the level as it still has the power to cap the CC.

Further major changes in local government finance in 1990 stem from a new system of capital control and new arrangements for housing. Under the Local Government and Housing Act (LGHA) 1989 the government now has powers to put a limit on all transactions involving credit allocation. In addition capital receipts will be taken into account in fixing the credit ceilings so that local authorities will no longer be able to finance additional capital expenditure out of their own funds. Further, central government will be able to compel local authorities to charge for particular services and also to set down rates of charge.

In the long term, the introduction of the new system of local finance, with only a quarter of revenue income raised from a locally determined tax, with capital spending under greater central control, must weaken the financial base of local authorities (Travers, 1986). Central government has now got control of local government finance.

Structural Change

One of the most significant changes in local government since 1979 has been structural. However, with the exception of the abolition of the Metropolitan Counties (1986) this has been achieved through a process of incremental adjustment. First, a vast number of QUANGOs or non-elected bodies has been created (see Chapter 1). Second, private organisations have been coopted into the provision of local services and, third, clients of the local government system have been unable to 'opt-out'. All these strategies have been used as ways of changing what local government does and how it does it.

As Chapter 1 has shown the government resorted to creating ad hoc agencies as a way of bypassing or outflanking local authorities. This enabled them to circumvent opposition, take direct control of policy and bring the private sector in. Urban Developments Corporations (UDCs), Enterprise Zones (EZs), the Financial Institution Group, Inner City Enterprises and Business in the Community were all planned to involve businessmen, to bring private capital into the local economy, and 'to alter local–central relations' (Duncan and Goodwin, 1988, p. 143). Some of these failed to meet the government's expectations and were disbanded, but others survived. Non-statutory bodies of civil servants and managers seconded from local firms formed 'task forces' to coordinate a range of schemes and programmes designed to deal with inner-city problems. They were effectively non-elected outposts of central government directly responsible to the Secretary of State for the Environment. The significance of these bodies lies in the fact that they wholly or partially replaced elected local government, as the main agent for urban development, with a range of non-elected, non-accountable and non-representative QUANGOs.

A different but comparable development has occurred in the area of housing where a parallel set of housing agencies has appeared with local authorities moving rapidly to a residual role in the provision of housing (see Chapter 8). In education, too, the government has sought to bypass local government by creating City Technology Colleges (CTCs), by transforming Polytechnics and Colleges of Higher Education into public limited corporations and by encouraging schools to 'opt-out' of local government and come directly under the DES (see Chapter 9).

Privatising local government has been a major strategy of central government since 1979. This has taken a number of forms including the sale of local authority assets, competitive tendering, contracting-out of services and deregulation. The policies of deregulation and competitive tendering have two main objectives. First, to impose the discipline of the market on local authorities by opening them up to competition and, second, to incorporate private sector producers more firmly into the local government system. Competitive tendering has brought private contractors into a whole range of local government activities and these will be extended as the 1989 Act is enforced. Deregulation in transport has also led to the creation of hundreds of new agencies as local authorities were required to create companies to manage their bus and airport operations.

Whilst central government has been the prime mover in the creation of local QUANGOs and privatisation Stoker (1989, p. 57) points out that 'Local authorities have also innovated and experimented . . . to provide themselves with better instruments and to provide opportunities for more direct involvement of service users in local provision'. Equally important has been their desire to bring in the private corporate interests and the greater involvement of the banks, building societies and private employers. They have spawned agencies like enterprise boards, community business and cooperative development agencies to coopt businessmen, and to seek to gain their active support. They have also actively enlisted and used the services of voluntary and private commercial 'welfare' bodies to meet the needs of the rapidly growing numbers of elderly and infirm.

Although most of these developments met with some resistance the most politically controversial structural change was the abolition of the Metropolitan Counties. The rationale, as set out in the White Paper *Streamlining the Cities* (Cm 9063) (DOE, 1983), was to simplify metropolitan local government and to reduce expenditure by removing the worst overspenders. Neither argument held up under investigation and it was widely accepted that the aim of abolition was political – namely to remove the most vocal opposition to the government and an important power base of the Labour Party. At the time the abolition campaign seemed to unite all strands of opposition and to constitute a government 'own goal'. However the abolition proceeded, and the government rode out the storm.

In place of the two tier system of the GLC and London boroughs over 70 separate administrative bodies became responsible for the local government of the capital. The 32 London boroughs now operate within a complex web of joint working arrangements and ad hoc agencies. In other metropolitan counties a similar complex system has evolved where in each area Joint Statutory Boards are responsible for police, fire and civil defence and transport. In addition a variety of committees deal with economic development, strategic planning, waste disposal, recreation and the arts. This highly fragmented and confused system of metropolitan government is further complicated by the existence in many areas of the new agencies referred to above. Clearly the institutions put in the place of the Metropolitan Counties cannot provide a base for coherent opposition, nor are they able to put forward policy alternatives. In addition they have been under central government control since 1986.

Structural change has produced a complex, fragmented and mixed system of public, private and hybrid agencies coexisting within the local government system. Many of the new structures have been designed to bypass local government altogether whilst others have been used to coopt the private sector in. They have clearly had an effect on central–local relations.

Central–local Relations

As argued in Chapter 1, relationships between local and central government have always defied a simple explanation. They have traditionally been diverse, multiple and often conflicting (Rhodes, 1988). There is however a widespread consensus that since 1979 there has been a major shift in the nature and direction of central–local relations (Jones and Stewart, 1983; Rhodes, 1988; Stewart and Stoker, 1989).

First, central government has increased its intervention on an unprecedented scale. As this chapter shows an immense volume of legislation has been used to remove powers from local government, to impose new responsibilities, to abolish a whole tier of local government and to give central government new powers to ensure that its own policies are carried out. In some instances the government has even placed itself above the law by excluding any challenge through the courts. Secondly, the government has interfered in the affairs of individual authorities to compel them to carry out its policies and to penalise financially any council which refused to cut its expenditure (rate-capping). Thirdly, it has assumed the power to determine what local authorities should be spending on particular services and to allocate its grant accordingly. Fourthly, it has resorted to structural changes and innovation to bypass local government and to centralise control in areas like urban development, housing and education. The Thatcher government has preferred to define what local authorities should be doing and how they should be doing it; this trend of detailed interference has become a major characteristic of a distinctive policy style.

In contrast to the corporatist, participative style of the past, the government have dispensed with most, if not all, of the consultative mechanisms. Major constitutional changes have been carried through without even a public inquiry (e.g. abolition of the GLC), whilst radical legislative proposals have been introduced with a minimum of time for interested parties to respond. Symbolically the Consultative Council of Local Government Finance, once a significant negotiating forum, has been reduced to an information receiving body. Even when the government appeared to be resorting to more conventional practices in setting up the Widdicombe Committee in 1984, it delayed taking any action for over two years and then ignored most of the recommendations.

The Widdicombe Report (1986) came out strongly in support of local government and of its role in a representative democracy. Although the government endorsed such views (DOE, 1988) it then proceeded to introduce changes in the internal organisation and procedures of local authorities which makes it more difficult for councillors to be full time, prevents councillors from being paid a salary and does nothing to attract people to stay or enter local councils. In addition, it limits the civil liberties and political rights of senior local government officers who are banned from standing as councillors, required to abstain from holding office in a political party and prevented from speaking or writing on controversial political issues. A statutory core of standing orders has also been imposed on all authorities and they are required to designate specific officers to hold responsibility for financial probity, legal property and management coordination. The government's stated commitment to strengthening local democracy does not fit with the changes it has introduced, which may be because it 'has a hidden agenda of subsequently remodelling the role of local democracy to incorporate a much stronger market/ customer dimension' (Leach, 1989, p. 120).

It is evident that the partnership which once dominated central–local relationships has become much more a principal–agent relationship. Although central government still relies on local government to carry out its policies central government has demonstrably increased its powers of control and direction over local government. In the first two Thatcher Administrations, when local authorities resisted both actively and passively most government attempts to increase its control the situation was characterised by ambiguity and uncertainty. But as the government persisted, coming back each parliamentary session with new responses, the cumulative impact became considerable.

The government has consistently pursued strategies of control and direction rather than consultation and negotiation. It has also used the media and its own rhetoric to gain public support for its attack on 'the enemy within' – that is, Labour controlled high spending councils. Local government has never been a popular institution in the UK although people have relied upon its services. It has therefore been easier to dismantle than the NHS as the main defence has come only from the local authorities themselves. The result is that local government's role has become increasingly one of administrative agent and what emerges in 1990 is a picture of increased centralisation in both British politics and government.

The End of a Decade

Local government has been transformed in the 1980s. How far that is
the result of the working out of a predetermined philosophy or the
consequences of a pragmatic set of responses to problems as they arose
is still in dispute amongst students of Thatcherism. Although local
government remains important and has responsibilities for almost the
same range of activities as in 1979, it has lost much of its autonomy.
Legislation has removed powers, imposed new mandatory duties and
increased central government's ability to direct, control and impose
policies. Financially it has been forced to curb its spending and has lost
the ability to decide its own expenditure. Central government now
determines not only the level of grant support but also the national
business rate. In addition it determines what local authorities can
borrow and how they can spend their capital receipts. Local
government has effective control of less than 25 per cent of its tax
revenue which can be capped.

The proliferation of local ad hoc bodies, appointed by central
government has also reduced local government powers and changed its
role, particularly in the areas of urban development, housing and
education. The abolition of the GLC and the Metropolitan Counties
has resulted in over 100 Joint Bodies and Committees being created,
many of them under central government influence and financial
control. There has been a significant shift from public to private
provision and from public to private ownership. Over 1m 'houses' have
moved from the public to the private sector along with other assets
including buildings and land. Contracting-out has resulted in private
companies collecting refuse, cleaning streets and maintaining public
buildings and parks. There has been a major growth in the private
provision of homes for the elderly and mentally handicapped, whilst
private capital has been attracted into urban renewal programmes and
difficult to let housing estates.

Up until 1987 it was not always clear what vision of local
government the Thatcher government had. The initial attack seemed
to be a part of a broader economic strategy to cut public expenditure
and to make the public sector leaner and more efficient. Yet the 'right
to buy' policy and engaging the private sector in urban regeneration
hinted at a more fundamental aim of social restructing, as did the
emphasis on more consumer choice. During the third Thatcher
Administration there is evidence of a clearer vision of the future of
local government summed up in the concept of the 'enabling council'.

In 1988 Nicholas Ridley set out a new radical view of local
government which challenges the traditional model of local authorities
as near-monopoly providers of standardised services to non-

discriminating clients. The 'enabling council' is seen, in contrast, as only one of a number of suppliers, contracting-out to other agencies and the private sector to produce and deliver services. It will be customer centred, seeking to understand its 'customers and client', responding to the electorate and identifying and serving the community needs. The image underlying the Ridley model is that of a marketing agency identifying markets and devising strategies to meet consumer demands. It is this view of a restructured local government which seems to be informing current government policies. The themes echoed in the government's policies since 1987 have been: the fragmentation of local government with local authorities sharing their service providing role; customer choice; competition; payment for services to reflect market conditions; local authorities regulating the provision of services by others; encouraging self-help and directing resources to areas of greatest need; reducing the power generally of 'producer' interests, including professional groups and trade unions; making local authorities more democratically accountable; and finally, forcing local authorities to become more efficient, effective and economical by pursuing good management practice. There is however another view of the 'enabling council'. This argues that the government's perception is a narrow one which sees local government as putting its business out, handing over activities, and enabling others to act on its behalf to provide local services. The alternative 'enabling council' is one using all the means at its disposal to meet the needs of the community. This may involve regulating, controlling, inspecting, advising, supporting, aiding, stimulating, guiding and also providing (Stewart and Clarke, 1988). It is not clear which, if either, of these views of the enabling council will dominate in the 1990s.

Changes in local government have been a direct consequence of accumulated political direction and intervention over a decade. They have also taken place in a turbulent environment in which demographic, social and economic changes have been occurring too. It is out of that context that the new system is emerging. The volatility of that environment as well as the uncertainty about the political future makes any prediction of local government in the 1990s a precarious activity. If the Conservatives are returned for a fourth term of office then their vision of the 'enabling council' with a residual regulatory role in a dismantled welfare state is likely to occur. They will push ahead with further privatisation and further centralisation. If a Labour government is returned it will have a preference for a more communitarian model of local government rather than an enabling–market model. With its commitment to reforming local government finance and returning more financial freedom the Stewart and Clarke model of the 'enabling council' is more likely to emerge.

What is clear is that local authorities, like other organisations in a rapidly changing environment, are going to have to be more flexible and responsive to their clients either as customers or taxpayers. They will also be only one of a constellation of public, private and voluntary organisations meeting the needs of the community for public and welfare goods and services. This model is similar to that found in countries of the EC, where there is a long tradition of cooperation between public and private agencies across the whole field of welfare and local concerns. The impact of 1992 may be that the more active European traditions of local government as the 'community governing itself' will take root here.

13

Equal Opportunities in a Cold Climate

CAROL LUPTON and DAVE RUSSELL

Introduction

When the editors of this book asked us to combine an examination of race and sex discrimination into one chapter, our initial reaction was one of concern. Those working and writing in these distinct areas have tended to resist the attempt, typically stemming from those who have little political commitment to the pursuit of either, to lump the two areas together. Such combination has served to underemphasise the different nature of the analyses and the different associated political strategies which need to be developed in respect of these disparate areas of social inequality. Such concerns notwithstanding however there are two central reasons why it may be useful to examine the state response to race and sex discrimination together. Firstly there are strong similarities in the statutory frameworks within which sex and race equality legislation has been developed in the UK and direct comparison helps to highlight the strengths and weaknesses of this legislation. The process of comparison moreover can serve to emphasise the contrasts as well as the similarities between these two areas of policy development. Secondly it is useful to consider race and sex-based inequality together because in their operation these two systems of inequality serve to overlap and reinforce one another, and to combine with class inequality to produce a double or triple layered marginality for certain social groups: white working class women, black[1] working class men, black working class women. Typically it is the combination of systems of inequality which operates to reduce the ability of these groups to utilise their legal rights to remove or redress the oppression they experience.

The Legislation

Unlike many other policy areas under scrutiny in this volume the legal framework within which equal opportunities policy operates was established before 1979 and has survived into the 1990s unscathed by Thatcherism. The years of the 1970s witnessed growing pressures for more effective state intervention to ensure the rights and expand opportunities for women and black people in Britain. The return of a Labour government in 1974 saw the introduction of two central pieces of legislation designed to increase the scope of earlier anti-discrimination legislation. At the same time similar fair employment legislation aimed at tackling the special problem of religious discrimination in Northern Ireland also appeared on the statute book (see Chapter 15). The 1976 Race Relations Act aimed to provide a more radical approach to race relations and a more effective means of redress against racial discrimination than had characterised the earlier legislation of the 1960s. The 1975 Sex Discrimination Act was designed to complement the operation of the 1970 Equal Pay Act and to extend the coverage of anti-discriminatory legislation to wider employment and training issues and to the areas of education, housing, and the provision of goods, facilities and services.

Both Acts broke new ground in anti-discrimination legislation by allowing individuals for the first time direct access to courts and industrial tribunals. A further innovation was the operationalisation of the concept of indirect discrimination. Unlike direct discrimination, where the motivation of the alleged discriminator becomes a central issue, the concept of indirect discrimination allows for the unintended consequences of particular policies or practices. Partly based on the American model of affirmative action this innovation was seen both as a way of avoiding the difficulties of proving intentional discrimination and also as a means of enabling action against institutional rather than individual forms of sexism and racism.

Both Acts established publicly funded semi-independent agencies charged with monitoring and reviewing the implementation of the legislation. The Equal Opportunities Commission (EOC) and the Commission for Racial Equality (CRE) came into operation in December 1975 and June 1977 respectively. Unlike the EOC which had no precursor, the CRE extended the law enforcement and public education roles performed by pre-existing agencies – the Race Relations Board and the Community Relations Committee. In addition to their advisory and negotiating powers and their responsibility for public education, the two Commissions were invested with considerable law enforcement machinery: they could conduct formal investigations on their own initiative, supported by the power to subpoena witnesses and to issue 'non-discrimination' notices enforceable through the courts.

The Impact of the Legislation

Together this legislation has formed 'the backbone of British civil rights law for more than a decade' (Gregory, 1987, p. 3) which no government has subsequently found necessary to improve. Evidence suggests however that the ensuing years have brought little in the way of real progress towards equality of opportunity for women or for black people in the Uk.

If we look at the position of women in the labour market, for example, the area where the legislation was designed to have a major impact, we find only limited and uneven progress. Initial improvements in women's labour market situation in the years immediately following the legislation faltered in the face of the economic recession of the late 1970s. Although more women entered the labour market, their concentration within a small number of employment sectors and within low-paid, part-time work continued. As the 1989 report by the EOC reveals men still receive significantly higher basic hourly earnings than women; the pay differential for non-manual employment indeed is wider now than at any time since the introduction of the Equal Pay Act. Although there are more women entering the professions, there is little increase in the proportion reaching the top: women still comprise only 2 per cent of the top wage earners in this country and represent a very small proportion of the membership of professional bodies. While there have been gains for a small minority of highly educated professional women, for the majority of women the 1980s has brought little real expansion of employment or training opportunities (EOC, 1989).

In a similar way evidence suggests that not much has been achieved by the various measures designed to outlaw racial discrimination and remedy racial disadvantage. The 1968 Race Relations Act had specifically widened the scope of earlier anti-discriminatory legislation to cover inequality in housing and employment opportunities, yet in these two crucial areas of racial disadvantage it is clear that progress has similarly been slow and unsatisfactory. Black people are still disproportionately concentrated in poorly-paid, low-status jobs and are twice as likely to become unemployed as are their white counterparts. Whilst an increasing number of black workers have made it into professional and managerial jobs, very few have been able to break through into the top jobs of the business or political world. No black face appears amongst the ranks of high court judges nor at the most senior levels in the Armed Forces or the Civil Service. Alongside continuing substantial inequalities in the field of employment, black people have also made relatively little progress in the housing market. Despite some improvement in terms of access to public and private sector housing, black minorities still tend to suffer lower quality housing and poorer housing conditions than do white residents. Black people take longer to be rehoused and are more likely to become homeless or trapped in inferior accommodation than are their white counterparts.

Why has so little apparently been achieved in the attempt to overcome race and sex discrimination? Why has state intervention designed to promote equality of opportunity for women and black people proved to be so ineffective? Three major reasons can be offered in response to such questions: difficulties of implementing the legislation; the limited and confused nature of the ideology which underlies and informs the legislation; and the increasingly hostile nature of the wider political and economic climate within the legislation has had to be implemented.

Implementing the Legislation – Individual Litigation

Although enabled by the legislation to pursue a complaint directly through the courts, the ability of individuals to obtain effective redress is constrained in a number of central ways. In practice the legislation involves a daunting array of loopholes and procedural hurdles which many individuals find difficult to overcome. Unlike almost every other aspect of employment legislation the initial burden of proof lies with the complainant; yet complainants have no powers to demand relevant information, no access to legal aid and no adequate system of support and representation. The courts and tribunals have themselves experienced difficulties in interpreting and applying the new legislation and research reveals a considerable degree of inclarity about the legislation on the part of tribunal personnel, most of whom are given no formal training (Leonard, 1987). Moreover no obligation is placed upon the tribunals to involve more women and black members in race and sex discrimination cases: only just over one-quarter of the tribunal panel of lay members in 1976 were women (Coussins, 1976). Above all the legal procedures fail to acknowledge or confront the existing imbalance of power within which the litigation takes place. As Atkins (1986) remarks about sex discrimination cases: 'the Act requires one woman to give evidence against a person who, in legal theory, is an individual with no greater rights than her but who, in reality, is often a large and corporate institution' (p. 61).

Not surprisingly perhaps the number of successful cases brought under the legislation has been disappointing: on average nearly two-thirds of all applications fail to reach a tribunal. Some are withdrawn because the employer concedes; many others are withdrawn as a result of a variety of pressures, most notably the advice of conciliation officers. Of those cases which do reach a tribunal moreover the great majority are dismissed: on average only just over 10 per cent of all sex discrimination cases and around 7 per cent of race discrimination cases brought to tribunals in the ten years following the legislation were upheld (Gregory, 1987). For those few which are successful the amounts awarded in compensation, particularly in the case of race discrimination, have been fairly low – rarely exceeding £1,000 – and little attempt is made by those involved in the tribunal system to ensure compliance with their decisions. Applicants themselves are left to collect any financial award and many employers utilise a variety of tactics to delay or avoid payment. Changes made to the tribunal system in 1980 moreover increased the possibility that complainants in unsuccessful cases will have costs awarded against them.

A major limitation on the legislative route to change is the problem of deep-seated attitudinal resistance. In the area of employment practice this resistance has come from both 'sides' of industry: employers and the representatives of organised labour. We know for example that given five years to adjust their employment practices to comply with the Equal Pay legislation, many employers utilised the full range of measures legally possible to limit its effect. Job segregation was made more rather than less extensive as employers hastily regraded and reorganised male and female workers so they could no longer be seen to be employed on comparable work (Snell, 1979). Evidence suggests moreover that many of those individuals who have successfully used the complaints procedures have subsequently suffered victimisation by employers (Coussins, 1976). The role of trades unions in the successful implementation of anti-discriminatory employment legislation can be central. Clearly those who are able to pursue their individual complaints with the help and support of their unions stand a much better chance of success; and the participation of unions in negotiating collective agreements or job evaluation schemes is vital. The response of trades unions to race or sex discrimination cases however has been equivocal; at best it has proved to be a decisive influence for change; at worst it has been actively unsupportive, defensively protecting the interests of white, male members. Despite perceiving the union as their first source of help, for example, under 10 per cent of all those pursuing race discrimination cases have been assisted by their union (Kumar, 1986).

Implementing the Legislation – Administrative Action

The EOC and the CRE serve a dual role in respect of implementation: they are enabled, although not required, to help an individual pursue a claim under the legislation by giving advice and/or by representing that individual at the tribunal hearing, and they have powers themselves to conduct formal investigations in order to ensure compliance with the legislation. Although structurally very similar – the EOC served as the prototype of the CRE – these two agencies adopted significantly different implementation strategies from the beginning. Generally the EOC made a very hesitant and uncertain start, pursuing few formal investigations, and offering help to individuals only on a very selective basis. EOC Commissioners seemed anxious to avoid any unnecessary confrontations and concerned to use formal investigations only as a weapon of last resort. Taking advantage of its greater resources and a pre-existing body of expert and experienced staff, the CRE began operations rather more vigorously – instigating a much larger number of formal investigations as well as assisting with a substantial number of individual complaints and developing an aggressive educational and promotional role. Where the EOC was criticised for its timidity and indecisiveness the CRE was seen to be more confrontational in approach and, in the face of a backlog of uncompleted investigations, faced concerns about its overambition (Gregory, 1987).

Despite their differences neither Commission has proved to be a very effective mechanism for enforcing the legislation. Most notably in the case of the EOC, some blame for this must lie with the Commissions themselves and the particular way they have chosen to interpret their duties and responsibilities. Whatever the limitations of their respective strategies however it is also the case that the operation of the Commissions has been hampered both by the resistance of the courts and by the active non-cooperation of the government. Generally the powers of the Commissions have been circumscribed by the procedural complexities of the legislation and by the strong concern of the courts to protect the rights of alleged discriminators. Courts and tribunals have been particularly resistant to the alien concept of indirect discrimination which has proved difficult to identify and even more difficult to establish. Central government moreover has consistently operated a very restrictive view of the Commissioners' responsibilities and powers, and studiously ignored their proposals for amending the legislation. Particularly in the case of the EOC the agencies have been constrained by the government's appointment of inappropriate and occasionally unsympathetic Commissioners. Above all however the operation of the Commissions and the progress of individuals through the courts have been circumscribed by central ambiguities surrounding the concept of 'equality of opportunity'.

Competing Conceptions of Equal Opportunity

Even amongst those who share a commitment to the pursuit of racial and sexual equality there is disagreement about the underlying principles and philosophy of equal opportunities, and about the best way of putting it into practice. Basically (EO) policies have developed in terms of a struggle between two fundamentally different conceptions of equal opportunities: the liberal notion of 'formal equality' and the more radical notion of 'substantive equality'.

Liberal Conceptions of Equal Opportunities – the Notion of Formal Equality

The liberal conception of (EO) places emphasis on the equal treatment of individuals from different groups and on the importance of judging people on their individual qualities or performance without regard to their sex or their racial/ethnic group membership. This approach insists that all individuals should be treated equally in a meritocratic 'colour-blind' or 'sex-blind' manner. The objective of EO policies should be the removal of any obstructions to free and fair competition between individuals, with 'fairness' being defined in terms of the absence of discrimination. The general approach is essentially regulatory and procedural; implementation involves the development of a managerial approach which proscribes certain forms of discriminatory behaviour and requires conformity to universally applied codes of conduct. Within this approach equality is typically identified with efficiency and good management practice.

Radical Conceptions of Equal Opportunity – The Notion of Substantive Equality

The broader more radical conception of equal opportunity is concerned with outcomes and with equal shares for women and for racially disadvantaged groups. It focuses on the crucial question of 'who gets what' insisting that equality of opportunity demands a more equal sharing of scarce goods and resources (housing, jobs, etc.). This position goes against the liberal principle of blind justice by arguing that people should be treated not as individuals but on the basis of their group membership. 'Fairness' is judged here by whether members of different sexes or racial/ethnic groups are distributed in proportion to their presence in the wider population, and some redistribution of opportunity may be sought by the establishment of 'targets' or 'quotas'. Like all redistributive policies, this sort of approach can be difficult to sell to those who have the least to gain from it and it can also be resented by black people or women who want to achieve things strictly on their own merit.

These two positions represent fundamentally distinct conceptions of equal opportunity, yet in practice they are commonly blurred. While it is arguable that the legislation is based mainly on the group perspective, its implementation has been severely hampered by a deep-rooted ideological commitment to individualism within the judicial system and the political culture of the UK. The legislation forbids in any case the full development of the radical version of EO: apart from enabling some positive action in respect of training opportunities, positive or 'reverse' discrimination is explicitly prohibited by the Race Relations Act and the Sex Discrimination Act (SDA). Unlike America the use of quotas is illegal in Britain with the one exception, provided under the SDA, of women's representation on the elected bodies of trades unions. Although the concept of indirect discrimination represented a move towards a more radical interpretation of equal opportunity, its effectiveness has been limited by the individualistic approach of the courts. While it is technically possible for someone to make a 'representative action' on behalf of a group, the success of such actions is limited by the lack of group procedures: the claimant must argue the position essentially as an individual and if successful will not be able to claim damages on behalf of others.

Tension between these two very different conceptualisations of EO has heightened throughout the 1980s as attempts to take more positive forms of action and to implement tougher versions of equal opportunities have sparked considerable resistance from inside and outside the EO camp.

Equal Opportunities and Thatcherism

A decade of Thatcherism has predictably turned out to have been a hard time in which to pursue equal opportunities for women and minority communities. Developing and implementing EO provision has been increasingly difficult in an ideological atmosphere where egalitarian principles have been steadily submerged by support for Thatcherite values of self-reliance and individual enterprise. The economic climate of the Thatcher years has also provided hostile conditions for EO initiatives. Economic recession and rising unemployment hit black workers concentrated in low-status, insecure jobs disproportionately hard, thus exacerbating the problem of racial inequality. Although increasing the number of women in paid work, the growth of the service sector and the drive by employers for greater flexibility has worsened the already disadvantaged position of many women workers – in particular the growing pool of low-paid part-time workers who most need but least benefit from EO policies. In such adverse economic circumstances and with employers in a powerful position little progress has been made on the EO front in the private sector. Altogether the voluntary promotion of EO in the private sector has been essentially limited despite evidence that the dominant liberal model of EO has become firmly established in the professional ideology of personnel management (Jenkins, 1987).

Perhaps to the surprise of some, the Thatcher governments have remained symbolically attached at least to the notion of formal equality, content to leave existing sex and race equality legislation on the statute book. Despite a commitment to the supremacy of the market and rolling back the state no effort whatsoever has been made so far to 'privatise' race relations or to pursue a full-blooded free-market solution to the problem of sexual inequality. Indeed Thatcherism in practice has offered little in the way of innovation or radical change with respect to EO. Against its own instincts, the Government was pressured into a marginal expansion during the early 1980s of its race related spending programmes as a result of the urban unrest which hit the inner cities. In the main however it has opted to neglect the issues of sex and race equality as far as possible, maintaining only a limited role for central government and off loading the brunt of policy implementation onto the two relatively powerless equality quangos. Equally importantly, the Thatcher government has, like its predecessors, maintained and in certain instances strengthened, the sexist and racist provisions written into government legislation in areas such as family policy and immigration control; areas which are outside the purview of the EOC and the CRE.

The Role of the EC

In the 1980s improvements in women's legal rights have come from the EC rather than the UK government. At the same time Mrs Thatcher's government has shown its true colours by consistently blocking key equality directives[2] issued from Brussels. For example, two important draft directives on part-time and temporary workers, which both had obvious implications for women, were opposed by the UK and a number of other member states. Another draft directive which proposed the introduction of at least three months' parental leave for either parent (but not both) was blocked by the UK alone. Nevertheless it has been Community directives on equal pay, dating back to the 1970s, which either directly, or through a series of legal cases based on them, have forced the Thatcher government to introduce changes in UK law which have strengthened the rights of women at work. The most important example is the changes to the Equal Pay legislation forced by a European Court judgement that UK legislation did not meet the requirements of the EC's directives on 'equal pay for work of equal value'.[3] Even so, in making this concession, the government still tried to limit the possible impact of the amendment by concurrently widening the terms on which employers could defend themselves against an 'equal value' claim (Gregory, 1987, p. 23). Moreover it should be noted that the EC lacks a legal framework for positive action, other than in the form of recommendations or codes of conduct – it cannot make positive action for women compulsory.

The EC does not play the same role in the sphere of race discrimination. A commitment to the principle that men and women receive equal pay for equal work was written into the original Treaty of Rome but race equality has never really figured on the EC political agenda. One practical effect of this is that the right to appeal on a point of law in UK race discrimination cases can go only so far as the House of Lords, unlike the situation with equal pay and sex discrimination where the European Court has adjudicated in a small number of vital test cases. The movement of the UK towards greater integration with the rest of the EC centres instead in the race field on immigration and nationality policies adopted by the UK government since 1971. It is possible to view these policies as part of a general European move towards more restrictive policies which are closing the EC's doors to migrants, immigrants and refugees from the Third World (Gordon, 1989, p. 26). The government's increasingly restrictive approach is at the same time part of a well-established British preoccupation with limiting the numbers of permanent black residents living in Britain with full citizenship rights. Such an overriding concern with the question of 'who belongs to the country?' has serious consequences: directly for black people born in Britain or legally entitled to permanent residence, and indirectly for the prospects of successful state intervention aimed at race equality. The underlying message of immigration policy – black people are a problem and more are not welcome in the UK – legitimises and reinforces hostile attitudes to black people and makes the struggle for race equality more difficult. Certainly it is clear that any steps taken since the 1960s to pursue race equality in the UK have taken a poor second place to the goal of developing effective immigration and nationality policies, designed to prevent Britain's black population from becoming 'too high', and also to bring Britain more in line with Europe.

The Role of Local Government

Despite the existence of a Thatcherite environment hostile to the advancement of EO practices the 1980s actually witnessed an expansion of EO policy programmes, occurring essentially at the level of local government. Prior to this local authorities generally had reacted only very slowly to the special responsibilities the 1976 Race Relations Act had given them for making appropriate arrangements to eliminate unlawful discrimination and to promote EO. The exclusion of any equivalent provision within the SDA together with the absence of any compulsion from central government meant that EO had at best only a peripheral place on local political agendas. However in the early 1980s a few councils – initially the GLC and some Labour controlled London boroughs – attempted to take EO more seriously. Soon many other local authorities took up EO in some shape or form, although in many cases this was done in a fairly tokenistic way: an attempt to jump on the EO bandwagon and demonstrate a commitment to change without much attempt to put that commitment into practice. Between 1982 and 1987 nearly half of all local authorities in the UK formally adopted EO policies, but the form and content of these policies varied greatly as did the level of political and financial support given to them. Under two-thirds had written policy statements and only just over one-third established formal political or organisational EO structures (EOC, 1988). Generally the development of EO policies within local authorities revealed a considerable gap between the symbolic gestures contained in strong policy statements and the effective implementation of that policy.

A few pioneering New Left councils however did make a determined attempt to implement more radical EO measures, prompted by a number of factors. First, urban unrest in the early 1980s served to catapult the issue of anti-racism onto local political agendas, especially in urban areas with significant black populations. Second, the size and strength of their black electorate prompted some councils into new initiatives. Local black councillors grew in number too and succeeded in raising the political profile of the race equality issue. Third, the new urban left sought to use EO as a means of widening the support base of the Labour Party to include minority communities, women and other marginalised groups. Fourth, growing pressure from autonomous local women's organisations and black community groups was important in drawing attention to issues of EO. Together these factors stimulated the rapid adoption of innovative EO measures pioneered primarily by the new Left councils in the early 1980s and through to 1987.

Policy Changes

The EO drive by the municipal left proceeded on a number of different fronts. First, the councils tried to improve their own record as employers through the establishment of good EO employment practices. Crucially, they also set out to adopt positive action measures permitted by the anti-discrimination legislation, including for instance the use of targets to increase the employment of black and ethnic minority staff, and to get more women in higher grade posts. Second, the councils were concerned to equalise service provision and to establish both equality of treatment and equality of outcome in terms of 'who gets what?'. To this effect ethnic records were introduced in order to monitor the allocation of housing and other services. Promotional work designed to improve communications with black and ethnic minorities was also launched (e.g. translations into ethnic languages, racism awareness training for council staff). Also, there was a resolve to develop consultation processes and to monitor service provision in order that council services should take more account of the needs of women and minority communities (e.g. the needs of single parent council tenants). Third, an attempt was made to increase the representation of women and black people in local government, especially through the creation of women's, race relations and EO committees, race units and advisers, women's officers, etc.

Policy Achievements

Some progress was made in terms of changing employment practices although often not much was done effectively to tackle group disadvantage. A few new Left councils like Lambeth and Hackney did make some advances during the early 1980s in getting their workforce to reflect more the multi-racial composition of their local populations (Solomos, 1989). However relatively little change was achieved in the employment profiles of the local authorities in question, with few women or black people becoming more visible in the higher grades of employment (Coyle, 1989). This was the picture even in those local authorities which best resourced and made the greatest commitment to EO. Notwithstanding their radical reputations, the recruitment and selection practices of many New Left councils failed very often to meet the requirements of radical EO employment policy to move beyond the confines of the liberal model of EO: beyond an emphasis on formalised and standardised procedures universally applied to all candidates.

Similarly earnest efforts to implement EO policies in service delivery had only modest success. Partly, this was because the race/sex equality units and various EO advisers were good at identifying needs but were seldom able to help meet them (Lansley *et al.*, 1989). On the whole they lacked much political clout; above all they were often marginalised and not properly linked into council structures. Women's committees and units for instance had relatively little influence over service managers in their day-to-day decision-making. They also suffered from the failure of council leaders to set priorities. Instead, EO initiatives of one kind or another were too often 'bolted on' to other policy programmes without clear guidelines about how things should operate in practice. Frequently, EO policy-makers tended to promise more than they were capable of delivering and too often they were not sufficiently realistic about the limited potential of many EO policies in such an inhospitable economic and political climate.

EO in Crisis

At the beginning of the 1980s local government was seen by the new urban left as a important 'testing ground' for new ideas and a platform on which to build an alternative to Thatcherism. The enthusiastic promotion of EO was an important part of the New Left's attempt to transform Labour town hall politics but as we move into the 1990s those early bright hopes seem to have evaporated. The progress of EO was certainly undermined by the attack on local government mounted by the Thatcher government. In particular this assault claimed as victim the GLC, the flagship of EO, and significantly reduced the power and resources of local councils in general. The limits placed by central government on the autonomy and spending power of local authorities have undoubtedly impaired their ability to implement EO policies and also made them less willing to innovate. More specifically the move to outlaw almost totally the contract compliance[4] policies imported from the USA by a growing number of councils has robbed local authorities of a weapon usually seen as an essential component in an effective EO armoury. This is despite the fact that the Thatcher government itself in 1982 empowered the Fair Employment Agency in Northern Ireland to implement just such a policy.

The legitimacy of the limited advances that have been made in EO policy was also damaged by a vicious popular press onslaught against anti-racism and town hall feminism. From the outset the tabloids presented women's committees and the like as a laughing-stock. Likewise anti-racism was seen by the right and the tabloid press as both ridiculous and menacing. The opposition to EO from hostile, external forces also encouraged internal forces of reaction within Labour groups to step up their resistance to EO. These included older, more traditional Labour councillors as well as 'macho class warriors' of the hard left who tended to see EO as a diversion from the socialist struggle. A tougher approach to racism and sexism also created tension inside the town halls amongst full-time officers, some of whom also began to talk about 'a climate of fear' and witchhunts (Lansley *et al.*, 1989).

Most importantly, Mrs Thatcher's third victory in the 1987 General Election presaged a new phase in the politics of EO and altogether the end of an era for the municipal left (Lansley *et al.*, 1989). The targeting of the 'loony left' was a key part of the successful Tory electoral strategy and subsequently since 1987 previously radical local authorities have been less willing and less able to advance controversial EO policies. The Labour Party has since been keen to distance itself from the discredited policies and activities of the left councils. In particular the new realism of the Labour Party leadership has caused it largely to disown anti-racism and anti-sexism, and to tone down its commitment to EO. In the harsher local government climate of the late 1980s, former trail-blazing councils such as Lewisham and Hackney, like others, have pragmatically dropped the race and women's units which provide soft targets for budget cuts. Moving into the 1990s it seems the acceptable face of EO is one set against radical positive action measures.

The Future of EO Policies

Arguably certain kinds of liberal EO policy are here to stay but the future for radical, more comprehensive EO policies looks bleak. Enlightened management in both the public and private sectors is still likely to retain a commitment to fair practice in employment and there are indications that even Tory-controlled councils accept certain elementary EO principles in other spheres of operation too. For instance, the Tory-controlled Wandsworth borough council recently became the first authority in the country to introduce a specific clause against racial harassment in its standard leasehold agreement for tenants exercising their right to buy. All in all there appears little prospect of the EO clock being turned right back but the original EO vision of the early 1980s pioneers does appear to be a thing of the past.

Perhaps it is a sign of the times that it is not racism or sexism that are presented as key problems any more, but anti-racism and anti-sexism! However, although the climate of opinion has undoubtedly shifted against anti-racism and anti-sexism, this can only in part be blamed on the media, or on the political and ideological successes of Thatcherism. The failure to develop popular and effective EO initiatives has also been due to the over-zealous and confrontational way in which these have often been implemented, and to the ill-conceived nature of some of the policies themselves (Mitchell and Russell, 1989; Lansley *et al.*, 1989). In this respect some recent developments in the implementation of EO policy should be seen as an attempt to strengthen rather than dilute its effectiveness. For example mechanisms to reconcile quality of service delivery with quality of access to those services, represent a progressive rethinking of EO practice rather than a step backwards (Coyle, 1989).

It is difficult to be more optimistic about EO when looking beyond Thatcherism. It is also hard to believe that a victorious Labour Party would be willing to 'break the mould' in the politics of sex and race even though on paper the proposals put forward in its policy review do hold out some promise of a more radical and determined use of central government power. We maintain that EO policies can most effectively be promoted by a far more extensive framework of legal and administrative powers together with a substantial increase in resources devoted to their implementation. Central government must give a strong lead in developing positive programmes and launch a direct and coordinated attack on sex and race inequality; it should not simply hive off responsibility to local government and the equality quangos. Some of the Labour Party proposals might appear to be on the right lines but its record in and out of office casts considerable doubt over whether its sponsorship of EO measures in the future would ever amount to anything more than another exercise in 'symbolic politics'. Certainly it is likely that a future Labour government would fight shy of adopting more radical, positive action measures or even allocating to the EOC and the CRE the resources necessary to put their present powers to better effect. Furthermore there appears little point in looking to Brussels for a more positive lead in the 1990s. The EC equality directives will continue to be a vital asset in the securing of women's citizenship rights but ultimately they are based on a limited conception of formal equality. The 'social dimension' to the impending Single European Market in 1992 will do precious little to usher in more positive action on EO.

Notes

1. The term 'black' will be used throughout to refer to both Afro-British and Asian people.
2. 'Directives' are Community policy decisions made by the Council of Ministers which must be carried out by member states although each is allowed to decide on its own legislation and method of implementation.
3. 'Equal pay for work of equal value' refers to cases where workers claim equal pay with men workers doing *different* jobs as opposed to the *same* or 'broadly similar' work. The basis of such claims is that the skills and competences of certain women's jobs are of a similar standing to men's in the same firm.
4. 'Contract compliance' refers to the practice adopted by many Labour councils of ensuring that all their contractors pursue EO policies, as well as meeting other conditions such as trade union recognition, good health and safety conditions, the provision of training and the employment of local people.

14

Government and Information

KELVYN JONES, FRANCES MILLARD and LIZ TWIGG

Introduction

The recent and rapid changes in the ways in which information can be gathered, processed, stored and transmitted have added a qualitatively new dimension to modern society and to the government – citizen relationship. In this chapter we shall examine some major elements of this transformation and ways in which the Conservative government has responded under Margaret Thatcher. After a general overview, we shall examine three case studies of information policy. Our thesis is that there is no 'government information policy' as such, but a series of ad hoc responses to particular issues and events. The main purpose of government policy has been to serve the interests of the government itself rather than to shape policy in accord with a particular philosophical or ideological perspective. Nonetheless, we can identify responses which are strongly in keeping with the authoritarian, centralist and cost-cutting tendencies of Thatcherism but which at the same time contradict Thatcherite emphases on individual citizen participation, responsibility and choice.

There are three major dimensions to the area of government information policy. The first concerns the holding of personal information about individuals by both public and private bodies, the extent to which such information is transmitted and safeguarded, and the right of the individual to know about and assess the accuracy of information being held. There are general issues of the right to privacy at stake here, while inaccurate or unproven information may threaten a person's social relationships, livelihood, or even life itself.

The second dimension concerns the extent to which government restricts or makes information available; it embraces a number of distinct areas, including censorship and regulation of the media and the degree of openness of government, and the limits of necessary secrecy where national security is concerned. This area, too, has profound implications for the rights of individuals in a democratic society: for freedom of expression, for the accountability of government to its electors, and for the ability of individuals to make their own choices. The controversy over food safety which emerged after Chernobyl in 1986 and again in 1988–89 provides a good example of the latter. As citizens we want to know the risks involved in the food we eat or the beaches we swim from.

The third element embraces the ways in which the government itself gathers and utilises statistics. The state is the biggest collector and purveyor of information. Its Government Statistics Service (GSS) is the main agency with the resources to provide a comprehensive national overview of what is happening in society and the economy. What statistics are gathered, how the information is obtained, and the way in which data are presented all influence the utility of that information in the policy-making process and the ability of scholars and citizens to evaluate the work of government.

In sum, the ways in which government collects, uses, regulates and disseminates information are of great significance. First, they raise important civil liberties' issues, particularly the right to privacy and freedom of expression. Secondly, they raise issues of individual responsibility and choice. Individuals can make rational decisions only if they possess adequate information. Thirdly, there are issues of the quality of government policy-making. Policy based on faulty, partial or biased information is far less likely to achieve its intended objectives. Finally, they raise issues of government accountability to the citizenry. An uninformed population cannot judge its politicians adequately. We will touch on these issues with a broad overview before turning to three specific examples.

The Thatcher Years – Continuity and Change

The Government and Secrecy

British governments have traditionally been secretive, whatever their partisan colouring; indeed, British government is frequently described as the most obsessed with secrecy of all democratic regimes. The existence of an unwritten constitution facilitates secrecy by providing enormous discretion to the executive branch under the guise of parliamentary sovereignty; many have argued that the powers of government should be clearly defined, with individual liberties enshrined in a Bill of Rights. The tradition of civil service anonymity has also contributed to the insularity of the bureaucracy. There are also specific instruments, such as section 2 of the Official Secrets Act (1911), which made it a criminal offence to reveal *any* 'unauthorised information'; or the system of D–notices, providing voluntary censorship of the media on defence-related issues. Governments also influence historical assessments of their records; they can limit or delay public access to government papers, and they practise the 'culling' of documents. In 1975 the Labour government even sought, albeit unsuccessfully, to prohibit the publication of the diaries of former Cabinet Minister Richard Crossman.

The Thatcher government is firmly entrenched in this tradition. Whether government secrecy has been greater than before is, however, difficult to establish. Certainly the Conservative government has closely controlled the information released to the public, and it has strenuously pursued civil servants who have engaged in 'unauthorised leaks' to the press. There are also a number of factors which have combined to make the issue of secrecy far more salient. The political context has undoubtedly shifted in favour of greater openness. A series of controversial incidents and events has made information a central political issue, and the international picture has changed. Almost all other Western-style democracies have some type of freedom of information legislation. Yet Thatcher not only resisted the reform of the Official Secrets Act until 1989, but also made use of section 2 (seen by all parties as wholly discredited since the 1972 Franks Report called it 'a mess'), more often than any of its predecessors. Two famous cases were the prosecution of Sarah Tisdall in 1984 for sending the *Guardian* official documents on the timing of the arrival of cruise missiles in Britain and that of Clive Ponting in 1985 for sending documents concerning the sinking of the Argentine ship the *General Belgrano* to an MP. The government also aroused controversy when it resurrected the principle of confidence to argue the new concept that civil servants owed a lifelong duty of absolute confidentiality to government; this was the grounds for prosecuting Peter Wright's book *Spycatcher*. The Security Service Bill (1989) places the security services on a statutory footing for the first time, but it does not provide for parliamentary scrutiny. Indeed, the Bill appears mainly designed to deter further government defeats before the European Court of Human Rights. One case pending is that of two Labour politicians who were formerly officers of the National Council for Civil Liberties (NCCL); it stems from the evidence provided by former MI5 employee Cathy Massiter that the NCCL was classed as a 'subversive' organisation. Generally, the politicisation of the civil service under Thatcher appears to have strained the common ethos shared by civil servants and politicians. Indeed, former permanent secretaries Sir Douglas Wass and Sir Patrick

Nairne have supported the Campaign for Freedom of Information, mounted in 1984.

The issue of environmental safety also came to the forefront. For example, the explosion of a Soviet nuclear power station at Chernobyl in 1986 generated great public anxiety about government secrecy over environmental matters. Initial assurances that the British public were in no danger from radiation subsequently proved false as sales of contaminated lamb were banned; and surveys of public opinion revealed high levels of distrust of government spokespersons. Seal deaths in the North Sea, revelations about the violation of EC safety standards for British water supplies, and outbreaks of food poisoning all contributed to the salience of information as a political issue.

The Thatcher government did at last move to reform section 2 of the Official Secrets Act in 1988, and this will form the basis of one of our case studies below. However, the government disappointed its critics by focussing on national security, thus failing to address the general issues of freedom of information and open government.

The Government and the Media

The Thatcher government has not appeared unduly worried about the press, which in any case has consistently displayed pro-Conservative tendencies. The government's campaign against *Spycatcher* certainly provided a cause for tension, as government-inspired injunctions affected a number of national newspapers. The protection by journalists of confidential sources also became an issue, as Jeremy Warner of the *Independent* was fined £20,000 for contempt of court after refusing to disclose material to a government investigation involving insider-trading. Concern also emerged over the falling standards of the tabloid press, leading to the right-to-reply controversy, and in April 1989 the Home Office announced an inquiry into the press.

However, the government appears more preoccupied with the broadcasting media, and the two sides have crossed swords on a number of issues. Two conflicting tendencies appear; both are represented in the 1989 Broadcasting Bill. On the one hand a preference for deregulation, commercialisation and pluralisation accords with the laissez-faire aspect of government thinking on the economy, its emphasis on widening consumer choice, and its campaign against the 'restrictive practices' of broadcasting trade unionism. The Bill does provide for deregulation. The proposed arrangements whereby companies take part in an auction for independent television franchises also reflect this dimension; the government did however make some concessions to critics who argued that the public service element of broadcasting would be eroded, as franchises would go to the highest bidder: the licensing authority gained a new role in assessing applicants' plans, and in 'exceptional circumstances' could reject the highest bid.

At the same time, regulatory tendencies are apparent, with justification offered on a number of grounds: to mitigate alleged bias, to ensure the maintenance of appropriate moral standards, and to assist in the battle against terrorism. The Broadcasting Bill itself extends the Obscene Publications Act to broadcasting and replaces the IBA with the Independent Television Commission (ITC), which is to license and supervise commercial broadcasting. The Broadcasting Standards Council, set up in 1988 to monitor general standards of taste in television and radio, is to be placed on a statutory footing.

A number of cases in the 1980s raised questions of freedom of expression, censorship and public accountability. The Falklands War was a period of particular tension between the government and the BBC. Then in April 1986 Norman Tebbit then Chairman of the Conservative Party initiated a period of sustained government criticism of alleged bias by his bitter attack on Kate Adie's reporting of the US bombing raid on Libya. A group of programmes illustrate government attempts to control the content of programmes: the BBC television series *The Secret State, Granada's Death on the Rock* and the radio series *My Country Right or Wrong.* In the first, the police raided the homes of journalists and the premises of BBC Scotland and seized documents and tapes. The programme in the series dealing with the Zircon communications' satellite was not shown as scheduled because an injunction was issued to prevent it. The programme aimed to highlight the fact that Parliament had not been kept properly informed about the development of Zircon. It had been made with the knowledge of the Ministry of Defence and with the cooperation of senior establishment figures; furthermore, the existence of Zircon was already in the public domain. No charges were brought against the BBC or individual journalists. *Death on the Rock*, dealing with the shooting of three unarmed IRA members by the SAS in Gibralter in 1988, was shown as scheduled. But it suffered a barrage of criticism as Margaret Thatcher led the way with accusations of 'trial by television'. Transmission of #My Country Right or Wrong# was also delayed, despite the fact that it had the approval of the Secretary of the D-notice committee.

Attempts to censor, delay or prohibit programmes have been most widespread of all in Northern Ireland, where plays, news programmes and documentaries have been subject to pressure on grounds of aiding or encouraging terrorism (see Chapter 15). The same justification was used for the introduction of an unprecedented restriction on peacetime broadcasting, namely the banning of interviews with members or supporters of named organisations operating in Northern Ireland. The ban included Sinn Fein, the political wing of the IRA. Critics pointed out that the ban would deny individuals the ability to judge the issues for themselves (Sinn Fein had 56 councillors and one MP at the time). All these incidents suggested increasing government encroachment on the broadcasting of information and raised fears that broadcasters would shy away from controversial issues because of anticipated government pressure.

The media have become embroiled in a different type of controversy over the use of advertising and public service information announcements. Critics maintain that increasingly the government has muddied the waters between impartial information and partisan propaganda. Certainly a preoccupation with 'presentation' has been a consistent recent theme of the Thatcher administration: controversial policies would be popular if they were effectively presented to the public. The government's spending on advertising increased dramatically between 1984 and 1989, from about £20m to £120m, excluding campaigns such as that by the water authorities to 'inform' the public about their activities. ·

Government and Administration

The emphasis on presentation has also generated worries within government departments themselves: in the spring of 1989 the information officers' union asked the prime minister's press secretary to draw up a code of ethics so that its members could avoid being asked by ministers to justify government policies rather than explain them. Neville Taylor, former Director General of the Central Office of Information (COI), expressed fears that the government's information service was in danger of becoming a partisan propaganda machine. The arguments over the quality of official government information have also been fuelled by the outcome of the cost-cutting and efficiency drives which have been one of Thatcher's hallmarks. One early casualty was the Royal Commission on the Distribution of Income and Wealth, set up to report periodically on changes in distribution trends. The main focus, however, has been the Government Statistical Service (GSS), which collects non-security information.

The GSS consists mainly of statistical divisions in separate government departments. It also includes the Central Statistical Office (CSO) which is the core of the service and came into being when Churchill, exasperated by conflicting figures from individual ministries, established the principle that 'the cabinet should never need to argue over the figures' (quoted in Civil Service Commission, 1988). In 1979 the GSS cost over £100m and employed more than 9,000 staff. On assuming the premiership, Thatcher invited Sir Derek Rayner to investigate ways of reducing government administrative costs. One area for particular attention was the GSS, where Rayner recommended reductions in spending by £25m and in staffing by 2,500. The Rayner Review (see below) initiated a process of continuing controversy over the alleged politicisation of government statistics.

Of course, it is difficult to maintain the Churchillian view that figures can be neutral arbiters in political debate. Statistics are created within a particular social and political context so that a political view of society, however implicit, is contained within apparently objective figures. Bias may be incidental or deliberate. For example, homelessness, like much official data, is not the result of a specially conducted survey but is a by-product of the administrative operation of state agencies. The homelessness figures represent those that have been registered with a local authority to be considered for housing. If the authority does not hear from them again within six months, the case is closed and a permanent solution is recorded.

Choice is also involved in the way data are collected and presented. Not surprisingly, civil servants have traditionally viewed their task as that of protecting their minister. Thus when Michael Meacher was a junior Labour minister at the DHSS, he had to provide a parliamentary answer to a question on the number of hypothermia deaths. His civil servants provided an answer based on official mortality statistics which showed that the numbers were small; he wanted to reply, based on survey evidence, that they were in fact much larger. He received a memo from a civil servant noting that 'any reply suggesting large numbers of old people are dying from hypothermia could be used to put pressure on government to increase heating provisions' (quoted in Lawrence, 1986). Thus, technical questions on what is hypothermia death are inseparable from political questions.

So the politicisation of statistics cannot be regarded as new. Nonetheless, critics see a qualitatively greater political interference since 1979 and accuse the government of 'cooking the books'. The Royal Statistical Society has also expressed grave concern and called for an independent National Statistics Council to be created.

The Government and Personal Information

Obviously the relationship between the government and its citizens is affected by all the issues discussed above. Here we focus on developments which affect the privacy of the individual and his/her control over the government's collection and use of personal information. The European Convention of Human Rights explicitly acknowledges a right to privacy, but in Britain there is no statutory acknowledgement of such a right. There are, however, common law traditions relating to confidentiality and strong cultural predispositions against interference in an individual's private life. In 1970 the government set up the Younger Committee to investigate whether legislation was needed to protect individual citizens (and also commercial and industrial interests) against intrusions into their privacy. The Committee found it difficult to offer a precise definition of 'privacy' and advocated instead a number of protective measures. It also laid down a number of principles for handling personal information.

These principles provided a benchmark for subsequent discussions. They were endorsed by the Lindop Committee on Data Protection in 1978. After its election in 1979 the Conservative Government, spurred by its desire to join the European Convention on Automatic Data Processing, began its consultations on Lindop's findings. The result was the Data Protection Act (DPA) 1984, another of our case studies below.

The DPA was one attempt to deal with some of the implications of information technology. It was followed by the Interception of Communications Act (1985), dealing primarily with the question of telephone tapping, but not with other modern forms of electronic surveillance, which remain unregulated. Over the next few years the government accepted a number of private members' bills aiming to increase individuals' access to information held on them: the Local Government (Access to Information) Act 1985; the Access to Personal Files Act 1987; the Access to Medical Records Act 1988; and the Environment and Safety Information Act 1988. The government also accepted the principle of public access to the Land Register, showing who owns land and property.

Nonetheless, there were also other areas of new or continuing controversy in regard to policies on the right to privacy, the storage and transmission of information, and the scope of legitimate surveillance of individuals. For example, the compilation of a national register for the poll tax created fears about the transmission of information among government departments and private institutions. Some questions on local registration forms were queried with the Data Protection Registrar (see below). The scheme for introducing football identity cards raised questions of individual files containing unsubstantiated information and details of alleged 'misbehaviour'. Local authority video surveillance of some city centres has been controversial. The proposal in autumn 1989 for a National Intelligence Unit also fostered anxiety about the use of personal information.

Three Case Studies

The 1984 Data Protection Act

The Content of the Act The government was anxious to accede to the European Convention on Automatic Data Processing in order to facilitate harmonisation of business practices and to protect commercial interests which without legislation would have lost out in international data processing traffic. At the same time there appeared strong civil liberties arguments in favour of legislation. The result was the DPA, which aims to protect individuals from the misuse of information held about them on computer files. The Act requires that holders and users of computerised information register the data base and its use with the Data Protection Registrar. All non-exempt users must comply with the following principles:

- Data must be obtained and processed fairly and lawfully.
- Data may be used only for specific, lawful purposes; these must be stated to the Registrar.
- Data may be used and disclosed to others only for the specified purposes.
- Data must be adequate, relevant and not excessive, i.e. relative to the purpose(s) specified.
- Data must be accurate and up-to-date.
- Data may be kept only for as long as needed.
- An individual may determine what information is held on him/her; where information is wrong, it must be corrected; where it is irrelevant or excessive it must be erased.
- Data holders must take adequate steps to prevent loss or destruction of files as well as unauthorised access.

These principles apply to all those required to register under the Act. For example, clubs may hold data on their members without registering, so long as members know and consent to personal details being kept. The use of computer files to pay wages does not require registration, but the data kept may not be used for any other purposes. National security files are also exempt.

The Act provides individuals with the right of access to their files, but here too there are exceptions. One may be refused access to one's file or part of it if, for example, the information is legally privileged or if another law regulates access. Thus a person seeking access to a credit file would apply under the Consumer Credit Act. Information held for tax collection or for the prevention and detection of crime may be refused. Indeed, the police are specifically exempt (when 'preventing or detecting crime') from the first principle of data protection; they do not have to obtain their information lawfully or fairly!

Broadly speaking, however, a person wanting access to his/her file should receive an intelligible copy within forty days of application to its holder. The addresses of the data users are listed in the Register available in larger public libraries. If information is refused or found to be inaccurate or irrelevant, then the injured party may apply to the court for redress and, in some cases, for compensation. The Data Protection Registrar (DPR) also has the duty to investigate complaints and may issue an enforcement notice.

An Assessment   The Act has been widely welcomed as adding to the statutory safeguards of individual civil liberties. Still, a number of criticisms have been made. The Act has not been widely publicised and it can be expensive to use, particularly where a data user has multiple register entries and charges the maximum £10 for each entry. It also appears that the limited resources of the Registrar make the Act quite easy to evade. By mid-1988 about 80,000 organisations had failed to register, despite a deadline of May 1986; only one firm had been prosecuted for non-registration.

Another criticism stems from the fact that the Act does not apply to information held on manual files. This means that firms like the Economic League, which maintains a blacklist of supposedly subversive individuals, are immune, though they have been shown to have provided inaccurate information to employers. The distinction between computer-held and manual files provides a means of bypassing the legislation because a manual file containing sensitive information can be used to back up a computer file. Most other European countries protect personal data however stored, and most report that complaints largely concern manual files.

As the poll tax (see Chapter 12) came into force, most councils were found to have violated the DPA by seeking unnecessary information, some including questions about relationships of household members. The first, Trafford Borough Council, withdrew its original form and promised the DPR that the offending information would be held only manually; but this too appears unlawful, as the questions should not have been asked in the first place. Unfortunately, legal cases are necessary to test fully the legality of the poll tax forms.

Another criticism concerns the exceptions provided in the Act. Parliament has accepted the validity of the data protection principles but has then exempted certain public bodies from some of them. It is also questionable whether national security files should be exempt from registration and whether information transmitted to the security services should automatically be exempt. It is perfectly reasonable to prevent those suspected of endangering national security from seeing their files. Yet there are examples of innocent individuals suffering because the security services held inaccurate information about them. Lindop recommended that such files be registered and that an individual with security clearance in the DPR's Office should oversee the accuracy and relevance of data held by the security services.

In sum, greater safeguards would be easy to build into the legislation, but the government has resisted them. Its approach appears to have been the minimalist one necessary for accession to the European Automatic Data Processing Convention. People are very concerned about these matters (Data Protection Registrar, 1988, Appendix 9), but the Government has not responded fully.

The Government and Official Secrets

The Reform of Section 2 Although prominent members of the Conservative government had added their voices to the chorus of criticism of section 2 of the Official Secrets Act, the government did not move until pushed. In January 1988 the backbench Conservative MP Richard Shepherd introduced a Private Member's Bill on the protection of official information. The government mobilised a three-line whip against it and promised to present its own reform proposals. Nonetheless, the Shepherd Bill was the occasion for a massive backbench revolt; it was only very narrowly defeated. The White Paper on the reform of section 2 was published in June, the Bill followed in December, and the new Act was rushed through quickly in 1989.

The then Home Secretary Douglas Hurd described the Bill as 'a substantial and unprecedented thrust in the direction of greater openness' and 'an earthquake in Whitehall'. Richard Shepherd saw it as 'illiberal' and 'repressive', and it must be said that this is the general view taken outside government circles. Whereas under the old section 2 *any* disclosure of official information was a criminal offence, the new Act specifies six categories of information remaining under the protection of the criminal law: security and intelligence, interception of communications, international relations, defence, that obtained in confidence from another state or international organisation, and that which results/is likely to result in crime or to impede the prevention of crime.

For former or current intelligence officers or others closely connected with the security services, the prohibition is absolute. They may *never* disclose anything about their work. This is also the case with information concerning 'authorised bugging', e.g. telephone tapping under a warrant obtained from the government. In the case of information falling within the other categories disclosure must cause or be likely to cause 'harm' or 'prejudice' or 'jeopardy'. A similar test of 'harm' applies to journalists reporting on security or intelligence matters but not on the interception of communications.

Obviously, a great deal of government information falls outside these areas, but this does not mean that civil servants will now be freer to disclose it. Instead of the criminal law, they will be subject to tighter internal disciplinary procedures. This is why, for example, the public still has no right of access to the safety records of particular cars or lists of factories whose safety certificates have been withdrawn. In this sense the Act is clearly not a charter for freedom of information.

An Assessment   The terms of the new section 2 have been criticised on a number of grounds. Firstly, the test of harm – where it is permitted – is very vague. Shepherd's Bill, for example, provided the more rigorous test of 'serious harm'. Secondly, there is no defence of prior publication; in other words, it will not be possible to argue that the release of information could not cause harm because that information had already been published. Thirdly, and most importantly, the government steadfastly refused to accept a 'public interest' defence, under which a person accused of releasing information could argue that the good resulting from the disclosure (say of a gross abuse of authority) was greater than any harm caused. The Labour Party, the Liberal and Social Democrats, David Owen's SDP, and a number of Tory backbenchers, as well as the Law Society, leading newspaper editors, and civil liberties' pressure groups all deplored the refusal to incorporate a public interest defence for breaching secrecy.

Clearly there remain many legitimate worries about the compatibility of the new legislation with the basic principles of freedom of the press and the need to prevent possible abuses of power by the organs of the state. The lack of a public interest defence is the vital issue in regard to press freedom, especially in the area of investigative journalism. Many civil servants and journalists who have in the past revealed negligence and wrongdoing by government would have no defence under the new provisions: Jonathan Aitken, publishing an official report on the Biafran War, and Clive Ponting, leaking documents on the sinking of the *Belgrano*, both won their cases on the basis of a public interest defence which would not now be admissible. Neither Peter Wright's nor Colin Wallace's serious allegations about the conduct of the security services could now be published, and nor could Andrew Boyle's *The Climate of Treason*, which exposed the spy Anthony Blunt. More open government is no nearer; indeed the pillars of secrecy appear strengthened.

The Rayner Review of the GSS

The Review We have noted above that the Rayner Review initiated a process of continuing controversy over the nature and validity of government statistics. Its findings, expressed in the 1981 White Paper, the *Government Statistical Services*, affected all three aspects of the final statistical product – what information is collected, how it is collected, and how it is made available to the general public. In deciding what was to be collected, one of the most important exercises of the review involved scrutinising every statistical collection system within the GSS, discarding those statistics which were not directly relevant and useful to government. As a result, some statistical enquiries have been reduced in size, carried out less often or cut altogether. The once annual *Census of Employment* is now carried out triennially and the sample size of the *General Household Survey* was reduced by 14 per cent to 12,000 households. Local authorities, for example, used to be able to analyse the work of home-helps by client groups, such as the elderly or maternity cases; but since the Rayner Review the statistical return has been discontinued on the basis that there is no longer a need for such analysis.

Ways in which information is collected were also scrutinised. Checking and verification procedures have been reduced and the streamlining of information systems to aid the introduction of information technology introduced. The unemployment count, for example, changed from being register-based to claimant-based. All those who register voluntarily at Job Centres but do not claim benefit are no longer included. It has been estimated that this lowered the total by at least 50,000 people. Financial cuts affected the amount and cost of statistical material made available to the public. Some statistical volumes were replaced with press notices and costs have been attached to once freely available publications.

An Assessment Critics from the 'left' argue that increased prices and new methods of dissemination, such as microfiche and computer tapes, have restricted the public's ability to comment on the government's business and performance. The now infamous Black Report of 1980 highlighted the social class gradients in health inequality and called for more statistical data to investigate the complex reasons for this phenomenon. The latest edition of *The Decennial Supplement on Occupational Mortality*, the main source for information on class differences in mortality, contained 50 per cent less information than the previous edition. Only five pages of commentary were devoted to social class in 1981 compared with 60 pages in 1971, and critics have accused the government of trying to hide the truth regarding class and health.

Throughout the review the GSS was assumed to serve only the needs of central government. The wider research field, including the universities, polytechnics, voluntary organisations and local authority research units, has largely been ignored. Indeed, some commentators from the 'right' of the political spectrum criticised the review for not recognising this wider market and have suggested that statistical information should be privatised and sold through recognised agencies. Furthermore, the issues regarding the responsibility of government to make itself accountable to the public are not raised by the review. The public are regarded as providing rather than needing information. The White Paper stated that one of the main reasons for the government's carrying out the review was 'to ensure that the burdens ... on the taxpayer and the form filler are no more than is essential for the efficient discharge of its functions'.

For Sir Claus Moser, a former head of the GSS, and Sir David Cox, a former President of the Royal Statistical Society, the Rayner Review is a watershed in the history of official statistics. Moser has said, 'Before the Rayner Review the purpose of the government statistical services was to serve several masters, first and foremost . . .the government; but also industry, academics, the public, indeed the whole nation. . .' (*Independent*, 9 October 1989). A whole range of controversies has arisen over the use and abuse of government statistics.

The unemployment calculations, amended by Rayner, changed 29 times between 1979 and 1989; only once did the change lead to an increase in the total figure. When Thatcher claimed that 88 per cent of claimants would be better off after changes in social security benefits in April 1988, the calculations took no account of inflation. National Health spending figures have also been queried. For example, even when figures have been adjusted for inflation, they have not taken into account that inflation in the health service is higher than for the general economy. NHS cost improvement programmes are assumed to yield recurrent savings, i.e. the level of savings achieved in the first year is assumed to continue in subsequent years, while these 'savings' are treated as additional revenue. Norman Fowler's famous computer list of large hospital schemes, presented at the 1986 Conservative Party Conference, was found to include a hospital car park. Poverty has also been an area where independent bodies have criticised the government. The Institute of Fiscal Studies issued a report noting that the DHSS had removed more than 1m people from the poorest category of the population by changing its method of calculation (IFS, 1989) and referring to 'fears that the changes were for political rather than bona fide methodological reasons'.

From the discussion above, it would seem that the Rayner Review, through the process of statistical scrutiny, has been used by government to alter politically sensitive information systems. It could be argued that this has been done in such a way as to minimise outside criticism of policy performance. This has been ensured by emphasising that the GSS is costly, so that any extension of responsibility to the wider interests of the general public is not financially viable.

Conclusion

From the general overview and each of the case studies presented within this chapter, it appears that the Conservative government has manipulated information policy to meet its own political needs. These needs cover the ability to define and control the release of security information (including regulation of the media) and to legalise the trade in personal information, whilst at the same time appearing to be concerned with the individual's right to privacy. Policy has also been introduced to allow government more control over statistical collection and presentation systems. This in turn enables it to optimise these processes for their own political goals. In all three of our case studies we observe the government's reluctance to acknowledge a wider public interest in greater openness.

As we hinted earlier, the ideological backcloths of the policy changes only partly conform to the Thatcherite emphases on individual freedom of choice, the promotion of individual responsibility, reduced public expenditure, and private enterprise. Indeed, where these ideological perspectives may be damaging or non-supportive, they have been replaced by authoritarian control.

The DPA and the Rayner Review show the two types of emphasis in complete contrast. The former illustrates how information policy has been presented so as to try to convince the general public that their personal privacy is being protected under the watchful eye of the DPR. As the assessment has shown, this policy is superficial in relation to this aim; in reality, its major impact has been to clear the way for full information trading with our European partners. Not only has the Act legalised the personal information industry, but it seems to be encouraging it. These developments seem to comply with the current Conservative philosophy of maximising the growth of free enterprise by removing all barriers to information trading.

In contrast, information policy surrounding the collection and processing of official statistics has restricted their utility to serve private enterprise. Under the guise of the need to reduce public spending, emphasis has been placed on customising data collection systems to meet only the needs of central government. The government argues that Exchequer funds are insufficient to extend the consideration of user-needs to a much broader field, including research bodies. Much official information, for example, would be of commercial benefit to the ever-growing numbers of market research companies, management consultants and other research agencies. Although commercial exploitation of certain officially collected information already takes place (e.g. the *Decennial Census* and *The General Household Survey*), many other datasets are not made available or are published in a form unsuitable for commercial research. Private health care companies, for example, may find hospital in-patient statistics extremely valuable for identifying potential 'markets' of sick people. While this type of information is made available for public scrutiny, much interesting detail – such as local area of residence or occupation – is omitted.

This leads to the question of why the GSS has not been made part of the government's privatisation programme (see Chapter 2), for which it appears a highly suitable candidate. The answer appears to lie in the determination to maintain control. The exact content of datasets would begin to move out of the government's control and could begin to reflect other, perhaps politically controversial, research needs. The presentation of information in a politically desirable manner would be less easy than it appears at present. In addition, other bodies, including various pressure groups, might politicise information for their own ends and use it as evidence against the government.

In this sense, then our case studies illustrate policies which serve government self-interest; they certainly do nothing much to impinge on government action. In the case of data protection the government has been able to bypass the reform when it might create some awkwardness for politicians. The 1989 Official Secrets Act similarly provides a better instrument to be mobilised in cases like Ponting's, while not reducing the scope of governmental secrecy. The changes instituted by Rayner were presented as an efficiency move, but they have led to greater government control of information affecting its own activities. Information policy has consistently favoured the state rather than the citizen.

15

Beyond Political Statement: New Thinking on Northern Ireland

FRANK LYONS

The Thatcher government's policy for Northern Ireland has, since 1985, been cast in the mould established by the Anglo–Irish Agreement, sometimes called the Hillsborough Accord. This chapter focuses on the Agreement, setting it in the context of British policy, from the beginning of the Troubles in the late 1960's; it outlines the responses from various sides of the debate within Northern Ireland and points to policy developments after 1985. Many of the problems facing the Government derive from the 1969 decision to send British troops to Northern Ireland, in what was officially described as a 'peacekeeping' role. Unrest and violence had erupted in response to civil rights demonstrations which challenged Protestant privileges. At the same time the Protestant community was itself split over attempts by Terence O'Neill, the Northern Irish leader, to modernise the economy. The deployment of troops ultimately created confusion over where political responsibilities lay. The security forces were, at that time, also being faced with the problem of the emergence of paramilitary groups, including the Provisional Irish Republican Army (PIRA). In August 1971 the government introduced a policy of internment without trial for those suspected of paramilitary involvement. This led to protest and a subsequent escalation of violence led to the establishment of the Direct Rule of Northern Ireland from London (Arthur and Jeffery, 1988).

Under the system of Direct Rule the people of the Province have lost many of their democratic rights, for policy-making is largely under the control of the Secretary of State for Northern Ireland and the Northern Ireland Office. Moreover, under the provision of the Northern Ireland Act 1974 legislation is made in such a way that there is neither accountability to the Northern Irish nor, on most occasions, is there debate of the policy in Westminster. The Northern Ireland Office is in fact staffed by London based civil servants rather than local officials in Northern Ireland. Subject to Direct Rule the Northern Irish have had no opportunity until recently to vote for the parties that have formed the government of the United Kingdom.

The elections of 1979 signified both continuity and change in overall British policy. The government continued the previous policies of Ulsterisation (the re-establishment of the Royal Ulster Constabulary (RUC) and the Ulster Defence Regiment (UDR) as the main forces of law and order) and criminalisation (the treatment of paramilitaries as criminals rather than political activists). In the early 1980's the criminalisation of paramilitary prisoners in the Maze prison led to hunger strikes in protest at the removal of their special category status. The prisoners gained international sympathy and Sinn Fein, the political wing of the PIRA, emerged with a new political strategy of putting up candidates for election. In other policy areas the Thatcher government developed 'new and close political cooperation' with the government of the Republic of Ireland. This led to a series of inter-government meetings from 1983 that culminated in the 1985 Agreement, signed at Hillsborough.

The Hillsborough Accord

It must be remembered that the Hillsborough Accord is an agreement between two governments and so the policy aims of both must be taken into account. A particular problem arises because the Republic of Ireland's government has twice changed since the signing of the Agreement. The Hillsborough Accord recognised the existance of two communities with separate cultures, histories and aspirations. Although this involved a shift from previous attempts to assimilate the two groups into one that recognised differences that might accommodate to each other, the Agreement established a framework for policy that recognized two communities rather than a cultural and political plurality. In this respect the objectives of the Agreement were as follows:

- To reaffirm the majorities' right to self-determination and the minorities' rights within the Province, whilst acknowledging their wish for a united Ireland.

- To guarantee the fair and equal treatment of both communities. As such, there were implications for equal opportunities in work, social and welfare provisions.
- To return the government of Northern Ireland to the people in the Province. This re-establishment of devolved government was to be done in a way that guaranteed that the interests of the two groups were represented. As such devolution was envisaged as occurring alongside joint London–Dublin supervision. This would involve some kind of power sharing arrangement, acceptable to both groups.
- To give particular focus to the problems of policing security, and the system of justice:

  – Cross-border police liason involving informational, technical and operational co-operation was proposed.
  – A broadening of recruitment to include more Catholics into the predominantly Protestant RUC was envisaged to overcome the situation in which one community polices the other.
  – The possibility of harmonising aspects of the systems of justice was considered, mixed courts made up of judges from the Republic and the North were considered possibilities. It was hoped that the bringing of terrorists to justice could be made easier if extradition from the Republic were made easier. The promoting of confidence in the administration of justice was seen as important. Here the problem is particularly focused on the 'Diplock' courts; in these courts a single judge assesses the evidence, juries having been suspended because they were seen as vulnerable to intimidation.

- An inter-governmental Conference was established to deal with relations between the two parts of Ireland in relation to the four areas: political issues, security and related matters, legal and justice questions and the development of cross border co-operation. In no way does this imply any obligation on the part of the Dublin government to accommodate British or Unionist criticism of Southern society or politics.
- The implication here is that until a power-sharing agreement, acceptable to both communities, is established the Republic will be consulted as the representative of the Nationalist community's interest.
- The workings of the Conference were to be reviewed in three years. The first review took place in November 1988 and as a consequence conference meetings are to be enlarged to include debate between ministers over industry, transport, finance, health and tourism. Meetings will be more frequent with the intention of focusing on day-to-day events rather than crisis management.

Policy Aims of the Republic of Ireland

South of the border there is a complex attitude to Nationalism. All too often the assumption is made by British observers that the Republic has an unreserved wish for Irish unity. Political ideals are however divided about the significance of Nationalism. In an *Irish Times* opionion poll in 1987 it was revealed that only a minority of citizens in the Republic were prepared to make material sacrifices for a United Ireland. In relation to other more pressing issues on the economy, welfare and the problem of mass emigration from the Republic, national unity remains of secondary but symbolic importance.

For all the major political parties in the South, national cultural identity is very important, and the beleaguered Catholic minority in the North is included within this sense of national sentiment. The parties differ however in their views about the means by which unity should be achieved. Dr Fitzgerald, who signed the Agreement and the Fine Gael and Labour parties, who were in a coalition government in 1985, emphasise the principle of *unity by consent.* For this coalition the Agreement meant a policy that gave an 'Irish dimension' allowing the Republic's government a consultative and watchdog role on behalf of the Catholics over the border. Dr Fitzgerald believed in the development of accommodation and the importance of the *nation of people* rather than placing emphasis on national territory and unification.

Dr Fitzgerald and Fine Gael included the Republic within the accommodationist strategy pushing unsuccessfully, as it turned out, for liberalising the restrictions of divorce and contraception. In a symbolic gesture the Republic was to be made more welcoming to a potential future Protestant minority.

Charles Haughey and the Fianna Fail party formed a minority government after the 1987 Election in which economic problems had been the key issues. At the time of the signing of the Agreement in 1985, Haughey had been openly nationalistic and found it difficult to accept those aspects of the Agreement that alluded to the separate status of Northern Ireland. He was particularly critical of that part of the Agreement that guaranteed the northern Protestant majority a right to self-determination within the Province. These rights were seen to challenge the rights of all Irish people to self-determination and the claims to a unified territory expressed in articles 2 (and 3) of the Republic's constitution.

Article 2. The national territory consists of the whole of Ireland, its islands and territorial seas.

Haughey's *territorial republicanism* has not been popular in the Republic where the people are anxious about reunification and remain committed to the Agreement. After the 1989 Election Haughey seems to have put aside his objections to Hillsborough. Now operating within a coalition government with the Progressive Democrats, Haughey has converted to an acceptance of devolution and the working of the institutions and procedures of the AngloIrish Agreement. However in the coalition government's joint programme, Northern Ireland only merits two paragraphs in the 32-page document.

Policy Aims for the Thatcher Government

Northern Ireland posed the Thatcher government more than just an internal security question. Radical right thinking emanating from the pro-NATO Institute for Defence and Strategic Studies argued the danger of Ireland as Britain's undefended western frontier. Further international public opinion has been critical of the failure of the British government to redress grievances in Northern Ireland by having a policy that is solely focused on counter-terrorism. Irish-Americans have been particularly concerned about discrimination in the 'old country'. Tom King, the Secretary of State (until 1989) attempted to rebut this criticism; when addressing American correspondents, in London in May 1988, he described the IRA as: 'Marxist republican terrorists, now receiving their only real support from Quathafi'.

Hillsborough was, in part then designed to deal with international criticism, possibly to help maintain a British presence in Ireland as well as leading to cooperation in combating terrorism. The London government hoped cooperation would include improvements in the extradition arrangement from the Republic to the United Kingdom. It was felt that terrorists, all too often had successfully found refuge in the South.

Hillsborough did not herald the development of new social policies, such as job creation schemes or house building programmes. For a government committed to market forces this is not surprising. Government (non-security) funding in Northern Ireland has been 40 per cent higher than funding in the mainland and in the early 1980s industrial subsidies were double that of other depressed regions in the United Kingdom. The absence of economic interventionist initiatives in the Agreement indicated a shift to the market that has become clearer since 1985. The privatisation of the shipbuilders Harland and Wolff and the plane-makers Shorts is in line with a policy that was more clearly stated in the Department of Economic Development's *Pathfinder* report which stressed the need to move from an employment to an enterprise culture. This strategy suggests that the economic solution for Northern Ireland does not lie in either state subsidies or in trying to attract subsidiaries of multinational companies but through facilitating the growth of small local initiatives.

Finally it should be recognised that Hillsborough had elements of a personal anti terrorist crusade for Mrs Thatcher. As well as the murder in 1979 by the Irish National Liberation Army of her friend Airey Neave, in 1984 the Conservative Party Conference had been bombed at the Grand Hotel in Brighton. Mrs Thatcher's personal commitment has become clearer since 1985, particularly in August 1988 after the Ballygawley bomb killed 8 soldiers and injured a further 27; Mrs Thatcher returned from holiday to overview new counter terrorist policy developments. Mrs Thatcher's position within the government and the Conservative party is however not uncontested. For a significant group of Conservatives, including Sir Geoffrey Howe, the Agreement has been welcomed as a step toward ultimate disengagement.

Responses to Hillsborough

Unionism

Unionists felt betrayed by the Agreement. Even whilst negotiations between London and Dublin were taking place it was denied to Unionists that they existed. The apparent lack of trust in Unionists was made all the more difficult to swallow when it was realised that the Nationalist John Hume of the Social Democratic and Labour Party (SDLP) had been consulted by Dublin. The Agreement itself seemed to Unionists to overturn everything for which the Union stood (Smith 1986). The critical problems were:

1. The ambiguity of the status of Northern Ireland within the Agreement where reference is made to 'the current status of Northern Ireland'. The ambiguity is seen as indicative of Britain's eventual intention to withdraw.
2. The 'rights' of the Republic to put forward views about Northern Ireland and the 'requirement' that the British government must listen is taken to indicate a level of joint sovereignty by Great Britain and the Republic over the Province.
3. In that the Agreement refers to the 'rights, duties and aspirations' of the two communities in the North, Unionists see this as legitimating the Republican aspirations of the minority in the North.

These three objections have been the basis of Unionists' refusal to have talks either about devolution or with the Nationalist SDLP whilst the Agreement remains in place.

Initially Unionist protest against the Agreement was intense, with mass demonstrations, the resignation of sitting Unionist MPs, the refusal of local Unionist councillors to set rate levels and an escalation of violence. (Bew and Patterson, 1987) Subsequently, although Unionist opposition remains as strong as ever there was growing disquiet about the direct action campaigns and the so called 'drift' in Unionism. This disquiet was in part spurred on by firstly, the growth of the 'Campaign for Equal Citizenship', a movement advocating the full extension of British laws and British political parties to Northern Ireland. Their aim is to reconstruct politics giving citizens the chance to opt out of the sectarian politics that dominates in the Province; secondly, the Ulster Defence Associations' document *Common Sense* argued for a devolved legislative government, a new set of constitutional laws agreed by Catholics and Protestants, a Bill of Rights and a system of proportional representation. This document, although produced by an ultra-loyalist group, acknowledged that all parties shared in responsibility for the troubles. In July 1987 the Unionist Task Force report *An End to Drift* was published. Based on a wide survey of Unionist views it concluded there was a need for negotiations and the seeking of 'alternative terms for the Union'. Consequently in the years to 1990 many Unionists have been seeking terms under which talks might be started. Usually focusing on the precondition that the Agreement be suspended prior to negotiations, the Unionists are however, often divided amongst themselves. Whilst some Unionists in local councils started devising their own systems of power sharing, others like James Molyneux of the Official Unionist Party (renamed the Ulster Unionist party in 1988) argue for full integration of the Province in the United Kingdom.

Nationalism

The constitutional Nationalist party the SDLP were both architects and beneficiaries of the Agreement. The involvement of the Republic in the Inter Governmental Conference, established by the Agreement, offers to the SDLP a far stronger voice in Northern Ireland than they would achieve through direct negotiation with the Unionists. John Hume the SDLP leader was consequently a strong supporter of Hillsborough. His support has shifted in the later 1980's with his growing emphasis on the 'Irish dimension', talk of 'new institutions of government' and 'an all-Ireland settlement'. Whilst the SDLP has backed away from full commitment to devolution, the SDLP has nevertheless been involved in talks with Unionists and Sinn Fein in attempts to create new dialogue. Sinn Fein, the political wing of the provisional IRA, sees the Agreement as a typical policy of, on the one hand an imperialistic British government that has no right in Northern Ireland and on the other, the policy of a Republican government that had betrayed nationalism. The Agreement led to a marginal decline in support for Sinn Fein and the transfer of allegiances to the SDLP. In the 1987 election their share of the vote fell from the 1984 figure of 13.4 per cent to 11.4 per cent.

Both Unionist and Nationalist leaderships can be seen as drifting away from grass roots opinion. In two 1988 opinion polls, reported in the journal *Fortnight* and in the *Belfast Telegraphy*, Catholic opinion was against the Agreement despite Hume's support of it. In a third *Sunday Life* poll, in February 1989, there was a majority support, including a narrow majority of Catholics, for the suspension of Hillsborough; a further 71 per cent indicated support for power-sharing devolution within the United Kingdom.

Policy Developments After the Agreement

Since the signing of the Anglo-Irish Agreement tensions have remained high. Despite warnings from Sinn Fein leader Gerry Adams that 'we must be careful and careful again' the policy of Provisional/Sinn Fein has not been marked by a decline in terrorist activity. In August 1988 they announced a new campaign and during that month alone killed 15 members of the security forces. They also made their first attack in mainland Britain since the Brighton bomb in 1984 and extended their campaign against British forces to Germany and Belgium. Nine Catholics, including paramilitaries and 3 civilians were also killed in August 1988. The bombings have continued, with off-duty members of security forces and their families making easy targets.

For the most part British government policies have continued to focus on security and the containment if not defeat of the Provisionals. Largely in response to the developing American MacBride campaign against discrimination in employment in Northern Ireland (by June 1989 12 American states and half a dozen cities had adopted the MacBride principles) the British government has adopted fair employment legislation for Northern Ireland. A third strand to government policy has been the recent emphasis on supporting cultural diversity amongst the Northern Irish themselves.

Movement Toward the 1988 Autumn Security Package

In December 1986 the quashing of sentences on 24 suspects convicted on the word of one time INLA member Harry Kirkpatrick ended the 'supergrass' system. This coupled with the RUC's action in limiting tension during the marching season and the announcing of a new code of conduct by the Chief Constable of the RUC suggested some progress in the general area of policing and security. There was no move to reform the one-judge 'Diplock' court system despite strong argument for either a three-judge court or the return of jury trials, excepting where there is evidence of the intimidation of jurors. There was no clemency shown toward the 'Birmingham 6' despite grave concern about the evidence upon which these alleged terrorists were convicted and despite similarities to the cases of the released 'Guildford 4'.

The credibility of the RUC was undermined by the failure of the government to act on the findings of the Stalker–Sampson inquiry despite admission that there was evidence of conspiracy to pervert the course of justice. Stalker had revealed that the RUC had been operating in a non-accountable manner with its 'shoot-to-kill' tactics in the early 1980s. Apart from the implication that the condoning of 'shoot-to-kill' is licensing murder, people in Northern Ireland are all too aware it is not just terrorists who have been victims. Between 1982 and 1986 more than 30 people, including 18 unarmed, had been shot dead by security forces. The continuation of 'shoot-to-kill' seemed to be confirmed by the killing of 3 PIRA activists in Gibraltar. The shootings, when arrest and trial were possible; the subsequent leaking of disinformation by the government; and the rebuttal of the UK government's version by the Spanish government has eroded any increased confidence in the security forces.

In July 1988 the RUC were given 'new stop and search' powers through the Police and Evidence Order. In the Autumn a whole new security package was introduced in response to the IRA's offensive as follows:

- Radio and television interviews with people connected with terrorist groups could no longer be directly broadcast on the grounds that such interviews would be offensive to the public after episodes of violence, and because as Mrs Thatcher argued terrorists must be denied the 'oxygen of publicity' (see Chapter 14). This measure in effect denied Sinn Fein media access to the 83,000 (or 40 per cent) of the nationalist community who vote for it. In doing so it may well have given them the sympathy of those mindful of this erosion of civil liberties. Equally it has removed the situation in which terrorists are made to account for their actions by interviewers in the media. In as much as the media itself interprets the legislation as a ban there has been in consequence a curtailing of reporting about Northern Ireland. Inquiries by British broadcasters to the Belfast Republican Press Centre have reportedly fallen by 75 per cent.

- The right to silence of defendants in Northern Ireland was ended (to be extended to mainland Britain) and circumstances were outlined in which courts would be permitted to draw inference of guilt from the silence of the accused.
- Monies held by suspected terrorists would have to be proven legitmate or confiscated.
- There would be a reduction in the remission of sentences for terrorist prisoners from one-half to one-third.
- The previously subject to renewal Prevention of Terrorism Act which applies in Great Britain was made permanent. This act gives police the power to stop, search and detain, without a warrant, anyone suspected of terrorist activities.

In November 1988 the European Court of Human Rights ruled that Britain had breached the European Convention by holding four men up to 7 days without charge under the Act. In December Britain derogated from this ruling arguing that an emergency existed thus excusing the government of its obligations.

Economic and Anti-discrimination Policies

The political situation in the Province is bound up with the economic climate in which the politics takes place. Described as a 'Workhouse economy' (Rowthorn and Wayne, 1988) it has a manufacturing sector that has been in decline for over twenty years. The unhealthy state of the economy leaves the Catholic working class population most disadvantaged. With 35 per cent unemployment they suffer 2½ times the unemployment rate of the Protestant working classes. The differential unemployment rates are the product of complex social processes in which sectarianism is only one factor. To some extent the sluggish economy has prevented equal opportunities strategies being effective; PIRA imtimidation helps account for the relative absence of Catholic employment in the government security services and regional unemployment has particularly disadvantaged Catholics living west of the Bann and those in Belfast, where 49 per cent of jobs in manufacturing were lost between 1973 and 1986.

The new Fair Employment Act, (Northern Ireland) 1989, offers employers a code of practice that is intended to ensure an equitable distribution of job opportunities. Employers are required to monitor the composition of their workforce and review their methods of recruitment to ensure the fair participation by Protestants and Catholics. If fair participation is not occurring the Fair Employment Commission can advise upon affirmative action and a timetable to remedy under-representation. A system of cash penalties for bad practice and cash compensations for victims of discrimination is included in the legislation. Although this act is the most radical fair employment legislation enacted in the United Kingdom, it has been criticised for assuming that the population of Northern Ireland must either be Protestant or Catholic. There are more than fifty separate entries in the census of religious denominations in the Province. Despite popular and mass media images, there are a whole range of economic and political identities beyond the bowler-hatted Orangeman and armalite-carrying terrorists. Those concerned about wider issues of citizenship or women's issues, for example, take issue with the government for focusing solely on sectarian issues in their policy.

The government has a policy with potential for dealing with cultural diversity. In 1986 the Standing Advisory Commission on Human Rights looked at the problem of community relations in Northern Ireland and as a consequence the Cultural Traditions Group was established in 1989 with a £1 million a year budget to help promote cultural pluralism and community relations programmes. The critical question about this initiative is whether spending money can promote mutual respect or will result in a dwelling on sectarian ideological differences. (Hawthorne and Smith, 1989).

Beyond Stalemate

Perceptions are that Mrs Thatcher has no coherent strategy for recovery in Northern Ireland as she does not seem interested in much beyond the containment of terrorism. The Anglo–Irish Agreement and subsequent security measures have not, however, defeated the PIRA, nor the other paramilitary groups, neither have they marginalised Sinn Fein.

Fair Employment policies cannot on their own redress the state of the economy but the government seems committed to little more than lessons in enterprise culture and various training schemes. The problem remains that the Province is, on the one hand, geographically located on the periphery of economic developments in the United Kingdom and Europe and, on the other, is not attracting the highly skilled workforce required for today's leading edge, high technology industries.

The continuation of the Agreement as the main strategy of the British government seems particularly flawed because it has failed in its security objectives; it has not produced devolution and the last four years of the operation of the Inter-Governmental Conference have been marked by a series of crises in relations between London and Dublin. The government's broader spectrum of policies seems equally destined to produce problems within Northern Ireland.

The crisis over the collusion between security forces and Protestant paramilitaries that emerged in 1989 is typical. Pursuing a policy of reforming the security forces the RUC Chief Constable Mr Hugh Annesley invited the Cambridgeshire Deputy Chief Constable John Stevens to investigate. The investigation led to court appearances by over twenty members of the security services (members of the UDR, prison officers, etc.). The investigation is however a two-edged weapon, no doubt encouraging some that reform is under way, revealing to others that loyalist corruption runs deep and offending those who feel their loyalist paramilitaries need information on nationalist paramilitary suspects. It is almost inevitable that policies developed in the Province that are progressive for one group will offend another. It is not surprising, that under such conditions, there has been a collapse in support for the Agreement. Whereas 33 per cent of the population in Northern Ireland were for the Agreement, after its signing in 1985, by 1989 only 21 per cent supported it and this included only 41 per cent of the Catholic population.

There are however potential ways forward beyond the present stalemate. Increasingly there are calls for government leadership and there has emerged a broadly based non-sectarian people's movement that proposes new thinking on Northern Ireland. The declining fortunes of the Conservative Party in the opinion polls, the spectre of fuller participation in the EC, and admiration for the democratic revolution in Eastern Europe suggests that new civil rights reforms may not be too far away.

The Conservative government may well be recognising these changing times, evidenced in their recent initiatives to encourage community programmes to promote cultural diversity. It would also help if policies were developed to help resist sectarianism by encouraging integrated schooling (Moffatt, 1988) and the development of new political identities. Further policies to help political normalisation would include a Bill of Rights, the phasing out of emergency legislation and economic planning directed at rebuilding the ghetto areas in which the Provos thrive.

People's movements are pushing for such changes and include the Campaign for Equal Citizenship which can be seen as in the same mould as the New Consensus movement that emerged in the Republic in October 1989. (Norris, 1989). Protesters in this movement, sickened by continuing violence in the North and recognising that the Republic's claims on the North might prove difficult to remove from their constitution are making a people's protest. Their politics disavow the PIRA's claim to be campaigning and murdering in the name of the Irish people.

16

Foreign and Defence Policy: The Impact of Thatcherism

FERGUS CARR

Introduction

The aims of this chapter are to depict Britain's current role in international politics and to establish the impact of Thatcherism upon foreign and defence policy. It is important to recognise that before 1979 fundamental changes had occurred in Britain's international position. Britain was a world power in 1945, presiding over an empire but by 1973 had become a regional, middle-ranking, European power. In the same period the international system had changed too. In military terms profound disparities developed between the superpowers and the arsenals of other states. The substance of international politics also changed with the growth of economic interdependence which has blurred the boundaries of foreign and domestic policy. These are the contexts within which policy-makers have had to act since 1979 and upon which they should be judged.

From Great Power to Regional Actor

Winston Churchill described British foreign policy as having three circles of interest, one encompassed North America, another Europe and the third the Commonwealth. Britain in the post-war era sought to maintain involvement in each of the circles which precluded a concentration of commitment to any one. Strategy was global in scope and supported by a nuclear deterrent from 1952. This international role could not be sustained as the external world changed and the resource base at home declined. Politicians however were often reluctant to change perceptions and the residue of the global role was to survive until the 1970s.

In 1956 the United States opposed the British invasion of Suez and with financial pressure induced a British withdrawal. The 'lessons' of Suez were that Britain could no longer act as an independent great power and an American Administration would oppose British interests despite the 'special relationship'. Whilst Macmillan could restore cooperation with America, notably in the Polaris Agreement of 1962, the significance of the relationship declined in the following decade. The reason was that 'Britain's residual capability as a great power was eroded, and with it Britain's special value to the United States', (Reynolds, 1986, p. 13). In 1955 Britain enjoyed a 19.8 per cent share of world trade, by 1976 it had fallen to 8.7 per cent. In the same decades Britain's Gross National Product (GNP) was overtaken by West Germany, Japan and France (Kennedy, 1989). Though spending a greater share of GNP on defence than West Germany or France, Britain's capabilities failed to match commitments. In the mid-1960s economic pressures led the Labour government to cut defence expenditure and then withdraw from Singapore and the Gulf. The end of the East of Suez role signalled the concentration of the British defence effort upon the North Atlantic Treaty Organisation (NATO) and Europe.

Britain had stood apart from the development of the European Community (EC). Labour and Conservative governments were suspicious of the loss of sovereignty that supranationalism implied. Both supported a united Europe, but a Europe of states and both resisted constraints upon the Commonwealth relationship. In 1961 Macmillan sought membership of the Community significantly regarding it as a means to attain a real Atlantic partnership (see Camps, 1964, p. 336). Labour's conversion came as Wilson reorientated foreign and defence policy in the mid-1960s but was less complete then the Conservatives in party terms. The Commonwealth had mitigated the loss of empire but its diplomatic and trade significance for Britain declined as Europe's grew in the post-Suez era. Commonwealth members criticised Britain for using force in Suez and then for not using it in response to the Rhodesian Unilateral Declaration of Independence (UDI) in 1965. Edward Heath concluded in 1971 that the idea that the Commonwealth might become 'an effective economic and political let alone military bloc had never been realised' (Mansergh, 1982, p. 197). In 1973 Heath led Britain into the EEC. Though Britain retains broad trade and commercial links, the EEC (now EC) has become the central focus. In 1985 the EC took 49 per cent of the UK's experts and supplied 49 per cent of the UK's imports (Julius, 1987).

An important feature of the contemporary British economy is its sensitivity to the processes of interdependence: a vulnerability to change in the international economy generally and to change in the economies of our trading partners. This vulnerability has been amply demonstrated in problems regarding issues such as exchange rates, interest rates, stock exchange activity, energy policy, etc. Interdependence is not new to Britain with its history of international trade and finance. What is new, is 'Britain's altered position within the international order, and the pace at which technical and economic developments are integrating national economies and industrial structures' (Wallace, 1986). Economic decline has reduced Britain's capacity to manage the processes of interdependence and consequently the autonomy of the state has been reduced.

The Policy Process

The foreign policy process is dominated by the executive. Parliament has little effective scrutiny in a policy area which rarely requires formal legislation. Questions, debates and Select Committee activity afford only an indirect influence. Policy-making is effected by the cabinet organised by the prime minister. The prime minister determines the agenda for Cabinet action, membership of Cabinet committees and appointment of the Foreign Secretary and Secretary of State for Defence. The freedom of action of these ministers is further determined by their relationship with the prime minister. Prime ministers have been described as 'super foreign secretaries' because of the scale of their involvement and interest in foreign affairs. Attendance at summit conferences and negotiations with other heads of government reinforces this role and highlights it in the media. Mrs Thatcher has proved to be no exception 'playing a supervisory role over important areas of policy' (Parsons, 1989).

The executive does face constraints in the policy process. Governments must still secure Parliament's, and ultimately the electorate's, confidence. Policy advice, information and coordination proceed through two senior ministries, the Foreign and Commonwealth Office (FCO) and the Ministry of Defence (MOD). Resources often are limited and with the huge costs of defence, financial scrutiny is at a premium. Governments furthermore inherit policy, commitments exist derived from membership of bodies like NATO or the EC. In defence policy weapon procurement decisions can bind governments for years ahead. The strategic and economic activities of other states further constrain policy choice and opportunities. Financial and industrial interdependence erode the capacity for autonomous decisions. In short the management of Britain's external relations is a complex and often difficult process. Foreign and defence policy however involve the most emotive of political values, sovereignty, independence and security. Since 1979 Mrs Thatcher has stressed these values. Policy has often been presented in stark terms, stressing the national interest and asserting autonomy. The prime minister 'expresses herself in terms of national objectives and national pride and exerts herself to promote national interests abroad and to protect national values at home' (Wallace, 1986).

Britain and the EC

British policy toward the EC since 1979 has in the main been negative and defensive in character. Until its resolution with the Fontainebleau Agreement of 1984 the dominant Community issue for Britain was budgetary. Mrs Thatcher made clear she would not accept net contributions, she demanded 'our money back' and declared the situation 'demonstrably unjust'. The cost of membership was not a new issue in British politics; what marked Mrs Thatcher's approach was her style. The Thatcher approach to negotiation has been described as 'direct, bruising' and 'unrelenting' (Nailor, 1986; Riddell, 1983). In the 'Battle of the Budgets' she clashed with other government leaders and reinforced the popular image of Britain as the reluctant European. Since 1984 attention has turned to an older issue, the threat to British sovereignty from Community institutions.

In 1985 at the Luxembourg European Council meeting measures were agreed which would form the basis for the Single European Act (SEA) which came into force in 1987. The SEA was designed to enhance the development of the Community. The target of 1992 was set for completion of the internal market; a treaty of cooperation in foreign policy established; greater use of majority voting in decision-making agreed, and a number of new policy areas incorporated into the EEC Treaty. The British response was to welcome completion of the single market and cooperation in foreign policy but to remain 'wary of greater integration'. The SEA however, gave an impetus to new measures of economic and social integration. The Hanover Council meeting in 1988 established the Delors Committee to explore the steps required to move toward economic and monetary union. The Delors Committee reported in April 1989 and envisaged a three-stage transition to a Community monetary policy, single Community currency and Eurocentral Bank. In May 1989 the Commission published a preliminary draft of a Charter of Fundamental Social Rights. Designed to protect workers from the possible negative effects of the single market it covers freedom of movement, living and working conditions, social protection, education and training (see Chapter 1). British reaction to the new European proposals has been negative. Mrs Thatcher has refused the 'socialist charter' and the 'bureaucratic regulation' from Brussels of social policy which she believes should remain the prerogative of each member state. In her Bruges speech of September 1988 Mrs Thatcher reaffirmed her belief in a Europe consisting of 'willing and active cooperation between sovereign states'. She warned that 'to try and suppress nationhood and concentrate power and the centre of a European conglomerate would be highly damaging' (Keesing's, 1989). At the 1989 Madrid European Council meeting British isolation was prevented by Mrs Thatcher's acceptance of Stage One of the Delors Report. Stage One involves elements Mrs Thatcher has endorsed; the completion of the single market and greater liberalisation of capital markets but it also requires full membership of the European Monetary System (EMS) by adoption of the Exchange Rate Mechanism (ERM). The prime minister insisted that she had not made a commitment to Delors Stage Two and Three and that Britain would launch an alternative proposal.

The British plan for 'freely competing currencies' has not however received support from Community Finance Ministers. Mrs Thatcher has also listed conditions which make British entry to the ERM highly unlikely before 1992. This could well leave Britain apart from the rest of the Community and has been opposed by Cabinet members concerned that without entry Britain cannot influence the movement to monetary union. Membership of the ERM was a key factor in Nigel Lawson's resignation as Chancellor; he has since called for entry at the 'earliest practicable time to join, rather than the latest.' To date Mrs Thatcher has not heeded this advice.

Britain and the Superpowers

In contrast to the EC Britain's relationship with the United States has been close and cooperative. Mrs Thatcher has declared British pride in being America's partner and that the two states have 'the same political dreams, the same ways of achieving them' (*The Times*, 17 November 1988). For Mrs Thatcher Anglo–American relations are 'special'. There can be no doubt that the prime minister enjoyed a 'special relationship' with President Reagan. The two leaders had a particular affinity, a 'political love affair' (Parsons, 1989).

The Anglo–American relationship is distinctive. The two states enjoy an intelligence alliance, bureaucratic consultation and a nuclear relationship (see Reynolds, 1986). The government renewed the nuclear relationship in 1980 with the announcement that Polaris would be replaced with another American missile, Trident (C4). When the United States decided not to proceed with the C4 but the more powerful Trident (D5) the British purchase was revised accordingly. A recent estimate of the cost of this decision is £9,043m (at 1987–88 prices and an exchange rate of $1.62 to the pound). Britain is home for numerous American military and intelligence bases. From 1983 until their removal following the Intermediate-Range Nuclear Force (INF) Treaty in 1988 America stationed 160 Cruise missiles in Britain.

The deployment of Cruise missiles came at a time of increasing domestic sensitivity to nuclear issues. America's exclusive control of the missiles heightened criticism from both inside and outside of Parliament which was not diminished by government assurances of consultative status. Government support for the United States has also been criticised for isolating Britain and distancing her from European allies. In 1985 Britain followed America's lead and withdrew from UNESCO against the wishes of her European partners. Of greater significance was the Westland affair which pitched a European consortium against an American company Sikorski, in producing rescue bids for the ailing British defence contractor. The prime minister and the Secretary of State for Trade and Industry, Leon Brittain, favoured the American bid as did Westland. Michael Heseltine, Secretary of State for Defence, preferred a European solution, perceiving EC collaboration as Britain's long-term interest. Heseltine resigned believing he had been unable to put his case fairly due to 'unconstitutional' Cabinet conduct (see Hennessy, 1989a).

Support of American military action has led to further criticism of the government's identification of British interests. In April 1986 American aircraft based in Britain bombed targets in Libya. While other European states distanced themselves from America Mrs Thatcher 'found it inconceivable to refuse the United States' request to use aircraft based in the United Kingdom'. In 1988 Britain found herself isolated again supporting America when the USS *Vincennes* shot down an Iranian passenger aircraft. In 1989 Britain vetoed an EC statement which did not support the American version of a fresh confrontation with Libya.

The Anglo-American relationship has not been entirely without discord. Mrs Thatcher's 'very considerable doubts' about the American invasion of Grenada, a Commonwealth member, in 1983 were met by Jeanne Kirkpatrick's retort that allies cannot have veto power over American security. The British commitment to nuclear deterrence has faced two potential challenges from the United States. The President's 'Star Wars' speech in 1983 launched the Strategic Defense Initiative (SDI). The strategy of defensive shields against ballistic missile attack threatened the principles of nuclear deterrence. British concerns were largely met when President Reagan accepted four points in negotiation with Mrs Thatcher in 1984. The points were to guide SDI and involved the principle that its objective was to enhance deterrence. In October 1986 the Reykjavik superpower summit concluded with President Reagan proposing the elimination of ballistic missiles in ten years. At Camp David a month later Mrs Thatcher received the President's confirmation that the sale of Trident would not be affected by the arms control process.

Until 1984 Anglo–Soviet relations were marked by some of Mrs Thatcher's most vigorous speeches. Relishing the role of 'Iron Lady', she depicted the 1980s as the dangerous decade. The prime minister warned of Soviet 'unrelenting ideological hostility' towards the West. In the wake of the Soviet invasion of Afghanistan Mrs Thatcher argued that Moscow's policy was to work directly or indirectly against Western interests 'wherever they could'. In 1983 the theme was stronger, the governing principles of the Soviet Union were 'force and dictatorship', Moscow was said to see 'the expansion of communism as inevitable' and the rest of the world 'its rightful fiefdom' (*The Times*, 30 September 1983).

Mrs Thatcher's visits to Hungary and the Soviet Union in 1984 marked the beginning of a change in Anglo–Soviet relations. The British government adopted what the prime minister has called a 'sensible dialogue', others a 'more balanced approach' or an 'end to megaphone diplomacy' (see White, 1988). The prime minister did not abandon her criticism of the Soviet political system but added negotiation on to the agenda. In her address to the American Congress in 1985 she made clear that 'despite our differences with the Soviet Union we have to talk to them'.

The arrival of Mikhail Gorbachev as Soviet leader in 1985 cemented the new Anglo–Soviet relationship. Mrs Thatcher has expressed her trust and respect for Mr Gorbachev. As contact has grown between the two leaderships, particularly at the summits of 1987 and 1989, Mrs Thatcher's support for the Soviet leader's domestic reforms has developed. The Prime Minister has described Gorbachev's pursuit of *glasnost'* and *perestroika* as a 'historic mission'. She has made clear that 'we very much welcome what Mr Gorbachev is trying to achieve in the Soviet Union. . . we must do everything we can to stretch out hands' (*The Times*, November 1988). Gorbachev's policies led to demands for economic and political reform in Eastern and Central Europe. In dramatic succession demands for reform engulfed the states of the Warsaw Pact in 1989. The leading role of the Communist Party has been challenged, multiparty systems and free elections promised in Bulgaria, Czechoslovakia, East Germany, Hungary, Poland and

Romania. Though the overthrow of Ceausescu was perhaps the greatest triumph of 'people power' against violent repression, change in East Germany has the greatest significance for European security. The opening of German borders, the breaching of the Berlin Wall and the promise of free elections in East Germany reopens the debates about the relationship of the two Germanies and the division of Europe. The question of German reunification and its strategic implications has made West Germany central to the future process of change in Europe. Mrs Thatcher has suggested caution, the need to 'take a measured view of the way ahead' because 'the very spread of change could put the goal of democracy in jeopardy' (*Independent*, November 1989) Mrs Thatcher's concern has been to maintain political order in Europe. Just as she has counselled caution in discussing the future of German politics so she has rejected the denuclearisation of Europe. A series of Soviet initiatives since 1988 have focused attention on Short-Range Nuclear Forces (SNF) in Europe. The prospect of reduction talks were particularly attractive to sectors of West German political opinion, if not the British leadership. The Brussels NATO summit of May 1989 agreed to negotiations on SNF to achieve '*partial* reductions', only after conventional force reductions in Europe were underway. Mrs Thatcher was less successful in her bid to have SNF modernisation, the West German government secured a deferment of the question until 1992. It remains to be seen whether Britain or West Germany becomes the dominant European influence on the future of American policy towards NATO and Eastern Europe.

Defence Policy

NATO forms the key contemporary British defence commitment. Significant non-NATO commitments include the Falkland Islands, Hong Kong, Belize, Brunei and the Sovereign Base Areas of Cyprus. It is defence roles in NATO however that account for 95 per cent of the defence budget. Britain is the sole European member of the alliance to contribute to all three levels of NATO strategy – strategic nuclear, theatre nuclear and conventional forces. This contribution is exercised in four main roles. (1) The nuclear role which consists of the strategic deterrent (currently Polaris to be replaced by Trident) and theatre nuclear forces; aircraft, short-range missiles and artillery. (2) The direct defence of the United Kingdom involving sea, land and airforces. (3) The defence of the European mainland of which the British Army of the Rhine (BAOR) and RAF Germany are the main components. (4) Finally the maritime role, concentrated upon the Eastern Atlantic and Channel areas.

Upon returning to office in 1979 the Conservatives pledged that defence would be the 'first charge on our national resources'. The government accepted NATO's Long-Term Defence Programme which called for 3 per cent annual increases in real terms in defence expenditure. By 1985–6 the defence budget was one-fifth higher in real terms than in 1978–79. Britain was spending more on defence in absolute and *per capita* terms than any other NATO member except the United States. Even so resources were becoming inadequate to match roles and the cost of weapon systems. Qualitative improvements to weapon systems have resulted in spiralling costs in excess of inflation. In 1981 John Nott, Secretary of State for Defence, was charged with conducting a review of policy.

The Government Review, *The Way Forward* stressed that 'we cannot go on as we are' but failed to take the politically difficult decision to cut a defence role. The government maintained its commitment to nuclear deterrence and the purchase of Trident. The direct defence of the United Kingdom was not to be cut. The continental commitment with its high costs was considered with 'especial care' but was seen as 'so important to the Alliance's military posture and its political cohesion'. The Navy was the recipient of 57 per cent of planned cuts. The Review found that the size of the surface fleet could no longer be sustained, it was to be cut from 59 destroyers and frigates to 50. A new Carrier, the *Ark Royal*, would be completed but only two of the three ships in this class would be retained. The old *Hermes* carrier and the assault ships *Intrepid* and *Fearless* would be phased out. The Naval Base at Chatham would be closed and a 'very sharp reduction' made in the scope and volume of dockyard work at Portsmouth.

Many critics, in particular those advocating a non-nuclear conventional defence strategy, believed the cuts in the surface fleet were the price for Trident. Other critics, but supporters of the nuclear deterrent, sought a review of the continental commitment. The outbreak of the Falklands War in 1982 and the key role of the Navy in the conflict intensified criticism of government policy.

Britain failed to deter the Argentinian invasion of the Falkland Islands in April 1982. Naval cuts, not least the withdrawal of the Falklands patrol vessel *Endurance*, 'signalled' a low level of commitment. A diplomatic unwillingness to compromise on sovereignty led to Argentinian frustration then military action. Lord Carrington, Foreign Secretary, resigned in the face of 'national humiliation' and Mrs Thatcher was left to rescue her government's domestic credibility. The United States chose first to mediate between her two allies but with the failure of Haig's shuttle diplomacy America turned to support Britain. The shooting war began in earnest when the Argentine cruiser *Belgrano* was torpedoed on 2 May with the loss of

360 men. It has been argued by critics such as Tam Dalyell that the prime minister ordered the sinking of the *Belgrano* to save her political position. The sinking, it has been asserted, prevented Argentina accepting peace proposals from Peru. Though the *Belgrano* was outside the Exclusion Zone, sailing away from the Task Force when hit, the balance of evidence suggests British motives were military not political (Freedman, 1988). There can be little doubt however that Mrs Thatcher could not settle for less than a reassertion of British sovereignty, whatever the means, diplomatic or military, employed. The military success of British forces in the recapture of the islands was translated by the Prime Minister into political success at home.

Government policy after the Falklands War went some way to restoring the Navy's position. The assault ships and the *Endurance* were retained in service. The carrier *Invincible* was not sold to Australia and three vessels in this class retained. The 1982 Defence White Paper, further confirmed a surface fleet of 55 frigates and destroyers would be maintained. The White Paper made clear however that the government regarded the Falklands campaign to be 'unique' in many respects. The main defence priority remained NATO and the rationale of the 1981 Review fundamentally correct.

The Falklands War added new costs to the already stretched defence budget, an estimated £3.5 billion in total if war and garrison costs are combined. The 1988 White Paper recognised that the ending of the commitment to real growth in the budget 'inevitably means that difficult choices have to be made between priorities in our forward plans'. The government has sought greater efficiency and competitiveness in defence management and procurement but it is unlikely that these measures will resolve pressure on the budget. The inexorable growth in defence costs ensures major difficulties in sustaining the four major roles of present policy.

Hong Kong

Unlike the Falklands dispute a diplomatic solution has been found to resolve the future of Hong Kong. The colony has been claimed by the People's Republic of China (PRC) and with British leases on a significant portion of territory due to expire in 1997 a solution was needed. Negotiations began following Mrs Thatcher's visit to Beijing in 1982 and resulted in the Joint Declaration of 1984. The agreement provides that the PRC will take control on 1 July 1997 and make Hong Kong a Special Administrative Region. Hong Kong will be given a high degree of autonomy, except in foreign affairs and defence. Its current economic and social systems 'are to remain unchanged and so will the lifestyle'. In 1987 Deng Xiaoping the Chinese leader confirmed that the capitalist system would be kept in Hong Kong for another hundred years.

The confidence inspired by the 1984 agreement has been undermined by events in China in 1989. The brutal repression of the pro-democracy movement in Tiananmen Square in June 1989 raises the question of future democratic and civil rights in Hong Kong. The colony does not have an elected government but since June 1989 its leaders have pressed Britain for greater democracy before 1997. Beijing will provide a new constitution, the Basic Law, for Hong Kong in 1990. The Basic Law will be executive dominated and unlikely to make more than 30 per cent of seats in a future local assembly directly elected. Hong Kong leaders have been calling for 40 per cent of seats to the existing Legislative Council to be directly elected by 1995 and some have demanded 50 per cent by 1997. Britain's problem is to maintain political and economic confidence in Hong Kong whilst working with China. The difficulty is that confidence could be eroded by either British resistance to democratisation or a rift with China over policies that would conflict with the Basic Law.

Britain has sought to ease transition problems by two measures. Firstly to double the intended number of directly elected seats in the existing Legislative Council to 20 in 1991. Secondly to offer to 50,000 key personnel and their families, a total estimated at 225,000, full British passports. This would grant the right of abode in Britain, unlike the British National Overseas passports held by the majority of the 3m plus Hong Kong Chinese. The decision stands in stark contrast to that concerning the mandatory repatriation of Vietnamese boat people who fail to secure refugee status from Hong Kong camps. For some Conservative MPs the key issue is however, immigration, and the government's decision is seen to undermine immigration policy. The seriousness of backbench opposition was underlined by the fact that its leading spokesman was the former Chairman of the Conservative Party, Norman Tebbit.

Britain and the Commonwealth

The Commonwealth's status and significance received a major boost in 1979 when the Lusaka Conference produced a solution to the problem of Rhodesian independence. White minority rule in Rhodesia had survived international condemnation, sanctions and diplomatic initiatives. The major African nationalist groups had formed an alliance, the Patriotic Front (PF) and launched a guerrilla war against Ian Smith's regime. In 1978 a Rhodesian 'internal settlement' led to the establishment of a new government headed by Bishop Abel Muzorewa. Though boycotted by the PF Mrs Thatcher was sympathetic to the 'internal settlement' and recognition of the Muzorewa government appeared a possibility in 1979. The Foreign Secretary, Lord Carrington, however convinced the prime minister that she should seek a broader settlement including the PF and acceptable to the Commonwealth and international opinion. It was at the Lusaka Commonwealth Heads of Government Meeting (CHOGM) that agreement was reached on the appropriate measures for a settlement, a ceasefire, a constitutional conference and free elections. The Commonwealth sent an Observer Group to report on the electoral process and armed forces to monitor the ceasefire. The success of these measures resulted in Zimbabwe achieving legal independence in 1980.

The unity of purpose achieved at Lusaka has not been replicated. Britain has not shared the enthusiasm of the majority of the Commonwealth for structural reform of international economic management. A preference for market solutions and a pragmatic approach differs from predominant Third World strategies. It has however been debates upon the adoption of an appropriate strategy toward the Republic of South Africa, that has caused the greatest strain in Commonwealth relations.

African, Asian and Caribbean opinion has strongly favoured the adoption of economic sanctions against South Africa. Since the mid-1980s Australia, Canada and New Zealand have sided with the majority leaving Britain isolated on the sanctions issue. Mrs Thatcher has called for the abolition of apartheid but consistently rejected the application of sanctions. At the United Nations in 1987 and 1988, Britain (with the United States) vetoed resolutions calling for mandatory economic sanctions. Mrs Thatcher has declared sanctions 'immoral' and argued that they would cause 'unemployment and starvation' amongst those they are supposed to help.

The British alternative to sanctions has been 'dialogue', encouraging the reform process rather than 'isolating' the Republic by sanctions. This strategy has failed to secure Commonwealth support. Rising levels of violence and civil unrest in South Africa predicated demands for stronger responses. Attempts at advancing dialogue have also failed. The Commonwealth Eminent Persons' Group (EPG) visited South Africa in 1986; its report concludes, there is 'no genuine intention on the part of South Africa to dismantle apartheid'. The Nassau CHOGM which initiated the EPG also secured agreement that South Africa should commence immediate reforms; release Nelson Mandela (since released) and other detainees; lift the ban on the African National Congress (ANC) (since lifted); and that there should be a suspension of violence on all sides. It was further agreed to ban the import of

Krugerrands, cease government loans to South Africa and support for trade fairs in the Republic. Unanimity was not maintained however with Mrs Thatcher's swift rebuttal that she had 'conceded only a teeny, weeny bit'.

Diminishing the Nassau Accord can be questioned for diplomatic tact but more seriously for the 'message' Pretoria would receive. British policy has consequently been subject to growing criticism. In 1986 32 countries withdrew from the Commonwealth Games in Edinburgh, Scotland. The then Indian Prime Minister, Rajiv Ghandi, had pointed to Britain's significant economic interests in South Africa and suggested that Britain had 'compromised on basic values and principles for economic ends' (Keesing's, September 1986). Mrs Thatcher's claim at the Vancouver CHOGM that she was converting the majority to her strategy did little to reduce tensions. It was British action at Kuala Lumpur in 1989 however that has brought the most open criticism from other Commonwealth leaders. The summit secured British agreement that 'existing sanctions should not be diminished until fundamental change has taken place'. Mrs Thatcher then issued a separate British statement which criticised the Commonwealth approach and declared that Britain's proposals for ending apartheid were more constructive. The Australian Prime Minister, Bob Hawke, found Mrs Thatcher's statement 'unacceptable'; the President of Zimbabwe, Robert Mugabe said it was 'despicable' but perhaps the Canadian Prime Minister caught the mood best by saying 'when we sign a document at 5.00pm, we do not repudiate it at 6.00pm' *(Guardian, 24 October 1989)*.

Conclusions

British foreign and defence policy in the 1980s has exhibited strong elements of continuity with the past. Indeed under Mrs Thatcher policy continues to reflect what might be termed the 'old consensus'. Defence policy has been characterised by its orthodoxy, adherence to nuclear deterrence, to NATO and to the Anglo–American relationship (see Freedman, 1989). Britain's European policy has been firmly on the defensive with regard to sovereignty reminiscent of past attitudes to the EC and the cost of membership. The image of the 'reluctant European' has persisted with the emphasis the prime minister has placed on Anglo–American relations as 'special'. In the area of Soviet relations it is arguable that change to a balanced approach brings policy back into line with the past (White, 1988). The significance of the Commonwealth to British policy-makers should not be exaggerated by the Zimbabwe case; the institution's importance has been declining in the post-Suez era. It would be wrong to conclude that there has not been change; the Falklands War stands out as an aberration in the trend toward a European defence role. Mrs Thatcher's style and approach are moreover distinctive. 'Battles' in Europe have been followed by abrasive encounters with the Commonwealth. It is, though, the relative absence of change which is the most interesting feature of the 1980s. The degree to which old roles, values and attitudes have been maintained is striking. It remains to be seen how long Britain can afford to sustain the past; to stand apart from measures to manage growing interdependence in the EC; to stand between Europe and the United States and to fund an increasingly costly defence programme.

Conclusion

In the Introduction a number of questions were raised about the overall characteristics of public policy under Thatcher. To what extent has policy since 1979 been based on a coherent ideological platform from which policy reforms and initiatives have arisen? To what extent has the radicalism of rhetoric under Thatcher been matched by radicalism in actual policy? This leads to an overall assessment of the degree to which public policy since 1979 has constituted a departure from the pre-1979 period of the so-called 'post-war consensus'.

The chapters contained in this volume hopefully allow the reader to reach some form of conclusion on issues such as these. Without ourselves offering a definitive response on each, there are certain points on which it is possible to reach a generalisation. Firstly, very much depends on the area of policy in question. The discussions contained in this book reach different conclusions on the impact of the Thatcher governments in specific policy areas. At the risk of over-simplification, one might group these conclusions under three headings. Firstly, there are those areas of policy which may be said to have undergone serious and even radical transformation during the Thatcher years. Under this category one could include privatisation policy, trade union reforms, local government and housing provision. Secondly, there are those areas of policy which may be seen as containing, if not the evidence of radicalism, then at least the potential for radical change in the near future. Under this grouping are education policy, social security, personal social services, and enterprise policy. In these cases, the reality of policy may not, as yet, have matched up to the rhetoric, but nevertheless, major reforms of strategy have been indicated in plans for the near future. The third heading contains those aspects of policy which may be seen as constituting a continuity, rather than radical break, from policy prior to 1979. Examples of this are foreign and defence policy, policy toward Northern Ireland, and law and order. This is not to deny that 'nothing has changed' in these policy areas – that would be most unlikely during any ten-year period of government – and it certainly does not imply that elements of a distinctive approach to policy have not been apparent in each. What it does mean is that there is every liklehood that had another party been in power, then the development of policy in the sense of the underlying direction of reform might very well have taken a similar form. To these categories we might also add an area in which policy has been largely absent, and in that sense environmental policy, as discussed in Chapter 5, is a good example.

A second set of questions relates closely to that of the degree of 'radicalism' of the Thatcher governments. It concerns the issue of how far one might be able to 'periodize' the Thatcher governments according to what have been changing priorities over the three administrations – for example, one might argue that industrial relations were a priority in the first, privatisation in the second, and social policy and local government in the third. Such summaries of the three periods of public policy must be treated with caution (see Jessop *et al.,* 1988, pp. 11–20), but they are interesting questions for the reader, on the basis of a study of the various aspects of policy, to consider. On the other hand, it does also raise the issue of whether, as Riddell and others have argued, the radicalism of the Thatcher governements, while less than apparent in the early years, has grown with the continuing period in office (Riddell, 1989, pp. 11–12). In turn the reader is asked to consider whether this is an example of an ideology coming into fruition, or rather a result of a diminishing opposition, both outside and inside of the Conservative Party, and as such a political rather than ideological process (see Chapter 1).

In addition to raising these questions, and hopefully providing the reader with the material to answer them, the book has also addressed issues relating to the future of public policy into the 1990s. Clearly, in a range of areas, new or emergent policies are on the agenda, which may set the tone for public policy in the new decade, and where these exist the chapter has discussed their potential impact in the area(s) concerned. In that sense the future of public policy is, at least in the medium term, reasonably predictable. However, that begs the question of the nature of the political horizon. At the time of writing, the prospect of a future government without Thatcher is no longer a distant possibility. The Labour Party appears in better shape, and has attracted more public support, as reflected in the opinion polls and in the striking by-election victory in Mid-Staffordshire, than it has for some considerable time. While the political cards may still be stacked against a future Labour government, even with the collapse of the centre parties witnessed in recent years, the nature of public policy under a possible future Labour government is increasingly under attention.

On that basis, we might then ask what evidence we have of the likely shape of such policy. Understandably, that picture is none too clear. Nevertheless, on the basis of statements already made, and given the documents which have emerged under Labour's Policy Review, a number of interesting points seem apparent. Firstly, that despite Labour's commitment to expanding state provision in a range of policy areas – particularly, it would seem, education and health – it will not enter the next Election with a open policy of massive increases in public expenditure. Labour has begun to make it clear that public expenditure increases will operate according to a ranking of areas of priority spending, and with full cognisance of the amount of resources available to the public purse. It would appear that a tight rein is to be kept on public expenditure. Secondly, the Review documents stress two approaches to policy not visible in early Labour strategies, inside and outside of government: decentralisation of services and greater attention to consumer wishes and rights in public service provision (see Labour Party, 1989). Thirdly, those same documents are not afraid to state the virtues of managerial effeciency and cost-effectiveness in the operation and accountability of public services and benefits.

These emphases indicate that the Labour Party has undergone some major reconsiderations of its own previous strategies for public policy, and moved toward an approach which, one is tempted to add, bear at least some of the hallmarks of public policy of the 1980s. One interpretation of this is that Labour has become convinced of at least some of the elements of the Thatcherism. Another is that, perhaps, had Labour itself enjoyed periods of office in the 1980s, it too might have gone down many of the paths which the Thatcher governments have travelled, not because of any emergent right-wing tendencies in the party, but rather because of the perceived need, already apparent in Denis Healey's stewardship at the Treasury during the 1974–9 Labour government, to cut back on public expenditure. Indeed there are some (see Riddell, 1983), who consider that the shift in post-war politics began before, not after, Thatcher came into office.

Of course, the key factor in the debate about the likely future of public policy is the political context as it develops in the early 1990s. That in turn rests on the public's perception of the effect of Thatcherite policies, primarily on the economic front, but also in sensitive areas such as education, health and the poll tax. The impact of such policies may determine not only the chances of electoral victory for Labour, but also the future of Thatcher herself as leader of the Conservative Party. In 1989 Mrs. Thatcher faced her first rival for the post of party leader in the shape of Sir Anthony Meyer, a little known Tory backbencher. The prime minister's supporters celebrated her massive victory over what was clearly a 'stalking horse' candidate, whilst her critics noted that she had failed to win the backing of one in six Conservative MPs. Whichever way, the campaign opened up the whole issue of the possibility of a Conservative Party without Thatcher – one which, should economic strategy and other measures be seen to fail, can only grow and grow. The choice for her successor, should that transpire, will almost certainly be made from a select list of candidates.

Kenneth Baker, now Party Chairman, would be a prime candidate, although since he is the architect of many Thatcher reforms in local government and education, his star seems likely to rise or fall with the fortunes of the government. Were he to succeed, despite his earlier preference for more modest policies, any radical direction of policy would most likely continue. The same would apply to another candidate, John Major, who, while notably pragmatic is certain respects (for example his support for British entry into the EMS), is still very much a Thatcher protegé. Both Baker and Major would be favourites to succeed Thatcher if the Tories were to win the next election.

An electoral defeat seems likely to swing the grassroot Tory opinion towards Michael Heseltine, certainly no Thatcherite. The greater the defeat, the greater the chances of him becoming leader. Heseltine has made no secret of his disapproval of many of Thatcher's policies, and her style of leadership (on the basis of which he resigned from the Cabinet when Defence Secretary in 1986). It is he, more than any other front runner, who has attempted to offer a vision of Conservatism markedly different to that cast by Margaret Thatcher. Were he to become the next leader of the Party, the politics of Thatcherism would be well and truly a thing of the past.

Guide to Further Reading

Chapter 1 Government During the Thatcher Years

Greenwood and Wilson (1989) provide what is perhaps the best general introduction to the issues raised in this chapter, and Drucker *et al.* (1988) or its replacement Dunleavy *et al.* (1990) offer a useful accompaniment. Concerning central government the White Papers *Efficiency in the Civil Service* (Cmnd 8293, 1981) and *Efficiency and Effectiveness in the Civil Service* (Cmnd 8616, 1982) outline the government's views on reform of the civil service's management methods and the Ibbs Report is essential reading. As regards local government, Stewart and Stoker (1989) offer a stimulating collection of essays. Nugent (1989) provides a clear and readable introduction to the EC.

Chapter 2 Economic Policy and Privatisation

Cairncross and Keeley (1987) is a very readable guide to economic developments under Thatcher for non-economists. Allen and Massey (1988) provides a useful overview of the changing industrial face of the UK in the 1970s and 1980s. Green (1989) offers a challenging interpretation of the economics and politics of Thatcher's economic strategy. Swann (1988) provides an accessible overview of changing views of the role of the state in production and regulation, and Vane and Caslin (1987) offers a fairly advanced account of the economic theory underpinning Thatcher's economic policy. Kay (1989) is a good text for providing a broad review of the main economic issues.

Chapter 3 Towards an Enterprise Culture? Industrial and Training Policy

A general introduction to the idea of an 'enterprise culture' may be found in Logan-Turner (1990). Useful, though somewhat difficult, discussions of industrial policy may be found in Gibbs (1989), and Thompson (1989). Duchene and Shepherd (1987) provides a European perspective on industrial policy; Parsons (1986) offers an overview of the development of regional policy since the 1930s. For up-to-date details of and debates about the government's training and enterprise schemes, see the Unemployment Unit's 'Bulletins' and 'Briefings', and the Department of Employment *Gazette*. For a discussion of the background to and political struggle around the introduction of ET see Lupton (1989).

Chapter 4   Trade Union Policy 1979–89: Restriction or Reform?

Gamble (1988), examines the politics of Conservatism during the 1980s and discusses the ideas of the 'new right' in British politics and their relationship to the Conservative tradition. MacInnes (1987), analyses the breakdown of consensus politics and the industrial relations consensus and the rise of the Thatcherite alternative, and also explores the effects of Thatcherite policies on industrial relations and people at work. Lewis (1986), is a wide-ranging collection of essays on all aspects of employment law set in their socio-economic, international and comparative contexts. Wedderburn (1986) is a scholarly and comprehensive analysis of British labour law which examines its development, the role of the law in society and the controversies surrounding employment. Farnham and Pimlott (1990) is a useful text for students who want to read more widely on industrial relations; it provides an up-to-date discussion of British industrial relations in their political, historical, economic and social context.

Chapter 5   Environmental Policy

The scientific background to environmental problems is introduced gently in Myers (1985). Some of the wider issues of environmental policy are developed further in O'Riordan (1976) and Sandbach (1980). More detailed studies of principles and practice are to be found in Mitchell (1989) and Sandbach (1982). The agriculture and countryside debate was fired by Shoard (1980); this remains a good if partisan introduction. A crucial source for following European legislation on the environment is Haigh (1989). Other reviews of environmental policy in the 1980s are Blowers (1987) and Lowe and Flynn (1989).

Chapter 6   A War on Crime? Law and Order Policies in the 1980s

For a detailed breakdown of the Criminal Justice Act 1987 and 1988 see Morton (1988). A useful overview of the development of penal policy since the Second World War is Ryan (1983). As regards developments in and issues concerning policing policy and practice, Reiner (1985) remains the outstanding text, and offers the reader a gentle introduction to the field. Benyon and Bourn (1986) contains a wide range of views on policing, with particular reference to the Police and Criminal Evidence Act 1984.

Chapter 7   Health Policy

For basic background reading, Allsop (1984), Ham (1985) can be recommended. The NHS Review itself, *Working for Patients*, provides the contemporary picture. Its background is covered by Timmins (1988), while an interesting series of reactions are reported in BMA (1989).

Chapter 8   Housing Policy in the Thatcher Years

Essential reading for anyone concerned with housing is the report of the Committee chaired by the Duke of Edinburgh – Inquiry into British Housing (1985). Minford *et al.* (1987) provide a thoroughgoing analysis of housing from a 'New Right' perspective. Housing Centre Trust (1987) offers a critical commentary on the government's own 1987 White Paper. Commentaries on the Housing Act 1988 may be found in Ginsburg (1989). An alternative housing strategy, from a Labour perspective, is mapped out in Clapham (1989).

Chapter 9   Education Policy: Education as a Business?

Hewton (1986) is a very readable, short text which addresses the question 'how does the education service deal with the problems of contraction?' Education has lost the political popularity it once enjoyed, has faced significant cuts in funding over the past ten years and exists within a difficult economic environment. These factors put the education service under great strain. MacLure (1988) is a section-by-section guide to the 1988 ERA, together with a commentary from the author. It is readable and comprehensive. McNay and Ozga (1985) is a collection of articles used as a part of an Open University Course (E333, Policy-making in Education). It offers a range of approaches to the study of educational policy-making against the background of the major policy developments of the mid-1980s. Although a little dated now, it still contains a wealth of material. The contributions by Kogan, Demison, Salter and Tapper and Parkes are particularly relevant.

Chapter 10   'A Caring Community'? Personal Social Services Policy in the 1980s

For a brief and very readable account of major issues of debate over community care, see Griffiths (1988). A more theoretical, and critical, account of community care can be found in Walker and Walker (1987); for illustration of the major questions in the area of child abuse and child protection, there is no substitute for consulting the official reports into specific incidents cases. (See Butler-Sloss, 1988, and Blom-Cooper, 1985, reporting on the Cleveland and Jasmine Beckford cases respectively.

Chapter 11   From Beveridge to the Dependency Culture: Social Security Policy

Alcock (1987) is a comprehensive history of the development of social security policy in post-war Britain up to the Fowler review; it also discusses the problems and contradictions of benefit provision. Becker and MacPherson (1988) contains articles by academics and professionals working with the poor on the impact of the April 1988 social security reforms and the social fund.

Esam and Oppenheim (1989) is a study of the effects of the poll tax and recent social security changes on the poor and how they will further lose out; it also explores the changing relationships between local authorities and local poor people. Green (1987) is a sympathetic introduction to neo-liberal thought; it concludes with a look at its political impact on a variety of policy areas including social security. Walker and Walker (1987) contains writings on the impact of government policies on the poor across several dimensions including unemployment, North–South divide, women and ethnic minorities. Ward (1985) is a collection of essays on such things as DHSS staff under pressure, the implementation of the housing benefit scheme, boarders, young people and fraud investigation.

Chapter 12   Local Government 1979–89: A Decade of Change

Duncan and Goodwin (1988) focuses on the changes in central–local relations since 1976 with a good analysis of inner city policies. Gyford, Leach and Game (1989) is an account of current local government politics based upon the authors' research for the Widdecombe Committee. Stewart and Stoker (1989) is a collection of essays which examines the changes in local government since 1979 and suggests scenarios of the future.

Chapter 13   Equal Opportunities in a Cold Climate

Bryan *et al.* (1985) is an important text which helps redress the marginalisation of black women in much literature on race and racism in Britain; it offers a good overview of the position and experience of black women in a number of different institutional areas. Beechey and Whitelegg (1986) offers a good introductory analysis of women's position in British society through an examination of four key areas – the family, employment, education and health. Gregory (1987) is the best available introduction to the anti-discrimination legislation, exceptional in that it combines together a lucid analysis of the sex and race legislation. Solomos (1989) is an excellent up-to-date textbook which is outstanding in its field. It argues a cogent case for the racialisation of British politics since the 1960s, and for the symbolic character of much that is done in the name of racial equality. Lewis (1988) is a polemical, New Right attack on anti-racism and the 'race relations industry', and it contains a controversial foreword by Enoch Powell.

Chapter 14   'The Right to Know': Government and Information

For a stimulating account of the Ponting Trial see Ponting (1985). Chapman and Hunt (1987) is a good overview of the issue of 'open government', and Wacks (1989) provides a detailed study of the law on personal information. Hooper (1987) offers a stimulating discussion of official secrets. On government statistics see Slattery (1986) for a broad coverage of the manipulation of information, and Radical Statistics Health Group (1987) for a specific analysis of health statistics. Cornwell and Staunton (1985) discuss the civil liberties' implications of data protection.

Chapter 15 Beyond Political Stalemate: New Thinking on Northern Ireland

Arthur and Jeffrey (1988) is a good introductory book which also contains, in an Appendix, the full text of the Anglo–Irish Agreement. It is also to be recommended for its summary of Catholic and Protestant politics. Bew and Patterson 1987) is an excellent article within a stimulating collection of essays that focus on the economic and social background to the troubles. Flackes and Elliot (1989) contains a chronology of events, dictionary of key characters, parties and organisations, and sections on election results, the security system, and so on. The journal *Fortnight* is an excellent source of political debate on Northern Ireland covering all perspectives on the current situation. Rowthorn and Wayne (1988) provides an excellent account of the economics in the North and the Republic; the text also gives a coherent argument for withdrawal, which can however be separated from the economic analysis.

Chapter 16 Foreign and Defence Policies: The Impact of Thatcherism

Kennedy (1981) is a study of the decline of Britain's power since 1865, an analysis of the relationship between Britain's changing economic position and its foreign policy. Divided into historical eras, the text offers a clear series of surveys within an overall theme. Northedge (1974) contains a comprehensive account of post-war British foreign policy; a standard general text which stresses the decline in Britain's international position and the growth of constraints upon decision makers. Smith *et al.* (1988) is a particularly useful publication which provides an introduction to competing analyses of British foreign policy. Specific issue areas in British external relations are discussed, including defence policy, external economic policy, East–West relations, Western Europe and North–South Relations.

Appendix 1
Legislation 1979–89

This Appendix provides a brief summary of the contents of the major pieces of legislation affecting local government in England and Wales which were enacted during the first decade of the Thatcher Government (1979–89).

General Local Government

1980 Local Government, Planning and Land Act

This Act is 'five acts in one'. It removed hundreds of controls over local authorities; repealed the Community Land Act and amended the law relating to planning; provided for the creation of urban development corporations (UDCs) and enterprise zones (EZs); introduced a new block grant and required local authorities to provide information and access to the public.

1981 Local Government (Miscellaneous Provisions Scotland) Act

This Act gave the Secretary of State virtual direct control over expenditure of each Scottish local authority. It gave powers to reduce grants for excessive and unreasonable expenditure and to prohibit council borrowing without permission. This paved the way for similar controls to be introduced in England and Wales.

1982 Local Government Finance Act

This increased central control by enabling the Secretary of State for the Environment to impose expenditure targets and to claw back grants from overspending authorities: the Act applied retrospectively; it also abolished supplementary rates and precepts and set up the Audit Commission to audit the accounts of local authorities and other bodies.

1982 Local Government and Planning (Scotland) Act

This gave the Scottish Office power to impose rate poundages on councils 'guilty of excessive and unreasonable expenditure' i.e. rate-

254

capping, once again a policy which was subsequently extended to England and Wales.

1982 Local Government (Miscellaneous Provisions) Act

This act amends a range of existing legislation relating to control of sex establishments, refreshment premises, fire precautions, land charge registers and sections of the Local Government Act 1972, Training Act 1973 and Highway Act 1980.

1983 Local Authorities (Expenditure Powers) Act

This removed certain restrictions on the powers of local authorities to spend money.

1984 Rates Act

This introduced rate-capping in England and Wales, two years after it had been used in Scotland.

1984 Local Government (Interim Provisions) Act

This 'paving' Act preceded the abolition of the Metropolitan Counties. It prolonged the lives of the existing councils for one year after an initial attempt to disband them. It established a Commission for safeguarding the interests of local government staff of the Metropolitan Counties and gave the Secretary of State authority to control the general expenditure powers of the councils prior to abolition.

1985 Local Government Act

This abolished the GLC and the six Metropolitan Counties and transferred their functions to districts or boroughs, and in some cases to newly created boards.

1985 Local Government (Access to Information) Act

This provides for public access to council meetings, reports and documents and requires councils to publish details of councillors.

1986 Local Government Act

This placed restrictions on the type of publicity local authorities can produce, restricted the sale of mortgage debt and outlawed the use of

deferred purchase arrangements to circumvent creative accounting by some local authorities. It also required all rating authorities to set a rate on or before 1 April.

1986 Rate Support Grants Act

This Act had retrospective effect and was passed to negate the High Court's decision in 1986 (*R* v. *Secretary of State for the Environment*) that the way in which part of the block grant system had been operated since 1981 was *ultra vires* ('beyond the powers').

1987 Local Government Finance Act

This Act retrospectively legalised government's past decisions relating to local government spending; it removed the right of appeal and judicial review of ministerial decisions relating to grant and accounting practices. It also required local authorities to keep separate accounts including a rate fund revenue account.

1987 Local Government Act

This was introduced to amend Part VIII of the 1980 Local Government, Planning and Land Act, and in particular to make new provisions for the payment of block grant in connection with education.

1987 Abolition of Domestic Rates (Scotland) Act

This Act replaced the rating system in Scotland with the CC. The policy was later applied to England (see below).

1988 Local Government Act

This Act requires local authorities to extend competitive tendering to listed activities; it gives the Secretary of State power to add to the list and to set financial objectives for local authority 'in house' contracts. Local authorities are required to disclose reasons for excluding contractors and to exclude all non-commercial matters when entering into contracts. The Act also in section 28 prohibits the intentional promotion of homosexuality whether by teaching or publication of material.

1988 Local Government Finance Act

This Act followed the government Green Paper *Paying for Local Government* (Cmnd 9714, 1986). It replaced the rating system with a new system of local government finance including the CC, the NNDR and a new RSG. It came into effect on 1 April 1990.

1988 Rate Support Grants Act

The Act set out the new procedures for calculating the block·grant for the remaining years of the rate support grant system, i.e. up until 1989–90. It was the thirteenth change in the period since 1979.

1989 Local Government and Housing Act

This is a compendious Act which followed the publication of the Government's Responses to the Widdicombe Report of *The Conduct of Local Authority Business*. It imposes political restrictions on senior local government officers and sets down new rules for the appointment of staff. It defines the voting rights of members of committees and prescribes their composition. In addition it establishes schemes for payment of councillors and for registering of members' 'interests'. It sets up Commissions for Local Administration to report on good and bad practice. Part III of the Act relates to economic development, Parts IV and V to revenue and capital accounts and to the introduction of credit ceilings for local government borrowing. Part II of the Act relates to housing and introduces a new financial system which gives central control over rents, investment, borrowing and repayment of outstanding debt.

Housing Legislation

1980 Housing Act

This introduced the 'right to buy' for council tenants of three of more years' standing. It enforced rent increases, transferred rent controlled properties to rent regulation and was designed to revive the private rented sector.

1982 Social Security and Housing Benefits Act

This transferred the responsibility for assessing and paying housing benefit to local housing authorities.

1983 Social Security and Housing Benefits Act

This introduced amendments to the 1982 Act.

1984 Housing and Buildings Control Act

This further extended the right to buy to tenants of development corporations and to those living in 'flats'. It also relaxed building regulations and building control.

1985 Housing Act

This Act, together with the 1985 Housing Associations Act and Landlord and Tenants Act (see below) consolidates previous housing legislation to give effect to the recommendations of the Law Commission. It has 23 schedules and covers all aspects of housing law.

1985 Housing (Consequential Provisions) Act

This Act supplements the 1985 Housing Act, providing for repeals of earlier legislation.

1985 Housing Associations Act

This consolidates certain provisions of the Housing Acts relating to housing associations with amendment to give effect to the Law Commission's recommendations. It defines terms, identifies powers and establishes the role of the Housing Corporation.

1985 Landlord and Tenants Act

This deals with information landlords must give to tenants, rent books, and the obligations of landlord. It also gives a reserve power to the Secretary of State to limit rents.

1986 Housing and Planning Act

This Act excepted from the right to buy dwellings suitable for elderly people, increased the discount and reduced the repayment period on council house sales and introduced government grants to new managers of public sector housing. It was generally designed to encourage more council tenants to exercise their right to buy and to facilitate sales of publicly owned dwellings *en bloc* to privately funded bodies.

1987 Landlord and Planning Act

This Act extends the rights of tenants where landlords wish to transfer ownership, and sets down information which must be supplied to tenants.

1988 Housing Act

This followed the White Paper *Housing: the Government's Proposals* (Cm 14, 1987). It removes the right of security of tenancy in rented accommodation; establishes a new body, Housing for Wales which, with the Housing Corporation can issue guidance to Housing Associations. It gives power to the Secretary of State to create Housing Action Trusts (HATs) to own, manage and dispose of public housing and to exercise the housing, planning control and public health functions of local authorities. It also provides for tenants to transfer with their existing homes to a new landlord.

1989 Local Government and Housing Act

This introduced a new system of housing finance with controls over revenue and capital expenditure (see above).

Education

1979 Education Act

This Act removed the duty to provide for 'comprehensive education' by repeal of the Education Act 1976.

1980 Education Act

The Act introduced 'parental choice', extended the role and composition of school governors, required all schools to provide published information, gave new powers to local government electors to object to reorganisation or closure of schools, reintroduced assisted places and enabled local authorities to provide nursery education, day nurseries and school meals. It also made teaching qualifications a requirement for Further Education teachers.

1981 Education Act

The Act made provision for children with special education needs.

1983 Education (Fees and Awards) Act

This gave the Secretary of State powers to set the fees for overseas students and the rules relating to discretionary awards.

1984 Education (Grants and Awards) Act

This made provision for new regulations covering the payment of education support grants to LEAs.

1985 Further Education Act

This enables LEAs to supply goods and services through Further Education establishments and to make loans to such bodies for that purpose.

1986 Education (Amendment) Act

This amended the 1984 Education (Grants and Awards) Act to provide for an increase in education support grants.

1986 Education Act

This Act amended the system for making grants to designated bodies and for the pooling of expenditure by local authorities on education.

1986 Education (No. 2) Act

This Act is based on the Green Paper *Parental Influences at School* (Cmnd 9242, 1984) and the White Paper *Better Schools* (Cmnd 9469, 1985). It relates to school government and covers the composition of governing bodies, the respective roles of the governing body, the LEA and the head teacher. Other sections refer to freedom of speech in Higher Education institutions, teacher appraisal, the abolition of the Central Advisory Councils and grants for teacher training.

1987 Teachers' Pay and Conditions Act

This Act suspended the Burnham procedures for collective bargaining of teacher's salaries and gave interim powers to the minister to establish a pay review body.

1988 Education Reform Act

This Act makes radical changes to the law relating to education. It introduces the national curriculum, extends parental rights, transfers the management of most schools to head teachers and Boards of Governors, provides for schools to opt out of local authority control and for the creation of CTCs. It also abolished ILEA.

Miscellaneous

1980 Transport Act

This Act made it easier for new and private sector operators to gain licences to provide bus services. The act also established three trial areas for deregulation.

1980 Child Care Act

This was a consolidation Act which brought together previous legislation relating to the care of children by local authorities or voluntary organisations.

1980 Foster Children Act

This was another consolidation Act which clarified the law in relation to fostering and complemented the 1980 Child Care Act.

1981 Disabled Persons Act

This Act placed duties on highway authorities, planning authorities and all local authorities to ensure that the needs of disabled people were catered for in accessing and using buildings and premises.

1981 New Towns Act

This legislation consolidated previous acts relating to new towns, set down the powers of the minister to create new towns and specified the powers of development corporations and the Commission on New Towns. It also provided for the dissolution of New Town Corporations and the transfer of their assets to local authorities.

1982 Children's Homes Act

This Act set down the rules relating to the registration, inspection and conduct of 'children's homes'. These included boarding schools but excluded community homes and other specified institutions.

1983 Representation of the Peoples Act

This consolidated previous legislation and set down the parliamentary and local government franchise, provisions for registration and rules governing the conduct of elections, publicity at elections, definitions of illegal practices and the conduct of the poll.

1984 Data Protection Act

All holders and users of computerised personal information including local authorities are required by the act to register their database and its use with a DPR. Eight principles are established to guide users. The public are entitled to access on payment of a fee.

1984 Registered Homes Act

This legislation was another consolidation Act which set down the rules relating to the registration and inspection of residential care homes and nursing homes. It relates to standards and minimum requirements for registration and deregulation and establishes registered homes tribunals for appeal.

1984 London Regional Transport Act

This Act replace the London Transport Executive with London Regional Transport, a public corporation which comes under the control of the Secretary of State for Transport.

1984 Public Health Control of Disease Act

This clarifies the powers and duties of public health authorities in relation to the control of diseases, inspection of lodging houses and control of burial grounds and crematoria. It gives powers to the Secretary of State to create port health authorities.

1984 Town and Country Planning Act

This Act, which relates to the disposal of Crown land with planning permission and the actions which may follow unauthorised development, applies to local planning authorities.

1984 Building Act

Yet another consolidation Act covering the powers and duties of local authorities in the control of building standards, etc.

1985 Transport Act

This Act extended the deregulation of passenger transport throughout Britain, excluding London. The system of licensing was abolished and replaced by a registration system. It required all Passenger Transport Executives and district councils operating bus undertakings to form themselves into companies which would operate as businesses. There was provision for the privatisation of the National Bus Company. The Act provided for local authorities to subsidise unprofitable but socially desirable routes.

1985 New Towns and Urban Development Corporations Act

This extended the powers of the Commission for the New Towns to take over and dispose of the property of the New Towns corporations and authorised the Secretary of State to terminate the Commission. It also amended the New Towns Act 1981 regarding the transfer of housing to district councils.

1986 Children and Young Persons (Amendment) Act

This was a further Act to amend the law in relation to children and young people in care. In particular it gave the Secretary of State power to make regulations covering to accommodation of children in care and the procedures to be followed by local authorities.

1986 Family Law Act

Another amendment Act covering the custody of children and restrictions on the removal of children from the United Kingdom.

1986 Disabled Persons (Services, Consultation and Representation) Act

This Act provides for the improvement of services for people with mental or physical handicaps and for the mentally ill. Local authorities are obliged to provide services to cater for the needs of the disabled including special education for children and young people and support for people leaving long-stay hospitals. The Act also gives further powers to the Secretary of State to make regulations relating to the representation of disabled persons by relations or other advocates.

1986 Airports Act

This legislation required local authorities operating an airport as a commercial undertaking to set up a public airport company and to transfer the ownership of the airport to the company.

1987 Fire Safety and Safety of Places of Sports Act

Following the fire at Bradford football ground in which nearly 100 people died, this legislation strengthened the law relating to fire precautions and imposed new responsibilities upon fire authorities in issuing safety certificates.

1988 Environment and Safety Information Act

This Act requires all authorities to establish public registers of notices served concerning health, safety and environmental protection. The public has the right of access to all such registers free of charge.

1989 Parking Act

This short Act amended the powers relating to parking under the Road Traffic Regulation Act 1984. It also covered offences and proceedings in connection with parking places provided by local authorities.

1989 Children Act

A further Act to reform the law relating to children; to provide for local authority services for children in need, to amend the law relating to voluntary organisations, voluntary homes, community homes and children's homes; and the law relating to fostering, child minding and day care for young children and adoption. It also sets out the Secretary of State's functions and responsibilities and extends the power to make regulations relating to all the areas covered by the Act.

1989 Pesticides (Fees and Enforcement) Act

A small Act affecting the powers of local authorities as environmental protection agencies.

Appendix 2

Rate-capped authorities 1985–6 to 1989–90

1985–6	1986–7	1987–8	1988–9	1989–90
Basildon	Basildon	Basildon	Basildon	Camden
Brent	Camden	Brent	Camden	Greenwich
Camden	Greenwich	Brighton	Ealing	Hackney
GLC	Hackney	Camden	Greenwich	Lewisham
Greenwich	Haringey	Gateshead	Hackney	Southwick
Hackney	Islington	Greenwich	Haringey	Thamesdown
Haringey	Lambeth	Hackney	Kingston upon Hull	Tower Hamlets
ILEA	Lewisham	Haringey	Lambeth	
Islington	Liverpool	Islington	Lewisham	
Lambeth	Newcastle	Lambeth	Liverpool	
Leicester	Southwark	Lewisham	Manchester	
Lewisham	Thamesdown	Middlesborough	Middlesborough	
Merseyside		Newcastle	Newcastle	
Portsmouth		Newham	Southwick	
Sheffield		North Tyneside	Thamesdown	
South Yorkshire		Sheffield	Tower Hamlets	
Thamesdown		Thamesdown	Walton Forest	
		Tower Hamlets		

In addition to these elected local authorities from 1986–7 all the Joint Boards appointed in the Metropolitan Areas following abolition and the ILEA were capped.

Bibliography

Advisory Conciliation and Arbitration Service (ACAS) (1987) *Annual Report 1986* (London: ACAS).

Advisory Conciliation and Arbitration Service (ACAS) (1988) *Annual Report 19867 (London: ACAS).*

Alcock, P. (1987) *Poverty and State Support* (London: Harlow).

Aldington, Lord (1986) 'Britain's Manufacturing Industry', *Royal Bank of Scotland Review*, 151, pp. 3–13.

Allen, J. and Massey, D. (eds) (1988) *The Economy in Question: Restructuring Britain* (Milton Keynes: Sage/Open University).

Allsop, J. (1984) *Health Policy and the NHS* (London: ACAS).

Anderson, D., Lait, J. and Marsland, D. (1983) *Breaking the Spell of the Welfare State* (London: Centre for Policy Studies).

Arthur, P. and Jeffrey, K. (1988) *Northern Inreland: The Political Economy of Conflict* (Oxford: Polity Press)

Atkins, S. (1986) 'The Sex Discrimination Act of 1975: The End of a Decade', *Feminist Review*, 24, pp. 57–70.

Audit Commission (1986) *Making a Reality of Community Care* (London: HMSO).

Aughey, A. (1989) 'The Politics of Equal Citizenship', *Talking Politics*, 2(1) (Autumn).

Barclay, P. (1982) *Social Workers: Their Role and Tasks: Report of a Working Party* (London: Bedford Square Press).

Becker, S. and MacPherson, S. (eds) (1988) *Public Issues Private Pain: Poverty, Social Work and Social Policy* (London: Insight).

Beechey, V. and Whitelegg, E. (eds) (1986) *Women in Britain Today (Milton Keynes: Open University Press).*

Bell D. (1973) *The Coming of the Post Industrial Society* (New York: Basic Books).

Benyon, J.and Bourn, C.(eds) (1986) *The Police: Powers, Procedures, and Proprieties* (Oxford: Pergamon Press).

Bew, P. and Patterson, H. (1987) 'The New Stalemate: Unionism and the Anglo–Irish Agreement', in Teague, P. (ed.), *Beyond The Rhetoric* (London: Lawrence & Wishart).

Birkinshaw, P. (1988) *Freedom of Information: The Law, The Practice and the Ideal* (London: Weidenfield & Nicolson).

Bishop, M. and Kay, J. (1988) *Does Privatisation Work?* (London: London Business School).

Blom-Cooper, L. (1985) Report of the Committee of Inquiry into the Death of Jasmine Beckford (London: Borough of Brent).

Blowers, A. (1987) 'Transition or Transformation? Environmental Policy Under Thatcher', *Public Administration*, 65, pp. 277–94.

BMA (eds) (1989) *The NHS Review: What it Means* (London: BMA Books).

Boyle, K. and Hadden, T. (1989)   *The Anglo–Irish Agreement* (London: Sweet & Maxwell).

Bryan, B. Dadzie, S. and Scafa, S. (1985)   *The Heart of the Race: Black Women's Lives in Britain (London: Virago).*

Butler-Sloss, L. (1988)   *Report of the Inquiry into Child Abuse in Cleveland 1987* (London: HMSO).

Cairncross, F. and Keeley, P. (1987)   *Guide to the Economy: Vol. 3* (London: Methuen).

Camps, M. (1964)   *Britain and the European Community 1955–1963* (Oxford: Oxford University Press).

Carson R. (1962)   *Silent Spring* (London: Hamish Hamilton).

Certification Office (CO) (1981)   *Annual Report of the Certification Officer 1980* (London: CO).

Certification Office (CO) (1989)   *Annual Report of the Certification Officer 1988* (London: CO).

Chapman, R. and Hunt, M. (eds) (1987)   *Open Government: A Study of the Prospects of Open Government Within the Limitations of the British Political System* (London: Croom Helm).

Christian, L. (1983)   *Policing by Coercion* (London: GLC).

Civil Service Commission (1988)   *Government Statisticians: Civil Service Careers* (Hampshire: Folio Advertising).

Clapham, D. (1989)   *Goodbye Coucil Housing?* (London: Unwin Hyman).

Commission of the European Communities (CEC) (1989)   *Background Report* (ISEC/B25/89) (London: CEC).

Connolly, M. (1989)   *Politics and Policy Making in Northern Ireland* (London: Prentice-Hall).

Cook, R. (1988)   *Questions of Health* (London: Labour Party).

Cornwell, R. and Staunton, M. (1985)   *Data Protection: Putting the Record Straight* (London: National Council for Civil Liberties).

Coussins, J. (1976)   *The Equality Report* (London: National Council for Civil Liberties).

Cox, C. and Dyson, A. E. (1971)   *The Black Papers on Education* (London: Davis-Poynters).

Coyle, A. (1989)   'The Limits of Change: Local Government and Local Equal Opportunities for Women', *Public Administration*, 67, p. 50.

Crenson M. (1972)   *The Un-Politics of Air Pollution* (Baltimore: Johns Hopkins University Press).

Crosland, A. (1956)   *The Future of Socialism* (London: Cape).

Daltrop A. (1982)   *Politics and the European Community* (London: Longman).

Damestick, P. and Wood, P. (eds) (1987)   *Regional Problem, Problem Regions and Public Policy* (Oxford: Clarendon Press).

Data Protection Registrar (1988)   *Fourth Report of the Data Protection Registrar* (London: HMSO).

David, M. (1986)   'Moral and Maternal: The Family in the Right', in Levitas, R. (ed)., *The Ideology of the New Right* (Corbridge: Polity Press).

Department of Employment (DE) (1981)   *Trade Unions Immunities* (London: HMSO).

Department of Employment (DE) (1983) *Democracy in Trade Unions* (London: HMSO).

Department of Employment (DE) (1987) *Trade Unions and Their Members* (London: HMSO).

Department of Employment (DE) (1989a) *Removing Barriers to Employment* (London: HMSO).

Department of Employment (DE) (1989b) *Trade Unions Immunities* (London: HMSO).

Department of Environment (DoE) (1983) *Streamlining the Cities* (Cm 9063) (London: HMSO).

Department of Environment (DoE) (1988) *The Conduct of Local Authority Business: The Government Response to the Report of the Widdicombe Committe of Inquiry* (Cm 433) (London: HMSO.)

Department of Health (DOH) (1989a) *Working for Patients* (the NHS Review) (Cm 555) (London: HMSO).

Department of Health (DOH) (1989b) *Children Act* (London: HMSO).

Department of Health and Social Security (DHSS) (1979a) *Inequalities in Health: A Report of a Working Party* (The Black Report) (London: HMSO).

Department of Health and Social Security (DHSS) (1979b) *Patients First* (London: HMSO).

Department of Health and Social Security (DHSS) (1981) *Growing Older* (Cm 8173) (London: HMSO).

Department of Health and Social Security (DHSS) (1985) *Review of Child Care Law*, Consultative Document (London: HMSO).

Department of Health and Social Security (DHSS) (1989) *The Law on Child Care and Family Services* (White Paper) (London: HMSO).

Department of Health/Department of Health and Social Security (DOH/DHSS) (1989) *Caring for People: Community Care in the Next Decade and Beyond* (White Paper) (London: HMSO).

Donovan, Lord (Chairman) (1968) *Royal Commission on Trade Unions and Employers' Associations: Report* (London: HMSO).

Downs, A. (1972) 'Up and Down with Ecology – the Issue Attention Cycle', *Public Interest*, 28, pp. 38–50.

Drucker, H., Dunleavy, P., Gamble, A. and Peele, G. (eds) (1988) *Developments in British Politics 2* (London: Macmillan).

Duchene, F. and Shepherd, G. (eds) (1987) *Managing Industrial Change in Europe* (London: Pinter).

Duncan, S. and Goodwin, M. (1988) *The Local State and Uneven Development* (Oxford: Polity Press).

Dunleavy, P., Gamble, A. and Peele, G. (eds) (1990) *Developments in British Politics 3* (London: Macmillan).

Equal Opportunities Commission (EOC) (1988) *Local Authority Equal Opportunities Policies: Report of a Survey by the EOC* (Manchester: EOC).

Equal Opportunities Commission (EOC) (1989) *Women and Men in Britain* (London: HMSO).

Esam, P. and Oppenheim, C. (1989) *A Charge on the Community: The Poll Tax Benefits the Poor* (London: CPAG/LGIU).

Farnham, D. P. and Pimlott, J. (1990) *Understanding Industrial Relations* (London: Cassell).

Field, F. (1989) *Losing Out* (Oxford: Basil Blackwell).

Flackes, W. D. and Elliot, S. (1989) *Northern Ireland: A Political Directory 1968–88* (Belfast: The Blackstaff Press).

Freedman, L. (1988) *Britain and the Falklands War* (Oxford: Basil Blackwell).

Freedman, L. (1989) 'Thatcherism and Defence', in Kavanagh, D. and Seldon, A. (eds) *The Thatcher Effect* (London: Clarendon Press).

Fry, G. (1987) 'The Thatcher Government, The Financial Management Initiative, and the New Civil Service', *Public Administration*, 66, pp. 1–20.

Gamble, A. (1988) *The Free Economy and the Strong State* (London: Macmillan).

Gibbs, D. (ed.) (1989) *Government Policy and Industrial Change* (London: Routledge & Kegan Paul).

Gilmour, I. (1977) *Inside Right* (London: Hutchinson).

Ginsberg, N. (1989) 'The Housing Act, 1988, and its Policy Context: A Critical Commentary', Critical Social Policy , 25.

GLC (1986) *Private Tenants in London: The G.L.C. Survey* (London, GLC).

Goldsmith, M. (1985) 'The Conservatives and Local Government 1979 and After', in Bell, D. (ed.), *The Conservative Government 1979–84: An Interim Report* (London: Croom Helm).

Gordon, P. (1989) *Citizenship For Some: Race and Government Policy 1979– 89* (London: Runnymeade Trust).

Gray, A. and Jenkins, W. (1986) 'Accountable Management in British Government: Some Reflections on the Financial Management Initiative', *Financial Accountability and Management*, 2(3).

Green, D. (1987) *The New Right* (Brighton: Wheatsheaf).

Green, F. (ed.) (1989) *The Restructuring of the UK Economy* (Brighton: Wheatsheaf).

Greenwood, J. (1989) 'Managing the Civil Service: From Fulton to Ibbs', *Talking Politics*, 1(1), pp. 56–61.

Greenwood, J. and Wilson, D. (1989) *Public Administration in Britain* (London, Unwin Hyman).

Gregory, J. (1987) *Sex, Race and the Law: Legislating for Equality* (London: Sage).

Gyford, J., Leach, S. and Game, C. (1989) *The Changing Politics of Local Government* (London: Unwin Hyman).

Haigh, N. (1989) 'EEC Environmental Policy and Britain *(London: Longman)* 3rd edn.

Ham, C. (1985) *Health Policy in Britain* (London: Macmillan).

Hawthorne, J. and Smith, D. (1989) 'Cultural Pluralism or Plain Sectarianism?' *Fortnight*, 278(November).

Hencke, J. (1988) 'Whitehall Eyes Swedish Model', *Guardian*, 29 November 1988.

Hennessy, P. (1989a) 'The Westland Affair', in Marshall, G. (ed.), *Ministerial Responsibility* (Oxford: Oxford University Press).

Hennessy, P. (1989b) *Whitehall* (London: Seeker & Warburg).

Hewton, E. (1986) *Education in Recession* (London: Allen & Unwin).

HMSO (1989) *The General Household Survey* (London: HMSO).

HMSO (1990) *Social Trends*, 20, (London: HMSO).

Holdsworth, T. (1986) 'Government and Industry', *Catalyst*, 2, pp. 59–67.

Holmes, M. (1985) *The First Thatcher Government 1979–83* (Brighton: Wheatsheaf).

Home Office (1990) *Crime, Justice and Protecting the Public* (London: HMSO).

Hooper, D. (1987) *Official Secrets* (London: Secker & Warburg).

Housing Centre Trust (1987) *Not a White Paper* (London: Housing Centre Trust).

Institute of Fiscal Studies (IFS) (1989) *Counting People with Low Incomes* (London: IFS).

Institute of Housing (1987) *Housing: The Government's Proposals. Response of the Institute of Housing* (London, Institute of Housing).

Jenkin, P. (1979) 'Interview', *Social Work Today*, 11(9).

Jenkins, K., Morris, B., Caplan, G. and Metcalfe, L. (1988) *Efficiency Unit: Improving Management in Government: The Next Steps* (Ibbs Report) (London: HMSO).

Jenkins, R. (1987) 'Equal Opportunities in the Private Scetor: the Limits of Voluntarism', in Jenkins, R. and Solomos, J. (eds) *Racism and Equal Opportunity Policies in the 1980s* (Cambridge: Cambridge University Press).

Jessop, B., Bennett, K., Bromley, S. and Ling, T. *Thatcherism: A Tale of Two Nations* (Oxford: Basil Blackwell).

Jewson, N. and Mason, D. (1986) 'The Theory and Practice of Equal Opportunities: Liberal and Radical Approaches', *Sociological Review*, 34(2).

Jones, G. (1985) 'The Prime Minister's Aides', in King, A. (ed.) *The British Prime Minister* (London: Macmillan).

Jones G. (1989) 'A Revolution in Whitehall? Changes in British Central Government Since 1979', *West European Politics*, 12, pp. 238–61.

Jones, G. and Stewart, J. (1983) *The Case for Local Government* (London: Allen & Unwin).

Jordan, A. and Richardson, J. (1987) *British Politics and the Policy Process* (London: Allen & Unwin).

Julius, D. (1987) 'Britain's Changing International Interests: Economic Influences on Foreign Policy Priorities', *International Affairs*, 63.

Kay, J. (ed.) (1989) *Privatisation and Regulation: The UK Experience* (London: Clarendon Press).

Keesing's (1989) *Keesing's Record of World Events* (London: Longman).

Kennedy, P. (1981) *The Realities Behind Diplomacy: Background Influences and British External Policy 1965–80* (London: Fontana).

Kennedy, P. (1989) *The Rise and Fall of the Great Powers* (London: Fontana).

King, D. (1987) *The New Right: Politics, Markets and Citizenship* (London: Macmillan).

Klein, R. (1983) *Politics of the National Health Service* (London: Longman).

Kumar, V. (1986) Industrial Tribunal Applicants Under the Race Relations Act 1976 (London: Commission for Racial Equality).

Labour and Ireland (1989) *Time to Go: Special Issue Labour and Ireland* (July–August).

Labour Party (1989)   *Meet the Challenge: Make the Change* (London: Labour Party).

Labour Research (1989)   'Equality in 1992 – UK Holds the Key', *Labour Research* (March).

Lansley, S., Goss, S. and Wolman, C. (1989)   *Councils in Conflict: The Rise and Fall of the Municipal Left* (London: Macmillan).

Lawrence, J. (1986)   'How Ministers Fiddle Figures', *New Society* 28 February.

Leach, S. (1989)   'Strengthening Local Democracy: The Government's Response to Widdicombe', in Stewart, J. and Stoke, G. (eds), *The Future of Local Government* (London: Macmillan).

Leonard, A. M. (1987)   *Judging Equality: The Effectiveness of the Tribunal System in Sex Discrimination Equal Pay Cases* (London: Cobden Trust).

Lewis, R. (ed.) (1986)   *Labour Law in Britain* (Oxford: Basil Blackwell).

Lewis, R. (1988)   *Anti-Racism: A Mania Exposed* (London: Charter).

Lister, R. (1989)   'Social Security', in McArthy, M. (ed.) *The New Politics of Welfare* (London: Macmillan).

Logan-Turner, R. (1990)   'Mrs Thatcher's Enterprise Culture', *Social Studies Review*, 5(3).

Lowe, P. and Flynn, A. (1989)   'Environmental Planning and the Thatcher Government', *ECOS*, 10(4), pp. 22–9.

Loughlin, M. (1986)   *Local Government in the Modern State* (London: Sweet & Maxwell).

Lupton, C. (1989)   'The Politics of E.T.', *Talking Politics*, 1(2).

MacInnes, S. (1987)   *Thatcherism at Work* (Milton Keynes: Open University Press).

MacLure, S. (1988)   *Education Reformed: A Guide to the Education Reform Act 1988* (Sevenoaks: Hodder & Stoughton).

McNay, I. and Ozga, J. (1985)   *Policy-Making in Education: The Breakdown of Consensus* (London: Pergamon).

Mansergh, N. (1982)   *The Commonwealth Experience* (London: Macmillan).

Marsh, A. (1979)   *Concise Encyclopedia of Industrial Relations* (Aldershot: Gower).

Marshall, T. (1981)   *The Right to Welfare and Other Essays* (London: Heinemann).

Minford, P., Peel, M. and Ashton, P.   *The Housing Morass* (London: IEA).

Ministry of Health (1956)   *Report of the Committee of Enquiry into the Cost of the National Health Service* (London: HMSO).

Mitchell, B. (1989)   *Geography and Resource Analysis* (London: Longman).

Mitchell, M. and Russell, D. (1989)   'Race and Racism', in Brown, P. and Sparks, R. (eds), *Beyond Thatcherism: Social Policy, Politics and Society* (Milton Keynes: Open University Press).

Moffat, C. (1988)   'Ulster Says More Mixed School Please', *Fortnight*, 263(July–August).

Moran, M. (1977)   *The Politics of Industrial Relations* (London: Macmillan).

Morton, J. (198)   *The Criminal Justice Acts 1987 and 1988* (London: Waterlow).

Mottershead, P. (1978) 'Industrial Policy', in Blackaby, F. (ed.) *British Economic Policy 1960–74* (Cambridge: NIESR).

Myers, N. (ed.) (1985) *The Gaia Atlas of Planet Management* (London: Pan).

Nailor, P. (1986) 'Foreign and Defence Policy', in Drucker, H. *et al.* (eds), *Developments in British Politics 2* (London: Macmillan).

National Association of Probation Officers (NAPO) (1988) *Punishment, Custody and the Community: The Response of the National Association of Probation Officers* (London: NAPO).

Neuberger, F. (ed.) (1987) *Freedom of Information . . . Freedom of the Individual* (London: Macmillan).

Norris, D. (1989) 'History Takes a New Track', *Fortnight*, 279(December).

Northedge, F. (1974) *Descent from Power: British Foreign Policy 1945–73* (London: Allen & Unwin).

Nugent, N. (1989) 'The European Community and British Independence', *Talking Politics*, 2, pp. 29–38.

OECD (1988) *Ageing Populations: The Social Policy Implications* (Paris: OECD).

O'Riordan, T. (1970) *Environmentalism* (London: Pan).

Parsons, A. (1989) 'Britain and the World', in Kavanagh, D. and Seldon, A. (eds), *The Thatcher Effect* (London: Clarendon Press).

Parsons, D. (1986) *The Political Economy of British Regional Policy* (London: Croom Helm).

Paton, C. (1980) 'Reviewing the N.H.S.: More Turbulence for the System', *British Medical Journal*, 297, pp. 1138–9.

Plant, R. (1988) 'Ideology', in Drucker, H. *et al.*, *Developments in British Politics* (London: Macmillan).

Pollard, A., Purvis, J. and Walford, G. (eds) (1988) *Education, Training and the New Vocationalism* (Milton Keynes: Open University Press).

Ponting, C. (1985) *The Right to Know* (London: Sphere).

Ponting, C. (1986) *Whitehall: Tragedy and Farce* (London: Sphere).

Ponting, C. (1989) *Whitehall: Changing the Old Guard* (London: Unwin Hyman).

Pryke, R. (1980) *The Nationalised Industries: Policies and Performance Since 1968* (London: Martin Robertson).

Radical Statistics Health Group (1987) *Facing the Figures* (London: Radical Statistics).

Rees, T. and Atkinson, P. (1982) *Youth Employment and State Intervention* (London: Routledge and Kegan Paul).

Reiner, R. (1985) *The Politics of the Police* (Brighton: Wheatsheaf).

Reynolds, D. (1986) 'A "Special Relationship?" America, Britain and the International Order Since the Second World War', *International Affairs*, 62.

Rhodes, R. (1988) *Beyond Westminster and Whitehall: The Sub-Central Government of Britain* (London: Allen & Unwin).

Riddell, P. (1989) *The Thatcher Decade* (London: Macmillan).

Ridley, N. (1988) *The Local Right: Enabling Not Providing* (London: Centre for Policy Studies).

Roskill, Lord (1986) *Fraud Trials Committee* (London: HMSO).

Rowthorn, F. and Wayne, N. (1988) *Northern Inreland: The Political Economy of Conflict* (Oxford: Polity Press).
Russell, T. (1978) *The Tory Party* (London: Penguin).
Ryan, M. (1983) *The Politics of Penal Reform* (London: Longman).
Salter, B. and Tapper, T. (1985) *Power and Policy in Education: The Case of Independent Schooling* (Brighton: Falmer Press).
Sandbach, F. (1980) *Environment, Ideology and Policy* (Oxford: Basil Blackwell).
Sandbach, F. (1982) *Principles of Pollution Control (London: Longman)*.
Savage, S. (1986) 'The Enemy Within: Law and Order Under the Tories', in Robins, L. (ed.) *Political Institutions in Britain: Development and Change* (London: Longman).
Seebohn, L. (1968) *Report of the Committee on Local Authority and Allied Personal Social Services* (Cmnd 3703) (London: HMSO).
Shoard, M. (1980) *The Theft of the Countryside* (London: Temple Smith).
Skuse, A. and Jones-Owen, R. (1983) *Government Intervention and Industrial Policy* (London: Heinemann).
Slattery, M. (1986) *Official Statistics* (London: Tavistock Press).
Smith, D. (1989) *North and South* (London: Penguin).
Smith, M., Smith, S. and White, B. (eds) (1988) *British Foreign Policy, Tradition Change and Transformation* (London: Unwin Hyman).
Smith, P. (1986) *Why Unionists Say No (the Joint Unionist Working Party)*.
Snell, M. (1979) 'The Equal Pay and Sex Discrimination Acts: Their Impact on the Workplace', *Feminist Review*, pp. 37–5.7
Social Security Consortium (1986) *Of Little Benefit: A Critical Guide to the Social Security Act 1986.*
Solomos, J. (1989) *Race and Racism in Contemporary Britain* (London: Macmillan).
Stewart, G. and Stewart, J. (1986) *Boundary Changes: Social Work and Social Security* (London: BASW/CRAG).
Stewart, J. and Clarke, M. (1988) *The Enabling Council* (Local Government Training Board).
Stewart, J. and Stoker, G. (1989) *The Future of Local Government* (London: Macmillan).
Stoker, G. (1988) *The Politics of Local Government* (London: Macmillan).
Stoker, G. (1989) 'Local Government for a Post-Fordist Society', in Stewart, J. and Stoker, G., *The Future of Local Government* (London: Macmillan).
Swann, D. (1988) *The Retreat of the State* (Brighton: Wheatsheaf).
Tant, T. (1988) 'Constitutional Aspects of Official Secrecy and Freedom of Information: an Overview', *Essex Papers in Politics and Government*, 52 (Colchester: University of Essex).
Tapper, T. and Salter, B. (1978) *Education and Political Order* (London: Macmillan).
Taylor-Gooby, P. (1985) *Public Opinion, Ideology and State Welfare* (London: Routledge and Kegan Paul).
Thompson, G. (ed.) (1989) *Industrial Policy: USA and UK Debate* (London: Routledge and Kegan Paul).

Timmins, N. (1988) *Cash Crisis and Cure: The Independent Guide to the NHS Debate* (London: Newspaper Publishing).

Titmuss, R. (1976) *Essays on 'The Welfare State'* (London: Allen & Unwin).

Travers, T. (1986) *The Politics of Local Government Finance* (London: Allen & Unwin).

Unemployment Unit (1989) 'Developing TECs', *Unemployment Bulletin*, No. 3.

Vane, H. and Caslin, T. (1987) *Current Controversies in Economics* (Oxford: Basil Blackwell).

Wacks, R. (1989) *Personal Information: Privacy and the Law* (London: Clarendon Press).

Walker, A. and Walker, C. (eds) (1987) *The Growing Divide: A Social Audit 1979–1987* (London: CPAG).

Wallace, W. (1986) 'What Price Independence? Sovereignty and Interdependence in British Politics', *International Affairs*, 62.

Walters, P. (1989) 'The Crisis of "Responsible" Broadcasting: Mrs Thatcher and The BBC', *Government and Opposition*, 42(3) pp. 380–98.

Ward, S. (ed.) (1985) *DHSS in Crisis: Social Security – Under Pressure and Under Review* (London: CPAG).

Wedderburn, Lord (1986) *The Worker and the Law* (London: Penguin).

White, B. (1988) 'Britain and East–West Relations', in Smith, M., Smith, S. and White, B. *British Foreign Policy: Traditional Change and Transformation* (London: Unwin Hyman).

Whitehead, C. and Kleinman, M. (1987) *Private Renting in the 1980s and 1990s* (London: Granta Publications).

Widdicombe, D. (chairman) (1986) *The Conduct of Local Authority Business. Report of the Committee Inquiring into the Conduct of Local Authority Business* (Cmnd 9791) (London: HMSO).

Wilks, S. (1983) 'Liberal State and Party Competition: Britain', in Dyson, K. (ed.), *Industrial Crisis* (Oxford: Martin Robertson).

Wilks, S. (1985) 'Conservative Industrial Policy 1979–83', in Jackson, P. (ed.), *Implementing Government Policy Initiatives: The Thatcher Administration 1979–1983* (London: RIPA).

Zander, M. (1986) *The Police and Criminal Evidence Act 1984* (London: Sweet and Maxwell).

Index